Welfare and wellbeing

Richard Titmuss's contribution to social policy

Edited by Pete Alcock, Howard Glennerster, Ann Oakley and Adrian Sinfield

The POLICY
PP
PRESS

First published in Great Britain in October 2001 by

The Policy Press
34 Tyndall's Park Road
Bristol BS8 1PY
UK

Tel +44 (0)117 954 6800
Fax +44 (0)117 973 7308
e-mail tpp@bristol.ac.uk
www.policypress.org.uk

British Library Cataloguing in Publication Data

A catalogue record for this book is available from the British Library

ISBN 1 86134 299 3 paperback

A hardback version of this book is also available.

Cover design by Qube Design Associates, Bristol.

Front cover: Photographs supplied by kind permission of Ann Oakley

Printed and bound in Great Britain by Hobbs the Printers Ltd, Southampton.

Contents

Sources of extracts

Introduction

Pete Alcock and Ann Oakley

Richard Titmuss was Professor of Social Administration at the London School of Economics (LSE) from 1950 until his premature death in 1973. He had a national and international reputation as a scholar and policy analyst, and his writings and philosophy have influenced generations of students of social policy both within and outside academia. He was the British welfare state's staunchest defender but also one of its most uncompromising critics; his analysis of its intended and unintended social divisions, always both scholarly and policy relevant, shaped a tradition which is still very much alive and well today.

Richard Titmuss

This volume, *Welfare and wellbeing*, is a collection of extracts from Titmuss's published work on social policy from 1942 to 1973. Our intention in compiling it is twofold: first, since most of his books are now out of print, there is a need to make his contribution accessible to those – students and otherwise – who have been frustrated by its inaccessibility. But, second, there are many areas in which what Titmuss had to say about public and private welfare has a new resonance today, as governments, academics and policy strategists grapple with the problems of public versus private spending, continuing inequalities in health and welfare, and many of the social divisions which first focused Richard Titmuss's thinking on the relationship between the state and the personal welfare of citizens.

Titmuss's academic career spanned over 30 years. In that time, the breadth, as well as the depth, of his work provided a guide to the parameters of the subject of social policy. Despite the many changes in both theory and practice since his death, his breadth of vision and substantive analysis remain as an enduring example of what the study of social policy can encompass. In the selections chosen for this book, we have sought to provide a sample of the key aspects of that vision and analysis, and to group these around some of the major issues which concerned Titmuss in his working life – and which still concern both students and practitioners today.

The family, poverty and population (Part 1) were among Titmuss's earliest foci of concern. He appreciated the need to understand the broad social context within which social policies must be constructed and implemented. Demographic trends and changing family and household structures underpin all policy planning. They are now being explored through a wide range of government and independent data sources which were not available to Titmuss in his early work. Debate about the existence of *The 'welfare state'* (Part 2) remains at the centre of social policy analysis, both empirically and conceptually. Titmuss was aware that we need to question critically what it is appropriate to study as part of the welfare activities of governments. His challenge to any narrow concern with directly funded public services remains a guiding principle for any understanding of the real scope of welfare provision, and his critical questioning of the simplistic notion of a 'welfare state' is still one of the most widely debated topics on university social policy courses.

Redistribution, universality and inequality (Part 3) were for Titmuss the issues which must drive decisions about policy planning. Who should receive welfare services and who should pay for them are questions which must be posed before any decisions can be taken about the structure and implementation of policy programmes. As the selections included in this book reveal, Titmuss was concerned with ensuring that an informed and principled approach to such planning underpins all policy analysis and development. As the selections in Part 4 on *Power, policy and privilege* reveal, however, he was also aware that the answers to these questions would be determined to a large extent by the vested and anticipated interests of social groups and other social agencies; as he insisted, our analysis of policy processes would be naive and ill informed if it did not seek to uncover and understand these.

As Part 5 on *International and comparative dimensions* makes clear, Titmuss was also an internationalist. His international work was varied in scope and context. He was invited as both advisor and visiting scholar to a wide range of overseas countries including, as Glennerster discusses in his commentary to Part 5, Tanzania and Mauritius. His ideas and his analyses were also taken up and developed by scholars in many other countries, most notably Martin Rein, S.M. Miller and Alvin Schorr in the United States, who came to visit Titmuss at the LSE department, and Hugh Heclo, now a leading social policy scholar in the United States, who was supported as a postgraduate student by Titmuss. Titmuss also promoted comparative analysis of social policy. His three models for welfare provision have underpinned most of the more recent development of comparative policy analysis, and his belief that we can understand better our own politics and policies by learning more about others remains the driving force behind international and comparative study.

Titmuss was the first Professor of Social Administration in the United Kingdom, and, as we can see in Part 6 *The subject of social policy*, he played a central role in its development in the United Kingdom and overseas. His influence on the study of social policy was immense – and remains so, as this book demonstrates. However, like most of those who have followed in his footsteps, Titmuss did not just *study* social policy; he also sought to *shape* it. He did this not only through ideas and argument, but also through participating directly in the formulation and implementation of policy and practice. He was an active member of a number of committees and commissions in the United Kingdom: for health visitors (1953-54), medical education (1965-68) and one-parent families (1970-73). He was deputy chairman of the Supplementary Benefits Commission and a member of the Community Relations Commission, as well as a range of other bodies from the Council of Toynbee Hall (the first settlement house, established in the East End of London in the late 19th century) to the Local Government Training Board Examinations Committee. This is evidence of his prodigious workload, as well as his sense of civic responsibility, his commitment to the inter-relation of research, policy and practice, and his determination to practise what he was preaching about the importance of altruism and reciprocity in the structuring of social relations. Combined with his writings and teaching, these public duties earned him a list of honours, including a CBE and a number of honorary degrees.

Almost 30 years after his death, Titmuss remains the single most important intellectual influence on the study and practice of social policy in the United Kingdom. Yet, as some critics have pointed out (for instance, Reisman, 1977), he did not produce a complete text outlining a theoretical and conceptual framework for the subject. There is no Titmussian general theory on welfare and social policy; and therefore no single unifying idea to act as a reference point for future analysts – in contrast perhaps to Titmuss's predecessor at the LSE, T.H. Marshall, whose treatise on the role of citizenship in shaping modern society is still used as the conceptual foundation of much modern welfare theorising.

It is perhaps a matter of regret that Titmuss did not write such a text, or that he did not have the opportunity to do so. But it is not evidence of any lack of concern for theoretical and conceptual analysis. Indeed, as can be seen in many of the extracts in this book, he was at pains to challenge the narrow pragmatism of much contemporary academic research and policy practice and to question the complacency behind those accounts which saw in the new post-war welfare capitalism the demise of grand political ideologies (for instance, Bell, 1960, and Lipset, 1960). There are clear and comprehensive conceptual frameworks in Titmuss's social divisions of welfare (see Part 2) and his models of welfare provision (see Part 5). That he did not develop these at length was in part because of the broader impact that they had already had in other aspects of his work and that of others; he felt that they were already quite well understood. But it was also because so much of his work, both in practice as well as in principle, was based upon the application of conceptual analysis to practical policy development and delivery. Titmuss did not write about welfare theory in the way that many have since; rather he took theoretical understanding into policy analysis.

In what was possibly his most sustained piece of applied conceptual analysis and policy research – his comparative study of blood donation in *The gift relationship* (1970), republished by LSE books (1997), Titmuss combines meticulous empirical detail with wide-ranging systemic analysis to demonstrate the strengths and weaknesses of different models of welfare provision, and the different conceptual biases implicit within these. In this entertaining and informative account can be found analysis of markets and public services, values and choices, and process and outcomes. And the combination of breadth of conceptual understanding with depth of empirical analysis has been an inspiration to many subsequent scholars. The original book was widely reviewed across the world and was also sought out by policy makers, including Elliot Richardson, the Secretary of Education and Welfare in Washington.

The gift relationship was one of Titmuss's last published works. His collection of *Social policy* lectures was published posthumously (Abel-Smith and Titmuss, 1974). It can be seen in some ways therefore as a general statement of his approach to the study of social policy. It was an approach which Titmuss had developed throughout his working life, from his earliest works on family and population, through his detailed description of wartime social services to his seminal lectures on social divisions and universal services. Curiously, though, his work may have had a more lasting impact on economics than on social policy – though few economists would admit it. One interesting study by a French economist (Fontaine, 2000) is suggesting precisely that. As we see in Part 2, fiscal welfare was a critically new idea. Economists took the idea over and called it 'tax expenditure' and it is now a fundamental and accepted part of public economics. Governments measure it and have changed their budget and economic statistics to include it.

Abel-Smith's work with Titmuss for the Guillebaud Committee (1956) on the finance of the National Health Service (NHS) was highly influential. The measure of health expenditure as a percentage of the gross domestic product, trends in real terms spending, the distributional effects of such expenditure, the impact of ageing – it is all there in the evidence and all are now standard tools in the economics of health. Titmuss's paper in *Medical Care* (1963) was raising questions about whether traditional market economics worked for goods like health care before economists provided a response and before the ground-breaking paper by Kenneth Arrow (1963) which suggested in formal terms that health care was indeed different. The whole set of ideas we now call 'market failure' post-date the criticisms

Titmuss made. Information failure and the imbalance of information between consumer and producer in health care and insurance markets more generally, adverse selection, cream-skimming, moral hazard – all these date from the 1970s in formal theoretical outline in the economics literature. How far Titmuss prompted economists to think like this is debatable. Arrow was probably the key influence. However, Titmuss did inspire some economists to think again about altruism as Fontaine shows. What we can say is that the nascent economic ideas Titmuss was groping for in the 1950s and 1960s became standard economics all over the world in the 1980s and 1990s. What a welcome irony he would no doubt have found that!

In all, Titmuss wrote over 20 books and over 80 academic articles and was visiting professor in half a dozen overseas universities. His ideas shaped the development of economic and social policy analysis throughout the world. The selections included in this book provide a guide to the range of ideas and analyses which he developed over his long working life, but they are only a guide.

* * * * *

Richard Maurice Titmuss was born in 1907, the second child of a farmer, and was brought up in the Bedfordshire countryside near London. In 1918 the family farm was broken up under Lloyd George's scheme for giving land to soldiers returning from the war. The Titmusses moved to Hendon in North London, where Richard's father started an unsuccessful haulage business. Titmuss left school at 14, was sent to a commercial college for a six-month course in book-keeping, and then became an 'office boy' in Standard Telephones, helping his father with the business accounts in the evening. When his father died at 53, leaving substantial debts, and the responsibility of two siblings and a depressed mother, Titmuss began a 16-year stint as an insurance officer in the County Fire Insurance Office in Piccadilly, London. From these unpromising beginnings, he moved in 1942 to the Cabinet Offices in Whitehall to write the social history of the Second World War. The move to a professorship at the LSE came eight years later.

The story of how an ill-educated young man, with few prospects, an impoverished background and heavy family responsibilities, managed to acquire sufficient skills and social contacts to transform himself from an insurance clerk to a university professor is mainly one of relentless hard work, combined with an astute eye for current policy issues, and an absolute obsession with teasing out the social realities behind official statistics (Oakley, 1996). Titmuss educated himself through voracious reading and political argument; he was a member of the Young Liberals before joining the Labour Party. While still working in insurance he managed to write, at snatched moments during the day and the evenings, many articles and five books. His

The Publishers sincerely apologise for an error that has appeared on page 5 of the book – Richard Maurice Titmuss should read Richard Morris Titmuss.

interests during this time were focused on the vital statistics of health and mortality, nutrition, eugenics, unemployment and foreign policy, disarmament and the peace movement. His first book, *Poverty and population*, appeared in 1938 (see Part 1, Chapter Two) and was published by Harold Macmillan, with a preface by the eminent physician, Lord Horder. It bore 'the authentic Titmuss stamp', asking questions of considerable importance which had not occurred to anyone before but thereafter seemed completely obvious (Gowing, 1975, p 6).

In the early years of the Second World War Titmuss worked in war damage insurance, a 'reserved occupation', and acted as adviser to the Ministries of Information, Health and Economic Warfare, the latter on German vital statistics. In connection with this work, he hired a German-speaking research assistant, Marie Meinhardt, a Jewish refugee from the Nazis. When Meinhardt died in 1986, she remembered in her will the exciting work with Titmuss and the help he gave both her and her husband to acquire British citizenship, and she left a substantial bequest to the Titmuss Memorial Fund at LSE, which is now being used to support many students who would otherwise be unable to complete their studies.

In 1941 Titmuss was recruited by economic historian Keith Hancock to contribute to a series of volumes on the history of the Second World War. *Problems of social policy*, published in 1950 (see Part 2, Chapter Four), told the troubled and fascinating story of the wartime social services which in many ways laid the foundation for the post-war welfare state. This commission, carried out while fire-watching in St Paul's Cathedral and growing vegetables on an allotment for the war effort, allowed Titmuss to roam freely through the statistics of the Ministries of Health and Education, the Home Office, the Assistance Board and the General Register Office, not to mention local authorities and many voluntary organisations. The book was extremely well received as a work of historical scholarship and incisive social analysis, and did much to establish Titmuss's academic reputation.

By the time *Problems of social policy* was published, Titmuss was working as Deputy Director of the Social Medicine Research Unit, a new group set up in 1948 by the Medical Research Council at the Central Middlesex Hospital in west London. The Unit's Director was a medically trained epidemiologist, Jerry Morris; together, Morris and Titmuss wrote a series of pioneering papers on social medicine, the new discipline to which Titmuss was increasingly seeing his own work as making a contribution (Oakley, 1991). The focus of the Titmuss–Morris papers was on social factors and disease, with a strong emphasis on the mechanisms through which poverty and social disadvantage operated to create the statistics of class-differentiated illness and mortality. The two men envisaged an ambitious programme of work in this area, but their plans were cut short when Titmuss was offered the chair at LSE in 1950.

He might equally well have been given one of the new chairs of social medicine, but social administration was another new field and Titmuss was chosen for both the first two social administration chairs – at Birmingham and the LSE. At the LSE he took over a department which went back to 1912 and was mainly concerned with the training of social workers. The rationale for the chair was that for the first time there were to be social administration options on an undergraduate sociology degree. The first years at the LSE were not happy, as Titmuss had to make difficult and sometimes unpopular decisions about the fate of various social work courses – all without any social work training himself (Donnison, 1973). However, by the early 1960s, he had managed to achieve an international reputation for the quality of the teaching and research carried out in the social administration department, which was the largest in Europe and about the same size as the largest in North America, and was attracting students and scholars from many countries.

Titmuss himself was more interested in teaching and writing than in university administration, which he regarded as a tedious and unpleasant activity based increasingly on the notion of universities as businesses. He took enormous trouble with his own lectures; one of two posthumous volumes, *Social policy: An introduction* (Abel-Smith and Titmuss, 1974) contains the last introductory course he gave at the LSE. Most importantly, he attracted to work with him at the school many who subsequently became well known in their own right. Indeed, during the early development of the study of social policy in the UK, many of the leading scholars and much of the leading scholarship came from Titmuss's department and the colleagues whom he promoted and supported within it. From here came Abel-Smith and Townsend's seminal research on relative poverty (Abel-Smith and Townsend, 1965; Townsend, 1979), Donnison's work on housing (1967), Atkinson's economic analysis of poverty and social security (1969), and Pinker's work on social work and social policy (1971).

The department which Titmuss led at the LSE became, and remains, the leading base for research and teaching in social policy within the UK, and across much of the rest of the world. It developed and has continued to house the most comprehensive library of social policy writing. It developed and has maintained a wide range of funded research programmes and centres. And it has encouraged and continued to support a stream of visiting fellows and overseas students who have carried on Titmuss's commitment to internationalism. The legacy that Titmuss left still sustains and inspires scholars and students in the department, not least through the establishment of the Richard Titmuss Chair of Social Policy currently held by Julian LeGrand.

During his years at the LSE, Titmuss published seven books and many articles and papers. Two of the seven books were collections of lectures and papers – *Essays on 'The welfare state'* (1958) and *Commitment to welfare* (1968). Three books were practical assignments: *The cost of the National Health Service in England and Wales* (1956, with Abel-Smith), *Social policies and population growth in Mauritius* (1961, with Abel-Smith and assisted by Tony Lynes) and *The health services of Tanganyika* (1964, with Abel-Smith and three colleagues for the African Medical Research Foundation). The other two books were written as a result of Titmuss's own interests in the topics of income and class inequalities (*Income distribution and social change*, 1962) and altruism and social and health policy (*The gift relationship*, 1970).

Titmuss was an intensely private man, sustained in his work through his marriage in 1937 to a social worker, Kay Miller, who devoted herself to supporting Richard and raising their only child, Ann. He was always absorbed in his work and eager to take on new challenges; he enjoyed fame, but was also well known for his ability to listen to, and support, those less advantaged. He was dogged by health problems, particularly tuberculosis in 1957, and was treated with drugs which caused partial deafness. In 1972 he was diagnosed with lung cancer. He died a few months later in the Central Middlesex Hospital, where he and Jerry Morris had 30 years earlier envisaged their grand plan for research on social factors and disease. His obituaries recorded his outstanding contributions to the field of social administration and public policy, and the difficulty of doing justice to the full breadth of his achievements. One, by a colleague, noted that, "Perhaps, in this knowing age, only a self-educated man who came, academically speaking, from nowhere would have so obstinately persisted in the belief that people can make the world a better place, simply by learning a lot about it, explaining its injustices cogently, and proposing saner arrangements for the future" (Donnison, 1973, p 81).

There is, as yet, no full-length biography of Richard Titmuss. A friend and colleague, Margaret Gowing, wrote a memoir for the British Academy (Gowing, 1975). A book by the economist John Vaizey, an early disciple of Titmuss's, contains a rather unkind picture of Titmuss and four other 'men of ideas' – Hugh Gaitskell, Iain Macleod, Tony Crosland and Edward Boyle – as impractical visionaries (Vaizey, 1983). Titmuss's daughter, Ann Oakley, has written a book about his life, work and family life before the LSE days (Oakley, 1996). The most comprehensive account of his thought is D.A. Reisman's *Richard Titmuss: Welfare and society* (1977; a new edition is expected).

* * * * *

A certain amount of editorial work has been necessary to produce this volume. While we have tried to maintain the cogency of Titmuss's argument and the style of his writing, we have made some cuts in the chapters reproduced here in order to reduce repetition and make for easier reading, and have changed a few words here and there in order to make the sense clearer; [ ] denotes editorial additions. Most of the tables, and all footnotes and endnotes have been removed, to be replaced by Harvard referencing style. References were not always Titmuss's *forte*; we have sought to complete these where possible, but have not always been able to track them down. He had a slightly irritating habit of sometimes quoting without indicating any source at all: for example, Dickens (p 18), Disraeli (p 104), Milne (p 28), and even "it was said" (p 83). We have tried to give page numbers for direct quotes, but sometimes the source has eluded us. Where first names are known, they are generally given; initials and titles have been removed.

Since the newest of these writings is over 30 years old, they contain a fair number of obsolete terms (for example, labour exchange, slide rules, the Soviet Union, the Common Market, the British Empire); we have kept most of these in the interests of historical accuracy. Tenses were another problem; we have changed some of these, but preserved most, again aiming to make Titmuss's meaning clear. Americanised English has been amended; inconsistencies in the dating of some Acts have been removed; and references to the wars of 1899-1902, 1914-18 and 1939-45 have been standardised as the Boer War, the First World War and the Second World War. Where possible, masculine pronouns have been pluralised or otherwise avoided.

This book has four editors, all of whom have been involved throughout the editorial process. In addition, we are very grateful to John Hills (Professor of Social Policy and Director of the Centre for Analysis of Social Exclusion [CASE] at the London School of Economics and Political Science) and Tania Burchardt (Research Officer at CASE) for their contributions to Parts 3 and 2 respectively.

We would not have been able to produce this book without the immensely careful and thoughtful copy-editing of Matthew Hough or without the generous support of the Titmuss Memorial Fund at LSE. Thanks to them and to all who have contributed to the enterprise of putting this book together.

The family, poverty and population

Commentary: Ann Oakley

The chapters in this first section of the book come from the early part of Richard Titmuss's career. Most of them were written before social policy had even started to become an official, academic subject, and before politicians and governmental decision-makers had begun seriously to entertain the idea of social science as a routine source of practical information to aid government policy. The themes of the chapters spell out a number of critical social issues which have subsequently become the focus of enormous policy interest and academic debate. In these early works, Richard Titmuss was anticipating the growth of the discipline to which his own name would be indissolubly linked, but he was also predicting policy concerns that would become an important focus of attention well into the 21st century: class inequalities in health and life-chances; the survival of The Family; the possibility of evidence-informed social policy; and the position of women.

* * * * *

Titmuss's origins as a social scientist lie in his work in the insurance industry, where the vital statistics of birth and death forged in him an enduring interest in the quantity and the quality of the population (Oakley, 1996). This was the focus of the first three of his books, *Poverty and population* (1938), *Parents revolt* (1942) and *Birth, poverty and wealth* (1943). Chapter One, 'The nation's wealth', comes from *Parents revolt*, a slim, angry volume printed on cheap war quality paper, co-authored with Titmuss's wife Kathleen. The book hypothesises a connection between the growth of acquisitive social values and the tendency of people to have fewer children. It argues that a nation's true wealth is not what we would today call its 'gross national product'; rather, the wealth of a nation inheres in the vitality of its people, and especially in people from *all* social classes. Written against the backdrop of the Second World War, it is not surprising to find the Titmusses noting that the whole enterprise of Britain's part in the war would have been impossible without the 'cannon fodder' supplied by large, working class families; differential fertility can be a matter of national convenience.

Parents revolt contends that, when national birth-rates fall, the welfare of nation states is threatened. More globally, the move away from parenthood may even signal the 'biological failure' of capitalism. The predictions of long-term fertility decline to which the Titmusses and others subscribed in the 1930s and 1940s turned out to have been wrong, but there was, of course, no way that people at the time could have anticipated the post-war 'baby boom'. Concern with fertility was already something of an academic industry by the 1940s and it has remained so, with the key questions being those about linking demographic patterns with human motives (Hazen and Frinking, 1990). Another continuing theme is the relationship between war, on the one hand, and policy concerns about health and fertility, on the other. The fear of population decline which fuelled *Parents revolt* was an aspect of a long-running, European-wide anxiety about the survival capacities of national populations. In part, this was a worry about the eclipse of elites by the masses; in part, a rather insalubrious eugenic fear of 'race' pollution (Teitelbaum and Winter, 1985). Disturbingly, some of these same arguments are resurfacing today in debates about sociobiology and the genetic determination of life-chances.

The indignation at social injustice palpable in *Parents revolt* was to inform much of Titmuss's later work, as it was also to constitute a critical driving force for the development of social policy. The themes of altruism and of the narrow-minded computation of public services in terms of economic costs and benefits – both key concerns in later social policy writings – make a fleeting appearance in 'The nation's wealth'. Titmuss's attack on 'the money culture' owed much to the influence of the socialist historian R.H. Tawney, whose book *The acquisitive society* (1921), came from a tradition of principled, ethical socialism. What Tawney argued – that modern society is organised around *functions* rather than *rights*, and that social policy ought not to encourage greedy individualism in 'men' – resurfaces again and again in Titmuss's writings. The materialistic mind-view, together with the very real concentration of capital in the hands of the rich, were always linked in Titmuss's writings with the appalling facts of class inequality in terms both of quantity and quality of life.

Chapter Two in this collection, 'The summation of poverty', from *Poverty and population*, is a forceful statement about the concentration of poverty, poor diet and premature death in certain social groups and regions. The book analyses regional statistics of illness, accidents and deaths, comparing the poorer with the richer. Titmuss calculated that there were some 500,000 preventable deaths of men, women and children in Britain every year. This, he said, constituted a national scandal in which no-one seemed to be much interested. By contrast, "... If one child is cruelly maltreated by its parents great newspaper publicity ensues and questions are ... asked in Parliament".

It was precisely this careful computation of statistics about social groups and life-chances – a legacy of his time in the insurance industry – that was one of Titmuss's most valuable contributions to the demographic and health literature. He was one of the first to develop methods for undertaking such analyses (Oakley, 1996). They played a prominent role in the book from which Chapter Three, 'A measurement of human progress' is taken – *Birth, poverty and wealth*. Here Titmuss anticipates much later work on child mortality in pointing out that the deaths of very young children are often the most sensitive indicator of social conditions; death rates in early childhood show the biggest social class differences. He points out that we cannot assume the progressive equalisation of life-chances in a 'civilised' society; on the contrary, the differential in infant mortality by social class had widened over the previous 20 years. Later researchers would agree with Titmuss on the two main causes of infant death identified in the book: poverty and 'insanitary urbanisation'. Personal and public health are closely linked; the material environment in which people live has a strong influence on their chances of health or ill-health. Just as the early public health reformers knew all about the connections between infectious disease and drains, so the 1980s revival of environmentalism in the form of the 'new' public health stresses the responsibility of government to ensure living conditions that promote, rather than prevent, health (Scott-Samuel, 1989). Most of the health gains attributed to medicine are in fact the product of healthier living conditions, rather than adjustments in individual life-styles (McKeown, 1976).

Inequalities in health have stayed on the policy agenda, though their place on it has shifted according to the colour of the government, and the focus of attention has moved between class, gender, ethnicity, and nationality. The *Report of the Independent Inquiry into Inequalities and Health* in the UK chaired by Sir Donald Acheson summarised the evidence (Acheson, 1998). Death rates are falling, but the gap between rich and poor is widening; in the late 1970s, death rates in social classes IV and V were 53% higher among men and 50% higher among women than among men and women in classes I and II; by the late 1980s, these figures had increased to 68% and 55%. A similar picture holds for life expectancy and for illness. For example, 21% of middle-aged professional men and women reported a limiting long-standing illness in 1996, compared with 47% among unskilled men and women. Diet, a concern of Titmuss's in *Poverty and population*, continues to show a pronounced and increasing class differential, with differences in nutrient intake related to income even *within* low income classes. Social factors are still the biggest threats to the health and survival of children (Roberts, 2000); a working-class child is twice as likely to die as a middle-class one (Woodroffe et al, 1993), and the gap between the most and least disadvantaged has widened in recent years for the main cause of child deaths – accidents (Roberts and Power, 1996).

* * * * *

Class inequalities are only one axis of social division. Before the 'second wave' of the Women's Movement in the late 1960s and early 1970s, there was little awareness in the social science and social policy domains of the importance of gender in differentiating life-chances. Socially patterned differences in the experiences and behaviour of men and women obtain in every domain of life (Costello et al,1998; Loutfi, 2001; Mirsky and Radlett, 2000). These mean that it is too reductionist (and certainly unhelpful from a policy point of view) to treat the sexes as homogenous; it also means that it can be misleading to view households or families as units – an established social policy tradition – when they are, in fact, assemblages of different individuals who tend to hold different perspectives. Most of Titmuss's own thinking and writing was no exception to this 'rule' of gender-blindness (Rose, 1981). However, in 'The position of women', Chapter Four, Titmuss stepped outside this limited frame of reference to consider some of the implications for the role of women of social and economic change in industrialised societies.

'The position of women' was originally a lecture given to the Fawcett Society, a campaigning organisation named after the suffragette Millicent Fawcett which is still alive and well today. The crux of Titmuss's argument in his Fawcett lecture was that childbearing and childrearing now occupy a much less significant portion of women's lives than they used to. His own calculation, of four years in an average lifetime in the early 1950s compared to 15 years in the 1890s, would probably work out as closer to two years today. Titmuss argued that this reduction of women's reproductive time meant that women still had around half of their lives in front of them when they had 'completed the cycle of motherhood', a period increasingly filled by employment. Thus, 'women's two roles' had become an accurate descriptor for an increasing proportion of the female population. Titmuss saw this change in women's position as nothing short of revolutionary; in so far as it was due to the Women's Movement, he deemed it, "... one of the supreme examples of consciously directed social change". However, the revolution in women's lives had, as it were, crept up on society unawares. While a widespread impact on the institutions of marriage and the family was to be expected, no one as yet knew the extent and consequences of disruption in traditional patterns of gender relations. In this sense, women's emancipation was a social problem. It was also a problem for women themselves, in two particular senses: first, in becoming 'working mothers', women were drawing the force of prejudice and moral disapproval on themselves; secondly, the elision of motherhood had not, so far, been accompanied by a removal of the barriers to women's participation in public life.

'The position of women' is itself a strange mixture of insight and prejudice. The latter is only to be expected in view of the social context in which Titmuss was writing, which was one of considerable opposition to the idea and practice of women's independence. The post-war period saw a burgeoning of domestic ideologies, as men reclaimed the jobs women had capably been doing during the war, day nurseries were closed, and 'Bowlbyism' hit the headlines, with its powerful assertions of the necessary damage to be done to children through maternal absence from the home (Riley, 1983). In these circumstances, it was hardly surprising that women's paid employment became a peg on which to hang all kinds of cardinal sins and errors, although evidence accumulating at the time suggested that most female employment was low status, poorly paid work, and was often a rather unrevolutionary extension of women's work inside the home (Jephcott et al, 1962).

While Titmuss's thinking was embedded in a traditional view of gender roles, it also absorbed and reflected, in its references to the works of Virginia Woolf and John Stuart Mill, a more overtly political critique of marriage and the family as oppressive institutions for women. The conflict between these two paradigms, one gender-blind, the other gender-sensitive, has marked much social science and policy analysis in the years since Titmuss published his pioneering essay (Hanmer and Hearn, 1999). Looking at the welfare state from the vantage point of women as a social group produces a different set of insights from those generated by the view which assumes the interests of men, women (and children) to be identical (Abramowitz, 1988). In particular, it leads to a more complex and context-sensitive understanding of family policy, and of the extent to which many social policies affect both The Family and real families (Land, 1978). As Ann Orloff (1993, pp 303-4) has put it, "Theorists may disagree about the causes of gender inequality and women's subordination, but few would deny that the character of public social provision affects women's material situations, shapes gender relationships, structures political conflict and participation, and contributes to the formation and mobilization of specific identities and interests". One way of demonstrating this is through comparative analysis of the architecture of family policies and their effects in different countries. Such analyses can show, for instance, different impacts on maternal employment and the economic wellbeing of families achieved through direct cash transfers as compared with other forms of policy support (Gornick et al, 1997).

The gender division of labour cross-cuts the class division of labour, and conventional, often implicit, ideas about men and women's work obscure the nature of women's work both in and outside the home. Housework, childcare and looking after the physical and emotional needs of male 'breadwinners' have a critical economic function as caring labour, a function which supports the whole edifice of capitalism and the welfare state (Delphy and Leonard, 1992). Significantly, too, much domestic labour provides an alternative, more altruistic model for social activity – just the sort of pathway to a more enlightened society the Titmusses may have had in mind when they wrote *Parents revolt* and which informed much of Titmuss's later work on health, welfare and social service provision.

Many of the questions raised in *The position of women* are still actively contended today: the meanings of women's employment for men, children and the family; the contest between family values and women's independence; the extent to which women's social position *really* has changed; the paradox of women's heavy dual burden and their apparently greater health and life expectancy compared to men (Coward, 1999; Graham, 1984; McRae, 1999; Oakley, 2001: forthcoming). In some respects – for example, the dynamics of power and economics within families – the academic debate has moved on, the statistical tools have increased in number and sophistication, and there is an enhanced expectation of evidence-based social policies in future (Anderson et al, 1994). But in other areas – for example, the meanings of maternal employment – the level of debate has stuck in channels which would be very familiar to the Titmuss of the 1950s (Benn, 1999; Hakim, 1995).

* * * * *

In a lecture given to the American National Conference on Social Welfare in 1966, Titmuss looked back to the early 1950s, when he wrote *The position of women*, and speculated on how many subsequent social trends were missed by social commentators such as himself at the time (Titmuss, 1968). No one, he decided, would have predicted the huge increases in child poverty and in income inequality that did occur; few would have anticipated the growth of racism, the anger of the civil rights movement, or the crises in many professional services. The lessons of history are that people get some things right, but they miss important clues because of their own values, or through hidden assumptions, for example that economic growth also brings social justice. These are exactly the reasons why the study of social policy as advocated by Titmuss is needed. They also provide the rationale for insisting that social growth as a goal is more likely to be achieved when policy making is informed by the kind of judicious social science Titmuss practised.

The nation's wealth

It is essential that we should first place the problem of population in the right perspective. Where lies the true wealth of a country? In answering this question, we shall have to rid ourselves of much of the mental debris accumulated in the 19th century which still obstructs our thoughts on fundamental problems. We must cut through the fog of tradition and, like the King in *Alice in Wonderland*, we must "begin at the beginning and go on till the end then stop". The reality of population is the root of all problems. It is the foundation of all else, the rock on which every social and economic problem is based. To assess sanely the future of man, we must have the right viewpoint; we must look at things in terms of men and women, and not in terms of money. We cannot discuss the problems of population objectively if we persist in using our present standards, which elevate material things above people and treat the national debt as of more consequence than the quantity and quality of our people. The history of all progress has been marked by the success of those who have refused to be obsessed by the fallacies of the past. Let us begin therefore by clearing from our path present-day society's overriding obsession.

We live in an age dominated and obstructed by the 'money complex', an age in which people are ever conscious of the presence of economic problems; an age in which people are forced more and more to regard money as the only means to security and the possession of material things. A hundred years hence, historians may say of us that the all-pervading mark of our generation was our abject servitude to the dictates of money and all that it spells. Such a forecast may bring an immediate protest from many readers. Some will revolt mentally and say that it is not true, and some who find it repugnant will do so because they are honestly trying to live a life in which money is not emphasised; others will find it distasteful because they find it hard to admit that, whatever the cause, money has dominated their conscious thinking. But let us be frank. Let us try to disabuse our minds and detach ourselves from the mass of moral platitudes which ooze in an unending stream from the churches, from Parliament and from the press to settle in the form of a smoke-screen of respectability over all our social institutions from Threadneedle Street to the local labour exchange.

It is not part of our social code to boast of acquisitiveness. In polite society, it is not fashionable to discuss the sordid means of distribution and exchange. Among the middle classes the most closely guarded secret is the size of money incomes, of salaries and wages.

"England", as George Orwell (1941) put it, "resembles a rather stuffy Victorian family, with not many black sheep in it, but with all the cupboards bursting with skeletons. It has rich relations who have to be kow-towed to and poor relations who are horribly sat upon, and there is a deep conspiracy of silence about the source of the family income." But if many in our society do not talk openly of money as money, they boast of all those things which money alone can buy. The possession of cars, of detached suburban villas, of expensive clothes, and the capacity to follow the whims and fancies of conspicuous waste are openly paraded as marks of the personal success of the individual. The ability to indulge in luxury consumption is regarded as a measure of social status. Outward display is, in our day and society, a sign of inward grace. This showmanship is reflected, as social habits are always reflected, in our novels, newspapers, plays, films and the way in which people spend their leisure time. Our newspapers carry columns of advertising, much of which is designed to inflame personal acquisitiveness, while the remaining space offers an extraordinary collation of patent medicines as the remedy for the feverishness induced by an acquisitive life.

The tremendous growth in hire-purchase, both in England and America, and a placarded, bill-posted landscape designed by high-pressure, super-safe, advertising automatons, are both expressions of our reverence for ostentatiousness; in pre-war Britain, £125 million was annually spent on advertising by press and poster, £25 million more than was spent by public authorities on education. News is normally a mixture of society scandal and society spending, or records of property crimes, while inordinate space is allotted to gambling ritual, described for those with money as financial intelligence and for those without as football pools. The films offer no help, for they usually depict happiness as synonymous with money and money as the measure of individual prestige. "As is well known to the wise in their generation", wrote Dickens, "traffic in Shares is the one thing to have to do with in this world. Have no antecedents, no established character, no cultivation, no ideas, no manners; have Shares".

A society based on the Christian ethic – on values rooted in the dignity and courage of the common man – would not, indeed could not, produce the pattern of wealth-ostentatiousness and the degree of money-consciousness that surround us today. A community which permits society journals, bug-infested children and super-magnificent cinemas, expresses the fundamental truth that wealth opens the door of opportunity while poverty keeps it closed from the cradle to the grave.

Those who are rich, the majority of whom have inherited their wealth, gently humour the poor; for the poor have work to do, while the poor admire the rich. Esteem is bestowed on those who get, not on those who give, and thus admiration is devoted to what is not admirable and happiness is sought where happiness cannot be found. It is difficult to believe that the conflict thereby induced can lead to anything but a frustrated society, a society epitomised in Mackinder's words as "the slumdom of the poor and the boredom of the rich".

The values we set on money-wealth as opposed to the wealth of human life are expressed in our physical environment. The most magnificent buildings equipped with gilded doors, panelled rooms, luxurious façades, deep carpets, noiseless lifts, uniformed attendants and all the vast, smooth, portentousness of the City of London are merely the repositories of a number of books containing a number of figures indicating the money-power of certain individuals over their fellow Christians. On the other hand, the meanest buildings in the saddest streets, bereft of furnishings and comfort and with standing room only, are the places where human 'labour' is exchanged. We have our cathedrals of wealth, redolent with calm, with spaciousness and with reverence, and we have also our labour exchanges characteristic of the drab inarticulate misery of the underprivileged.

Let us not pretend that these examples are exaggerations. We have been so saturated in money-thinking, so impregnated by the economic principles of the 19th century, which held that the accumulated result of innumerable private greeds was the only road to national wellbeing, that we often fail to regard objectively the evidence around us of the treatment of wealth in contrast to the treatment of man made in the image of God. The physical fact and the mental fear of unemployment have forced millions to mould more firmly their individual lives and their individual thoughts to the compelling power of money, for money to them spells security even if the safety to be purchased is short-lived. Unemployment was the outstanding social phenomenon of the 1920s to the 1940s, and while only 10-20% of insured persons were out of work in Great Britain on any given date, the proportion who experienced some spell of unemployment in, say, five years amounted to at least half the insured population. If we add to these the wives, children and other dependants, then something like 20 million individuals actually experienced unemployment to some degree, with all the social degradation and the debasement of the dignity of man that loss of work entails. The men and women of Britain learnt one lesson and the lesson drawn, which has indeed been forced upon them by the newspapers, the films and all the outward and visible signs of a tinsel society, is that status in the community is measured by money; to be rich is to be important.

Many people are concerned about the size of the national debt, about the high level of taxation and about the cost of rebuilding our bombed and shattered cities. Sir Kinglsey Wood, the Chancellor of the Exchequer, clearly had in mind a restriction in our already inadequate social services when he said in the House of Commons on 2 November 1941, "The size, form and cost of the war debt will clearly have an important influence on post-war policy". Lord Derby wants our educationalists to prepare for "the commercial battle for the world's markets which will follow this war", while Admiral Sir William Goodenough warns us through the columns of *The Times* (12 September 1941) that "competition in seaborne commerce after the war will be tremendous", and asks us, "for God's sake" to prepare to meet that competition. These eminent and admirable people are thinking backwards; they are mentally in the middle of the 19th century. They still believe, like Sir Robert Kindersley, President of the National Savings Movement, that wars are won by the biggest bank balance. Sir Robert seems unaware of the fact that, had the working people of this country returned from 1900 the same birth-rate as the well-to-do, we should not have had sufficient manpower to wage this war. If the common people had restricted the size of their families in the same way as the well-to-do, Hitler's *Wehrmacht* might now [1942] be goose-stepping down Whitehall.

It is perhaps to be expected that in the environment we have attempted to sketch, the thoughts of many should, as they turn to speculate on the pleasanter aspects of peace, tend to concentrate on the material things of life. These people are conditioned by their environment which in many ways, large and small, insidious and blatant, forces them to dwell on the physical things, the observable phenomena, the bricks and mortar of existence. It is in essence the atmosphere which, distilled as it is by the economic structure of our society, *compels* the individual to translate all human activity into the language of money. Curious as it may seem today, the provision of drains, of water-closets and clean water was advanced not to enhance human freedom but because, in terms of economics, they were a paying proposition and would protect the rich from contracting much infectious disease; witness the influence of the cholera epidemics. The economic argument also bespattered the provision of other social services such as health measures, factory legislation and state education. All these things spelt higher production and increased efficiency in the battle for world markets. Unemployment during the Depression of the 1930s was unctuously debated in terms of banknotes; the case for public works was not argued on the grounds that absence of work was an affront to democratic decency and the dignity of man but whether in terms of national finance public works would 'pay'. We did not ask 'Is it right?' but 'Will it pay?', and as it was not deemed profitable for the state to build houses, to clothe children and to feed mothers, it was decided to pay a lot of men a little money for doing nothing.

The highest economic authorities have told us that the foundations of our society were dissolving and that the country would crash in ruins almost overnight unless we close the net deficit in the national budget of £70 million – a figure which in 1942 we spend in six days and still regard as inadequate. It was even decided that Britain could not afford £1.5 million a year for extended services to reduce maternal mortality, a sum we spend in three hours of war! Even more fantastic was the announcement that Britain could not afford the sum of £30,000 once in ten years to find out in the 1931 Census at what ages British mothers bore children and a few other questions absolutely imperative to any study of the population problem. As there was no apparent financial profit to be gained from such expenditure, it was eliminated immediately.

The same insane values governed our thoughts at the beginning of the war; we were assured in official literature and by official spokesmen that 'Britain must win' by reason of our superior wealth. In war, as in peace, our yardstick was money. If, as we sometimes do, we attempt to measure the progress of our society over a period of x years, we immediately begin to think in terms of the level of real wages, the cost of living, the national income and so on. If we try to assess the change in different divisions of society, we automatically turn to the share in the national income, the trend in the ownership of property by the different classes, the savings of the poor and the accumulations of the rich. These techniques of assessing social progress have their rightful place, but their use to the exclusion of all other means is symptomatic, suggesting once again that unconsciously we are so saturated in money standards that we cannot visualise the use of any other mode of estimating social change.

The summation of poverty

According to an editorial in *The Times* (13 February 1936), "One half of the population is living on a diet insufficient or ill-designed to maintain health". Assuming this generalisation applies to the whole of the country, there is ample justification in the regional distribution of causative factors of inadequate diet to assess the proportion in the North and Wales at, if not above, three-quarters. That such a supplementary estimate is well grounded is evident from the cited facts which illustrate poverty resolved into the unnecessary and untimely deaths of 150 men, women and children every day in the North and Wales throughout at least the ten years to 1938, culminating in a total social waste of over 500,000 human beings. These figures not only confirm the opinion expressed by *The Times* but, as the expectation of life at birth and at all ages is considerably lower in the North and Wales than in the South East, read in conjunction with all the other relative indices, they point to the fact that the incidence of inadequate diet must be extensively above that for the whole of the country.

Remember that these are not just statistics but the *lives* of men, women and children. These conditions applied in 1936, a year of relative prosperity. The fact that premature deaths to the extent of 54,000 should occur during such a period is a condemnation of past complacency and a reflection of our disregard for human life. If these lives had been suddenly and sensationally terminated in some tremendous catastrophe, revulsion would have swept the country. We have seen that, if one child is cruelly maltreated by its parents, great newspaper publicity ensues and questions are quite rightly asked in Parliament. But allow these men, women and children, through poverty and a revolting environment, to sink slowly from one stage of degradation to the next and ultimately to take prematurely their allotted places in the Registrar-General's return, then nothing stirs to ruffle the insulated calm of the nation.

It is not only those who die but the thousands clinging to a precarious existence who, wracked by poverty and aged before their time, will contribute in the years ahead to the total of premature mortality.

High maternal mortality, the excessive mortality among infants, children and young people, the severe incidence of nutritional defects and tuberculosis among young people, and of deaths from heart disease in the thirties, the premature ageing and the defect-shortened lives, and all the amassed evidential statistics from many and varied sources mean that we are losing one quarter of our population every generation. After every alternative reason has been discarded, these factors point to the presence of intense poverty on a scale so considerable and so widespread, but at the same time so veiled and hidden by British stoicism and complacency, that public opinion has hitherto refused to recognise as conceivable the existence of such conditions in the heart of the British Empire in the 20th century.

A measurement of human progress

Infant mortality provides society with the first major index of the reaction of a new human life to its surroundings. It is a measure of human beings' ability and willingness to control their environment. The characteristics of a community begin to impress themselves as soon as the child starts its separate existence apart from its mother. This existence begins with explosive force. At no period in after-life does there occur any shock like that accompanying birth. For in the great systems of the body, in the physiological processes of respiration, circulation, heat regulation and digestion, there is an instantaneous and drastic change, and the failure of the child to meet these new demands or of the community to provide adequate protection can only result in death. Infant mortality is indeed the price of adaptation paid by each generation when entering life and the toll of infant deaths is a broad reflection of the degree of civilisation attained by any given community. "Health", declared René Sand (1935), "is purchasable.... Each country, within certain limits, decides its own death rates." In British Gambia in West Africa, life for the native is both brutal and brief, with infant deaths at the rate of 370 to every 1,000 births. At the other extreme, there are districts of New Zealand where the rate has fallen to below 20. Or we may compare Glasgow and its rate of 109 in 1936 with pre-1939 Amsterdam and a rate of only 30. These wide differences in the risk of death bear out Sir Arthur Newsholme's view (1909-10) that "Infant mortality is the most sensitive index we possess of social welfare and of sanitary administration, especially under urban conditions".

"Progress", wrote Herbert Spencer, "is not an accident" and it is no accident that the infant death rate for England and Wales fell from over 150 to around 50 in one hundred years. It was not, however, until about 1900 that the rate began to fall rapidly and the ensuing thirty years witnessed the greatest decline. It is instructive to note that public attention, as seen in the flow of commissions and inquiries after 1900, was directed to high infant mortality chiefly by the disclosures of physical ill-health and inefficiency during and after the Boer War; the first detailed statement of infant mortality in the Registrar-General's reports appeared in 1905. There is perhaps something rather shocking in the idea that it took a war to focus public attention on a wastefully high infant death rate. Whatever our reaction, it remains true that our concern for national health has followed the course of our military fortunes. Just as the Boer War focused attention on the physique and health of the nation (impelling the Inspector-General of Recruiting to speak of "the gradual deterioration of the physique of the working classes from which the bulk of the recruits must always be drawn"), so did the 1914–18 war [First World War], with its revelations of ill-health and the first appearance of the phrase 'a C3 nation'; and once again, the present war [Second World War, 1939–45], pressing closely on the whole population, sharply reminds us that we tend to forget communal fitness when the threat of mass destruction is not upon us. We have yet to formulate a standard of positive health as an absolute good in itself unrelated to industrial or military considerations. To do so, however, demands an understanding of the fundamental causes of ill-health and premature death.

The termination of an individual life is the product of an enormous number of complex and inter-related forces: from a government's policy in international affairs to the local methods of refuse disposal and from a coal-owner's decision to close the pits to a mother's intake of calcium. Reducing this diversity to identity, to find the causation of infant mortality, we can distinguish two main factors operating in the past to produce a high death rate: one can be summed in the word 'poverty'; the other is insanitary urbanisation.

As an illustration of the latter we may compare Norway's infant mortality rate of 105 during 1851–55 with Glasgow's rate of 109 in 1936. In the middle of the 19th century, Norway and Ireland were considered to be, in comparison with England, poor countries. While ignorance, lack of personal hygiene and a higher degree of poverty contributed to produce a rate above 100, these countries did not suffer from the dirt and infection manufactured by industrialisation and rapid urban growth. During 1891–95, just before a rapid decline in the rate occurred in each country, England and Wales had a rate of 151, Ireland 102 and Norway 98. The purely economic differences between these countries were, however, masked by the factor of population density and, for that reason, by standards of sanitation involving air and water-borne infection. While Ireland and Norway were, in the main, poverty stricken at the end of the 19th century, their poor were not crowded together in an insanitary environment. The people of England and Wales, who at that time probably stood at a somewhat higher standard of living, were nevertheless subjected to the factor of high population density. This factor, when superimposed on poverty, thus contributed to produce an infant death rate 50% higher than that obtaining in poorer, but sparsely populated agricultural communities. If, however, the urban populations of the three countries are compared, we find Dublin with the highest rate of 169, then Oslo with 158 and lastly London with 156. In the reversal of the rates for English, Irish and Norwegians, we see the influence exerted in the 19th century by the forces of density and industrialisation. It was William Farr (1843) who first pointed out that mortality was a function of the density of the population.

In Farr's day, the public health administrator was faced with two main problems: poverty and drains. Although both were indubitably present, only one was recognised as a problem – poverty was part of the natural order of things – and all the emphasis was concentrated on drains. While the Royal Commissions on sewage policy succeeded one another with monotonous regularity, the treatment of the impoverished sick was dominated by the simple Poor Law [1834 Poor Law Act] maxim that "people must not be encouraged to be ill by the knowledge that they could be treated free at the expense of the state". To most, poverty, or the unequal distribution of wealth, was quite natural in an age when every man was taught to promote his own self-interest. The poor were part of the landscape. The phrase 'the labouring poor', so beloved of official reports in those days, is rich in social implications (Simon, 1890). Equally expressive was Young's tranquil observation, as of one enunciating a commonplace, that "everyone but an idiot knows that the lower classes must be kept poor or they will never be industrious". In such an age when, under the leadership of the new class of self-centred, self-confident, God-fearing and money-worshipping entrepreneurs, Britain was becoming the workshop of the world, it was not perhaps unnatural that to many the provision of drains conflicted with the principle of self-seeking. "The beneficient private war", to quote Sir Henry Maine, "which makes one man strive to climb on the shoulders of another and remain there" was hardly conducive to equality in the realm of clean water, drains, water-closets and other sanitary necessities. It is necessary to read the lives of men like Farr, Chadwick and Simon to understand how long and bitter was the battle for drains. Just as the mass of the working class suffered from an unequal distribution of wealth, so, until the turn of the 20th century, did they have to endure pail closets, privy middens and ash-pits.

It was not until the rich were forced to the conclusion that sanitation was economic sense and would save them, the rich, from contracting much infectious disease (witness the influence of the cholera epidemics) that water-closets and clean water were provided. Thus the winning of the battle for drains and the effective control over sanitary urbanisation were the chief factors in the lowering of infant mortality to one third of its former level. It has now been abundantly proved that mortality need not increase at all with the density of the population so long as other influences are not active at the same time. This is notably true so far as infant mortality is concerned and it may be said that, in most advanced countries, infants have now little to suffer from the struggle for adaptation to an urban mode of life. Stocks (1934), for instance, has shown that up to middle life the importance of crowding per room as a factor in mortality would appear to be almost double that of density per acre. He arrived at this conclusion by measuring the change in mortality according to the two types of density, one factor being held constant in each case. To distinguish between the two factors of density is important; the one (per acre) is an index of success or failure in combating insanitary evils such as water-borne infection, the other (per household) is a measure of the effects of overcrowding per se (including the transmission of disease by droplet infection) and/or other social factors with which overcrowding is inextricably related.

Improved sanitation having amputated the 19th century peak in infant mortality, there now became apparent the contours of a new peak largely formed on the dynamics of poverty. It was not until 1911, however, that the first official attempt was made to measure the different rates of mortality in different social classes; the earliest investigation of occupational mortality among adult males relates to 1851. Before this, a few unofficial investigations had been made, mainly actuarial in purpose, to find out the expectation of life of different social groups. Such work, however, had to be done with the most inadequate statistics and the results were not very reliable. As early as 1815, Milne concluded, "There can ... be no doubt but that the mortality is greater among the higher than the middle classes of society".

The Commissioners for Inquiry into the State of Large Towns and Populous Districts (1844) were told that a 'gentleman' in London lived on average twice as long as a 'labourer', while the corresponding figures for Leeds were 44 and 19 years, and for Liverpool 35 and 15. In York City, during the years 1839-41, the average age at death for 'gentry and professional persons and their families' was 48.6; for 'tradesmen and their families' 30.8; and for 'labourers and their families' 23.8.

Bailey and Day (1861) found that the mean duration of life at birth in peerage families was greater than that for the general population, greater indeed than for Farr's 'Healthy Districts' of England and Wales. The difference was apparently largely due to lower death rates during childhood. This class difference was again confirmed when Ansell (1874) found that the expectation of life at birth in the upper and professional classes was 53 years, indicating an advantage of about 10 years over the expectation for the general population.

Thus it would seem that, even in those early days, wealth triumphed over the handicap of inferior drains. To enquirers at that time, such as Farr and Chadwick, concerned with the riddle of varying death rates, nothing was known of the functions of nutrition, but to the more far-sighted it seemed that some important factor, other than drains, was at work.

Twenty-two years were to pass before Sir Francis Galton (1883) published his conclusions as to the parts played by heredity and environment in determining human qualities. The study of heredity preceded nutritional research, for it was not until 1897 that Eijkman, concerned with the outbreaks of beri-beri in the jails of the Dutch East Indies, carried out his classical experiments with chickens and decided that some important factor was missing from the polished rice the native prisoners were receiving. Since these studies, there has accumulated a vast amount of evidence on the relative influence of nature and nurture, and the period following the First World War produced results which emphasised the great importance of the quality of nutrition.

In a few parts of the world [in 1943], infant mortality has been reduced to below 20 deaths per 1,000 live births. Dublin (1928) suggested that a rate of 30 was feasible. One might suggest that there are no medical, social or economic reasons why advanced communities should not achieve a rate of 15 [the rate in 2000 was 5.6 per 1,000]. The saving of 100,000 lives of English infants every four years would be no small achievement.

It would be as well therefore if those who have visions of a democratic approach to the problems of population realise in time that these cannot adequately be solved without reference to handicaps and inequalities in infancy. They should also appreciate that these handicaps and inequalities are not isolated phenomena but an integral part of an unequal society, pervading and invading all human activities from the cradle to the grave. If the beginning be sordid, can life be full, abundant and generous?

The position of women

In a period when the possibilities of social progress and the practicability of applied social science are being questioned, it is a source of satisfaction to recall some of the achievements of the Women's Suffrage Movement in Britain. The development of the personal, legal and political liberties of half the population of the country within the span of less than eighty years stands as one of the supreme examples of consciously directed social change.

There have been numerous historical and biographical studies of the Movement and of Millicent Fawcett and its other leaders. Many of these studies have analysed the political, legal and vocational consequences, though largely within a middle-class ethos. Few have been concerned with the working-class woman and particularly with the conditions of life of the working-class mother (McGregor, 1955). Yet, during the 20th century, far-reaching changes, social, economic and technological, affected her status and role as a wife and mother, as a home-maker, as a contributor to the economy of the family, and in a variety of situations in the cycle of married life. Social historians and sociologists have been curiously neglectful of such studies and have allowed the subject of the position of women in modern society to be dominated by the psychologist, the psychiatrist and the sexologist.

* * * * *

The purpose of this chapter is twofold: first, to draw together some of the vital statistics of birth, marriage and death for the light they shed on the changes that have taken place since the beginning of the 20th century in the social position of women; and secondly, to suggest that the accumulated effect of these changes now presents the makers of social policy with some new and fundamental problems.

The fall in the birth rate in Western societies is one of the dominating biological facts of the 20th century. Commenting on the British statistics, the 1949 Report of the Royal Commission on Population noted the rapidity of the decline in family size after 1900. Viewed within the context of the long period of industrial change since the 17th century, it is the rapidity of this fall which is as remarkable as the extent of the fall since 1900. By and large, these trends have been shaped by changes in family building habits of the working-classes in the 20th century. The first phase of declining family size among non-manual workers, and particularly middle and upper-middle class groups, took place earlier. The absolute difference in the average size of completed families of non-manual and manual workers, which was 1.15 for 1900–09 marriages, fell by one-third to 0.76 for 1925–29 marriages. From a mid-Victorian family size of six or more, the average size of completed working-class families of marriages contracted in 1925–29 had fallen to just under 2.5. For all classes, the proportion of couples having seven or more children during the second half of the 19th century was 43%; for marriages contracted in 1925 this proportion had fallen to 2% (1949 Report; Glass and Grebenick, 1954). It would probably be true to say that at the end of the 19th century about half of all working-class wives over the age of 40 had borne between seven and fifteen children.

I mention these more recent data simply to point the contrast between 1956 and fifty years earlier. This contrast, remarkable as it is in average family size, is even more so in terms of the number of pregnancies; that is, when allowance is made for the losses from stillbirths, miscarriages and deaths in infancy experienced at the beginning of the 20th century.

When this is done, it would seem that the typical working-class mother of the 1890s, married in her teens or early twenties and experiencing ten pregnancies, spent about fifteen years in a state of pregnancy and in nursing a child for the first year of its life. She was tied, for this period of time, to the wheel of childbearing. In the 1950s, for the typical mother, the time so spent would be about four years. A reduction of such magnitude in only two generations in the time devoted to childbearing represents nothing less than a revolutionary enlargement of freedom for women brought about by the power to control their own fertility.

This private power, what Bernard Shaw once described as "the ultimate freedom", can hardly have been exercised without the consent, if not the approval, of the husband. The amount and rapidity of the change together support such a proposition. We are thus led to interpret this development as a desired change within the working-class family rather than as a revolt by women against the authority of men on the analogy of the campaign for political emancipation.

* * * * *

What do these changes signify in terms of 'the forward view', namely the vision that mothers now have and have had about their functions in the family and in the wider society?

According to the Registrar-General (1914, Part I, English Life Table No 7 for 1901–10) the expectation of life of a woman aged 20 was 46 years. Approximately one third of this life expectancy was to be devoted to the physiological and emotional experiences of childbearing and maternal care in infancy. In the early 1950s, the expectation of life of a woman aged 20 is 55 years (Registrar-General, September 1956, Appendix B). Of this longer expectation, only about

7% of the years to be lived will be concerned with childbearing and maternal care in infancy.

That the children of the large working-class families of 1900 helped to bring each other up must have been true; no single-handed mother of seven could have hoped to give to each child the standard of care, the quantity of time, the diffusion and concentration of thought that many children receive today. In this context, it is difficult to understand what is meant by those who generalise about the 'lost' functions of parents in the rearing of children. Certainly the children themselves, and especially girls, have lost some of these functions. Despite the help that the mother had from older children, she could not expect to finish with the affairs of child care until she was in the middle-fifties; only then would the youngest child have left school. By that time too her practical help and advice would be increasingly in demand as she presided over, as the embodiment of maternal wisdom, a growing number of grandchildren. In other words, by the time the full cycle of child care had run its course, the mother had only a few more years to live, an analogous situation to the biological sequence for many species in the animal world. The typical working-class mother in the industrial towns in 1900 could expect, if she survived to 55, to live not much more than another twelve years by the time she reached the comparative ease, the reproductive grazing field, of the middle fifties (Registrar-General, 1914, Parts I and II).

The situation of the 1950s is remarkably different. Even though we have extended the number of years that a child spends at school and added to the psychological and social responsibilities of motherhood by raising the cultural norms of child upbringing, most mothers have largely concluded their maternal role by the age of 40. At this age, a woman can expect to live another 36 years (Registrar-General, 1956, Appendix B) and, if we accept the verdict of the sociological fundamentalists Parsons and Bales, the anthropologist Margaret Mead and others, she has also been largely divested of her role as a grandmother by the professional experts in child care. Although this may be true of middle-class white populations in the United States, there are no systematic studies in Britain to support such a conclusion. On the contrary, Young and Willmott (1957) have shown that in Bethnal Green, London, mothers rarely cease to play an important role in the lives of their children and grandchildren.

What these changes mean is that by the time the typical mother has virtually completed the cycle of motherhood, she still has practically half her total life expectancy to live. Should she have only had boys, instead of girls or children of both sexes, the necessary adjustments in outlook may seem more obvious and the diminution in role sharper. This is a new situation for the generality of women in most societies of which we have any reliable records. It presents an industrialised society, based on an extensive division of labour, on the early acquisition of occupational skills, on the personal achievement of status through educational and other channels which steadily narrow after the first ten years of adult life, with a host of new social problems. They are problems in the sense that these can be situations in which uncertainty and conflict develop over the individual's future role. What is socially approved behaviour is to recognise the need of the young adolescent for a growing measure of independence. Yet to relinquish the reins of motherhood is no longer, as it was in 1900, a seemingly natural process of life closing in; of adjusting to the disabilities and tiredness of a long cycle of childbearing. Many mothers of today are not worn out by their forties, nor may it be supposed that they are any more psychologically prepared to become more dependent on their husbands. For that is what the adjustment could spell to some wives as they consciously relinquish the independence-giving and emotionally expressive maternal role. What was in the past an almost unconscious process is now becoming a conscious one. This is to be expected as a natural corollary to the development of self-consciousness, as part of the intellectualisation of childrearing, in the parental role (Parsons and Bales, 1956).

These questions are being formed by the conjunction and combination of many forces, including changes in family building habits and changes in the rates of dying since the 19th century.

It is common knowledge that there have been great reductions in mortality since 1900, particularly in infancy and childhood where rates of dying have fallen by approximately 75%. What is less well known is that death rates among women have been declining faster than among men. A comparison of the standardised mortality rates (which allow for differences in the age structure of the male and female populations) shows that the rate among men in 1955 exceeds that for women by about 50% (Registrar-General, 1955, Part I, Table 3). This excess has accumulated steadily throughout the 20th century. If rates of mortality are any guide to the general level of health of a population then these trends suggest that, since 1900, the health of women has improved, and is still improving, at a considerable faster rate than that of men [see Table 1].

The relative gains, as measured by death rates, of women over men apply to all age groups, but the really striking changes have taken place over the age of forty-five [Table 1]. This is shown by the

Table I

Age	25-34 %	35-44 %	45-54 %	55-64 %	65-74 %	75-84 %	85+ %
1896-1900	15	22	29	24	17	13	9
1951-55	28	28	62	91	65	37	20

percentage male excess at 10-year age groups for two periods (Registrar-General, 1955, Part I, Table 4).

Easily the greatest gains have been registered by women aged 45 to 74. There is no justification here for a lower pensionable age for women. Their expectation of life at 60 exceeds that for men by nearly four years, which means that they are covered for national retirement pensions for about nine years longer than are men. Thus, with a pension running for nineteen years from 60 (Registrar-General, 1954, Part III, Table 30), and if a family allowance and an income tax child allowance runs to age 18, there are 37 years of 'dependency' recognised by the state in social policy.

A large part of these gains to mortality by women has been achieved since 1931. To quote the Government Actuary (Registrar-General 1951, Life Tables, p 11), in reporting on mortality changes between the censuses of 1931 and 1951: "At ages over forty, however, the experience of the two sexes has diverged. For women, there has been a continued substantial lightening of mortality, extending to age eighty and beyond. For men, on the other hand, the improvement has been much less; at age sixty the 1951 rate is almost the same as that of twenty years earlier. At that age the women's rate of mortality in 1950-52 was about 45 per cent less than that forty years before, while the men's rate was only 22 per cent less".

These conclusions are more pronounced in the case of married women (and to a somewhat less extent for widows) for all ages up to 70, in contrast with the experience of single women. Not only do married women show much lower rates, but the gains they have made since 1930-32 are more substantial. Even single women show much lower rates than married men after the middle-forties.

Working-class women still show, however, substantially higher rates of mortality than the national average for all women. The expectation of life at age 45 for Glasgow women was four years lower that that for London women of the same age in 1950-52 (Registrar-General, 1951, Life Tables, Table V4; Registrar-General for Scotland, Life Tables, Appendix II, Table 3). But, even so, all the declines registered by women (in contrast with the trends for men) can only be summed up, to use the words of the Registrar-General for Scotland, "as sensational" (1950-52, p 12).

This phenomenon is not peculiar to Britain. The relative gains by women over men since 1900 appear to be even more sensational in the United States, a fact that has been explained by J.C. Maloney (1950, p 51) in these words: "In this patriarchal American culture males preserve their masculinity complex. Striving to live up to the expectations of maleness, men blow out their coronaries and cerebral arteries, making wealthy widows out of their wives. Men die five years before women in this country and women possess 83 per cent of the wealth".

Whatever the reasons may be for the relative, if not the absolute, worsening in mortality rates for men (Morris, 1957), such comments do not explain the dramatic improvements shown by the rates for women. So far as Britain is concerned, a reasonable hypothesis would be that these improvements are in large part attributable to the decline in the size of the family since 1900. This receives support from the remarkable change, after 1930–32, in the relationship between the mortality of single women and that of married women. In Scotland, for instance, while the rates of single women in youth and early middle age fell by something like 25% between 1930–32 (when they were lower than those for married women) and 1950–52, the rates for married women in the same age range fell by about 60% by 1950–52. This fall put the rates for single women about 60% in excess up to the age of 42 (Registrar-General for Scotland, 1950–52, p 12).

Among married women, not only have the hazards of childbirth and the frequency of confinements been greatly diminished, but the number and proportion of mothers worn out by excessive childbearing and dying prematurely from such diseases as tuberculosis, pneumonia and so forth are but a fraction of what they were in 1900. Above all, the decline in the size of the family has meant, in terms of family economics, a rise in the standard of living of women. This has probably been of more importance than any change since 1900 in real earnings by manual workers. Nor would it be hard to argue that this factor was far more influential up to the Second World War than any additional benefits derived from the expansion of the social services and improvements in medical care.

Yet, when one turns to the history of the Women's Suffrage Movement in Britain, it is odd to find that little attention was given to the problem of continuous childbearing with all its attendant evils of chronic ill health and premature ageing. The social freedom of working–class women to control their own fertility was not an issue of any importance. Nevertheless, the Victorian myth about the biological inferiority of women was still powerful. For example, the manifesto of 1889, signed by Beatrice Webb, Mrs Humphrey Ward and others, protesting against Women's Suffrage, observed: "We believe that the emancipating process has now reached the limits fixed by the physical constitution of women" (Strachey, 1928, p 285). Such an argument could hardly be brought forward today by those who oppose the principle of equal pay for women.

Before I turn to the subject of marriage, I would make one general point about the long-term consequences of these trends in mortality and fertility. At the beginning of the 20th century, when the total population of England and Wales was 32.5 million, there were 661,000 men aged over 65 and 1.3 million women aged over 60, a total of 2 million or 6% of the population. In 1956, there are 2 million men aged over 65 and 4.4 million women aged over 60, a total of 6.4 million people of pensionable ages, or 14% of the population. According to the Registrar-General's projections (1955, Appendix B) we are likely to have by 1975, approximately 750,000 more men aged over 65 but 1.25 million more women aged over 60. About 18% of the population will then be of pensionable ages. While this proportion is not abnormally high for a more or less stable population, it does contain a preponderance of women. The problem of social policies for old age today and tomorrow is thus mainly a problem of elderly women, a fact that is generally overlooked by those who consider that private occupational pension schemes for men will answer all the questions of income maintenance in old age.

* * * * *

When the Women's Movement was in full flood, most thoughtful observers believed that to release women from the domination of men, exercised through what John Stuart Mill (1869, p 81) called "the foul means of marriage", would lead to fewer marriages in the future. No student of society would have had the temerity at that time to forecast the remarkable changes which the institution of marriage has undergone since those days. On the subjective plane, it can be said with some degree of truth that the mutual relationships of husband and wife are very different from the picture of married life which emerges from the literature and social investigations of Edwardian times. The extent to which fertility has come under control by married couples is evidence of this. New patterns in the psychological management of married life have been slowly evolving; the idea of companionship in marriage is being substituted for the more sharply defined roles and codes of behaviour set by the Victorian patriarchal system with, to quote Virginia Woolf (1938, p 135) "its nullity, its immorality, its hypocrisy, its servility".

It seems that we are at some, as yet undefinable, stage in the process of 'democratising' marriage. It follows therefore that, as the size of the family has declined, we have gradually come to expect more and more of our marriages. "We are more inclined now than we used to be to demand a capacity for response between the partners, to look for intellectual and temperamental compatibility, as well as purely material welfare, in addition to the ordinary social and parental satisfactions. The more we demand in these respects, the more frequently, perhaps, we shall have to count our failures, but also the higher may be our level of achievement" (Slater and Woodside, 1951, p 126). Perhaps that is why the 1951-55 Royal Commission on Marriage and Divorce saw that its primary task was to seek out "ways and means of strengthening the resolution of husband and wife to realise the ideal of a partnership for life".

No doubt the political and legal emancipation of women has

contributed to these changes in what is expected from marriage. A more socially equal relationship was foreseen by the leaders of the Women's Movement, but what they could hardly have envisaged is the rise in the popularity of marriage from about 1911. Here we turn from the debatable field of value judgements about the quality of married life to the statistics of marriage, distinguishing between the amount of marriage taking place in a given population and the age at marriage.

As to the first, it is clear that for about forty years before 1911 marriage rates among women were declining. Somewhere around this time a change occurred; the amount of marriage began to increase. An increase of nearly one third between 1911 and 1954 in the proportion of women aged 20 to 40 married represents, as the Registrar-General has said (1910-15,Vol II), "a truly remarkable rise". Never before, in the history of English vital statistics, has there been such a high proportion of married women in the female population under the age of 40 and, even more so, under the age of 30. From 1911 the proportion at age 15 to 19 has risen nearly fourfold; at age 20 to 24 it has more than doubled. Such figures as these hardly support the conclusion of the 1951-55 Royal Commission on Marriage and Divorce that "matrimony is not so secure as it was fifty years ago".

More marriage has been accompanied by a great increase in the years of married life experienced by married couples. Declining death rates have not only lengthened marriage and, with earlier childbearing, very substantially lengthened the years of married life during which there are no children to be cared for, but they have brought about a striking fall in the proportion of marriages broken by widowhood and widowerhood under the age of 60. It is highly probable that the proportion of broken marriages under the age of 60, marriages broken by death, desertion and divorce, is in total, smaller in 1950 than at any time in the 20th century. The greater the amount of marriage, the greater will be the chances that men and women, with impaired health and handicaps, physical and psychological, and unstable personalities will be exposed to the hazards of married life and childrearing. In other words, a wider range of personality and character variation may now be drawn into the ambit of marriage and parenthood. Formerly, this segment of the population (some part of which could be distinguishable by the incidence of acquired and inherited physical handicaps) might not have entered matrimony. No interpretation of divorce statistics or of the facts about 'broken homes' can be satisfactory unless account is taken of this factor and of the strikingly high rates of remarriage of divorced men and women. By 1955 this was in the region of three-quarters with about 7% of marriages terminated by divorce (Registrar-General, 1955, Part III, pp 2-3).

Married life has been lengthened not only by declining mortality but by earlier marriage. It is a fact of the greatest social importance that in the first half of the 20th century, a trend towards more youthful marriage was in progress. In 1911 24% of all girls aged 20 to 24 were married; by 1954 this proportion had risen to 52%. As a result of this trend and rising marriage rates, the proportion of women still single at the age of 35 falls to only about 13%. There are fewer unmarried women aged 15 to 35 in the country than at any time since 1881 when the total population was only 60% of its 1956 size. Yet "the last generation in this country to reproduce itself completely was born as long ago as 1876 or thereabouts" (Registrar-General, 1946-50, p 83).

What broadly emerges from this incursion into the statistics of marriage is a remarkable increase in the amount of marriage in the community; more and more youthful marriage, especially among women; a concentration of family building habits in the earlier years of married life; and a substantial extension in the years of exposure to the strains and stresses of married life. All these changes have taken place during a period of increasing emancipation for women. Paradoxically, therefore, fewer social and legal restraints and more equality and freedom for women have been accompanied by an increase in the popularity of the marriage institution.

* * * * *

To survey the changed position of women in English society from the standpoint of the vital statistics of birth, marriage and death raises a great many questions. It is possible to discern from the bare facts the outlines of new social problems which, as yet, we have hardly begun to contemplate, while other problems, long recognised, have now to be seen in a different frame of reference: the problem, for instance, of the dual roles of women in modern society; of the apparent conflict between motherhood and wage-earning which now has to be viewed in relation to the earlier and much more compressed span of life during which the responsibilities of motherhood are most intense. With an expectation of another thirty-five to forty years of life at the age of 40, with the responsibilities of child upbringing nearly fulfilled, with so many more alternative ways of spending money, with new opportunities and outlets in the field of leisure, the question of the rights of women to an emotionally satisfying and independent life appears in a new guise.

Yet practically all forms of educational and vocational training, along with entry to many pensionable occupations, are shut to the woman who has reached the age of 40. Motherhood and date of birth disqualify her, while the unthinking and unknowing may condemn her in moralising terms for seeking work outside the home. Few subjects are more surrounded with prejudice and moral platitude than this; an approach which perhaps deepens the conflict for the women themselves about their roles as mothers, wives and wage-earners.

More and more middle-aged mothers are seeking to find some solution to the social, economic and psychological problems which face them or may do so in the future. Dimly they may be perceiving the outline of these problems in the years ahead where the days of child upbringing are over.

Between 1946 and May 1955 the number of married women in either full or part-time gainful employment rose by 2.25 million to 3.75 million or 48% of all women at work (*The Economist*, 14 July 1956, p 131). The biggest source of recruitment has been married women over thirty years of age (*Ministry of Labour Gazette*, June 1954). The most important group, relatively and absolutely, are those aged 40 to 50. There are, at the beginning of the 1950s, over one million married women of these ages at work, or one in three of all married women in this group (*Ministry of Labour Gazette*, August 1952). Of all married women under the age of 50 at work in 1951 at least one fifth had children at school age.

Making allowance for seasonal and other work changes, it is probable that the lives of about four million families in Britain in the mid-1950s are affected by the paid employment of the wife or mother outside the home. This development has no doubt contributed substantially to the standard of living of a large proportion of working-class families, as it has to that of the nation as a whole. Mothers and wives are likely to be affected first by any rise in unemployment.

In the field of employment opportunities, as in so many other fields, new issues for social policy are taking shape as a consequence of these changes in the position of women in society. The problems for state policy which the Woman's Movement of 1900 brought to the fore were largely political; those raised by the women's movements of today are largely social.

The 'welfare state'

Commentary: Tania Burchardt

I t is perhaps difficult for contemporary readers to appreciate that at the time of Titmuss's earliest writings, the term 'welfare state' was not in common parlance, social policy did not exist as an academic subject, and the idea of using fiscal instruments for social ends was anathema to most politicians and commentators. The concerns Titmuss explores in the four extracts which form this part of the book reflect the newness of 'the welfare state' as a concept: scoping and defining what constitutes a welfare state, addressing arguments for and against state control of welfare provision, and puzzling over its rapid development in Britain. There is a refreshing urgency and immediacy about the arguments; although some would not be out of place in the debates of today, it is important to bear in mind that in many cases they found their first expression in Titmuss's lectures and articles.

* * * * *

In 'The welfare state: Images and realities', originally presented at the University of California in 1962, Titmuss traces the history of the term 'welfare state', noting that it came into common use in Britain only in the 1950s – several years *after* the Beveridge report, the foundation of the National Health Service (NHS) and the passing of the National Assistance Act. The confusion over its meaning was such that Titmuss avoids it where possible, preferring to use the term 'social services'. In the United States, 'welfare state' was a term of abuse; former President Hoover described it in 1949 as "a disguise for the totalitarian state". This difference in meaning and emphasis can be seen reflected in the use of language today: 'welfare' in the US refers to social assistance and carries connotations of dependency, while the 'welfare state' in Britain encompasses universal services with much higher degrees of public support, such as the NHS. Thus the main American parties competed at the polls in 2000 on the basis of who would cut more through welfare reform, while in Britain the competition the following year focused on who could maintain high levels of spending on health and education (albeit, for the Conservative and Labour parties, without raising taxes).

Titmuss identifies two kinds of meaning of 'the welfare state' in 1960s Britain. One differentiates it from other kinds of state (communist, pre-industrial), while the other refers to a state within a state – that part of government activity which is concerned with promoting the welfare of citizens. The comparative approach to definition gets short shrift from Titmuss: "No Western democracy ... is today publicly committed to an official policy of more unemployment, less education, no social security provisions for the needy and no tax deductions for the needs of dependants", hence all the countries of the non-communist developed world could be categorised as welfare states. Amalgamation into a single category is unhelpful; the particular causes of social problems in each country, and the policy responses to them, need to be investigated individually. Titmuss contributed to this goal through his in-depth studies of Mauritius (Titmuss et al, 1961) and of Tanganyika (Abel-Smith et al, 1964), and the development of his own typology of welfare provision. The urge to learn through international comparisons and, in particular, to classify states according to their welfare provision, has by no means faded away (as discussed further in Part 3 of this book).

The second approach to defining the welfare state addresses questions of scope. Titmuss emphasises the impossibility of considering social welfare in isolation from economic policy. For Beveridge, full employment was a precondition of a successful social security system. Similarly, for Titmuss, management of the economy, including levels and regional distribution of employment, was an essential part of the context in which social welfare operates. Economic policy might have goals other than the promotion of social welfare, but its impact fundamentally defined the task with which social policy was charged. This point, though apparently uncontroversial, has frequently been overlooked in subsequent analysis of the functioning of welfare systems. The now widely-accepted delineation of the welfare state as consisting of education, health, social security, housing and social services – outlined by Titmuss in 'The welfare state: Images and realities' – has focused attention on the strategy and delivery of these services, at the cost of obscuring the significance of the wider economic context. There are of course notable exceptions (for example, Glennerster and Hills, 1998), but the fact that these authors are obliged to rehearse the argument in detail indicates that it has not been generally acknowledged.

* * * * *

Having emphasised the folly of considering welfare services in isolation, Titmuss goes on to show that, even within the five core areas of welfare provision, analytical attention is generally focused too narrowly on state cash benefits and state-provided services. He argues that fiscal welfare (through tax reliefs and allowances) and occupational welfare (benefits in cash and in kind through employers) should take their place alongside direct state provision in the 'divisions of welfare'; all represent collective interventions to meet individual need. The definition of 'welfare policy' should be based on objectives and outcomes, not on the mechanisms employed to achieve them. This thesis found its fullest expression in 'The social division of welfare', originally a lecture given in honour of Eleanor Rathbone, the champion of family allowances, at the University of Birmingham in 1955. It was one of the most influential aspects of Titmuss's work on welfare, in both academic and policy circles.

An important implication of bringing fiscal and occupational welfare within the scope of 'welfare', is the effect on the analysis of the distribution of contributions and benefits across social classes. This is explored in more detail in Part 3, but in this chapter Titmuss argues that the middle classes are the primary beneficiaries of fiscal and occupational welfare. He shows that the effect of child tax allowances is to give three times as much to a high-earner with two children than to a low earner in similar circumstances. Moreover the total tax expenditure on dependants' allowances had, by 1955, grown to over half the total Exchequer expenditure on direct cash benefits. Adding to this the wide range of benefits provided by employers (including occupational pensions, which themselves attract tax relief), it becomes clear that the fiscal and occupational divisions of welfare could no longer be regarded as insignificant.

Policy interest in the divisions of welfare has been enduring. Its most immediate impact was in the Labour Party. Taxation had been seen as a tool of redistribution by means of allowing greater expenditure on public services, but in the early part of the 1960s, the realisation that taxation could also be used – for better or worse – directly to affect income inequality began to influence Labour Party policy (Whiting, 2000). The role of the tax system and of employers in meeting individual need is still very much a live issue today. Labour's introduction of 'stakeholder pensions' is an attempt to spread one aspect of occupational welfare to lower-paid workers, while combining private sector management, tax finance and individual contributions. Recent employment legislation, largely via the European Union, has strengthened provision for maternity, paternity and parental leave, extended rights to part-time workers and established minimum holiday entitlements. Such regulation would certainly fall within Titmuss's definition of welfare as social provision to meet individual need. Perhaps most significant is the rapid expansion at the turn of this century in the use of tax credits as an alternative way of delivering social security benefits to the low paid. In this respect, Titmuss's concerns about the regressivity of fiscal welfare have come full circle: once the potential of tax allowances and reliefs to affect the distribution of income has been realised, they can be targeted to benefit the better-off (as was the case with relief on mortgage interest and private medical insurance premiums) or the worse-off (as for Working Families' Tax Credit).

In academic circles, the focus which Titmuss adopted in 'The social division of welfare', namely, the financing of collective provision to meet individual need, has been broadened in two main ways. The first is a consideration not only of different ways in which welfare is financed, but also how it is provided. Thus, directly tax-financed services may be provided by voluntary or profit-making bodies – a route which became more prominent during the 1980s and acquired the name 'contracting out' (Papadakis and Taylor-Gooby, 1987). Alternatively, providers may remain in the public sector but be reorganised to respond to market-like incentives – the so-called quasi-market introduced to the National Health Service in 1991 (LeGrand and Bartlett, 1993).

The second development in the study of divisions of welfare is the addition to Titmuss's taxonomy of individual provision to meet individual need, whether in the form of direct purchase of services or private insurance. Thus the divisions of welfare can be drawn in many different ways (Burchardt et al, 1999): according to provision (state, occupational, private, voluntary sector, informal), finance (tax, employer contributions, individual purchase), or who makes the decisions about level and type of provision (state or individual – compulsory or voluntary. The three questions tackled by Titmuss have continued to be debated across this wider field: quantifying the contribution made by different divisions of welfare, identifying winners and losers, and arguments about which mechanism is the most appropriate solution. The ideological pendulum swung towards individualised provision in the Thatcher years (for example, Booth and Dickinson, 1997), but shifts in expenditure were relatively small (Burchardt, 1997). With the change in government in 1997, interest in changing the balance of finance from state to individual subsided, though debate around the use of private and non-profit organisations in the delivery of welfare intensified (IPPR, 2001).

* * * * *

Aside from addressing questions of definition and scope of the welfare state, the first two extracts in Part 2 also explore its raison d'être. Leaning on Durkheim, Titmuss argues that, as capitalism develops, specialisation of labour increases and individuals become more interdependent. The labour of others, and their participation in market exchange, is essential to produce and distribute the full range of goods and services any one individual needs. One consequence of this greater interdependency is collective recognition of, and response to, individual need: the range of situations in which social support is regarded as appropriate, and indeed necessary, expands. Retirement is created (Hannah, 1986); the period of education prior to labour market entry is extended; and unemployment, injury and illness are acknowledged as 'legitimate' states of dependency. The examples

Titmuss uses come from the first half of the 20th century, but the process has continued through the succeeding decades: the states of lone parenthood, disability and low pay have all come to be acknowledged and attracted specific social security provision and regulatory legislation (the 1991 Child Support Act, the 1995 Disability Discrimination Act and the introduction in 1999 of a national minimum wage, for example). A similar argument appears in Esping-Andersen's *The three worlds of welfare capitalism* (1990). The controversial decommodification index, on which the book's typology of welfare states rests, is a measure of the extent to which individuals are able to survive without selling their labour.

Titmuss argues that welfare provision can therefore be seen as a necessary corollary of economic development. Criticisms that welfare spending was absorbing too great a proportion of national wealth, or was over-burdening the middle classes, which were prevalent at the time he was writing, were thus misplaced. In 'The social division of welfare', Titmuss identifies four assumptions on which such arguments rest: (1) that the objectives of the 1942 Beveridge Report have been achieved, (2) that the aggregate effect of welfare provision has been a transfer of resources from rich to poor, (3) that it is possible to calculate the distribution of costs and benefits, and (4) that it is feasible to abstract welfare provision from the wider economic and social context.

As we have already seen, Titmuss rejects the second, third and fourth of these assumptions. He also queries the first, while acknowledging that in this respect, the complacency of the supporters of state welfare about what has been achieved has sometimes made them their own worst enemy. Titmuss marshalled a considerable body of evidence to show that several of Beveridge's giants were still at large. Poverty remained a problem, especially among the elderly whose National Insurance pensions were inadequate and who were reluctant to take up the stigmatising means-tested benefits as a top-up (a problem still with us today). The goal of equal opportunity through free education had not been achieved, despite the 1944 Education Act: the proportion of children going on to higher education was low by international standards, and they were drawn almost exclusively from the middle and upper classes. Moreover new social problems were continually emerging – the task set for welfare services is never static.

* * * * *

Among the social and economic forces shaping the functions of welfare, Titmuss singled out for particular attention the role of war. His meticulously researched account of social services during the Second World War, *Problems of social policy* (1950), formed one of the volumes of the official history of the war; the final chapter, 'Unfinished business', is reprinted here as Chapter Four. 'War and social policy' (originally delivered as a lecture at King's College London in 1955 and reprinted here as Chapter Three) takes a longer historical perspective, touching even on the progressive policies of the Ancient Greeks during the Persian invasion of 480 BC. In modern times, Titmuss outlines four stages in the relationship between waging war and the development of welfare provision. In the first stage, during the early and mid-19th century in Britain, the growing scale of war prompted concerns about population quantity. In the second stage, as the techniques of war became more demanding of soldiers both physically and psychologically, attention shifted from quantity to quality. More recruits were rejected as unfit or accepted only to be invalided out of active service in due course. This is an example of the creation of a previously unidentified state of dependency, as discussed in 'The social division of welfare', leading to a corresponding development of social services to meet the new need.

The Boer War (1899-1902) marks the beginning of the third stage, according to Titmuss's account. Here, concern about the fitness of fighting men is generalised to the whole population and, in particular, to the next generation of potential soldiers. Reports of physical deterioration among the working class, and of the widespread incidence of childhood disease and malnutrition, led more or less directly to the establishment of school medical and feeding services in 1906. Similar concerns and a further widening of the availability of general health services followed during and after the First World War.

The fourth stage is reached when direct participation in war is no longer restricted to soldiers but involves civilians in large numbers, as was the case during the Second World War. Social measures are then made available as of right to the whole population. This is the phase to which Titmuss devotes most attention. By the end of the war, government had greatly extended its responsibility for health and wellbeing of the population, for example, through provision of school meals, the National Milk Scheme, the Vitamin Welfare Scheme (all arising from national food policy), and the widening eligibility for, and generosity of, pensions. This was despite the chronic lack of manpower and resources – the vast majority of which were, of course, directed at the war effort itself. Moreover, the responsibility which the government had assumed was universal, not targeted on the poor. The spirit of provision was the antithesis of the stigma attached to social assistance which had been prevalent since the Poor Law and throughout the depression of the inter-war years. One result, and quite contrary to expectation, was that many important health indices showed a significant improvement after 1941, compared to pre-war figures, despite food shortages, bombing, lack of medical resources and the unquantifiable strains of living in a country at war.

Though Titmuss recognises that the absence of a severe winter, the largely fortuitous avoidance of any epidemic of illness, and a reduced birth rate all contributed to unexpectedly good health outcomes for the population, he argues that full employment, food subsidies, fair shares, price control and welfare schemes – all the result of government action – were a powerful combination of influences. Some developments took place, as in previous wars, as a result of the need for more men and for more work. Other policies were the result of the recognition of hitherto hidden needs, which were exposed by the additional demands of war life and by the mixing of classes during evacuation and sheltering from bombing raids. The universality of provision was seen as fitting the general mood of social solidarity; bombs did not respect distinctions of social class and, if dangers were to be shared, resources should also be. Civilians and soldiers alike needed to feel that Britain was a society worth fighting for. Finally, Titmuss observes that conflicts of interest and ideology, which had prevented or delayed the development of state welfare in the preceding years, were swept aside in a rare display of consensus. By the end of the war, the state had demonstrated itself to be an extremely effective manager of economic resources, giving reformers a precedent on which to base the argument for peacetime state-controlled social services.

Titmuss himself notes that later historians may be better placed to evaluate the long-term effects of the war on social policy and indeed they have not been slow to take up that challenge. The explanations offered for the development of state welfare in *Problems of social policy* have been questioned in two main ways. The first is whether the Second World War really did lay the foundations for a successful, modern welfare state. On the one hand, the development can be seen as a more gradual process. Harris (1992, 1997) suggests the genesis of the expansion in state welfare was embedded in the depression of the 1930s; the war was merely the catalyst for reforms to meet needs which had become increasingly apparent over the preceding decades. Others trace the welfare state heritage back even further and see the post-Beveridge welfare state as the culmination of a gradual process beginning perhaps with the enactment of political and civil rights in the middle ages (Marshall, 1950; Papadakis and Taylor-Gooby, 1987). On the other hand, there are those who accept that the post-war settlement did mark a turning point in the development of welfare, but argue that this was a wrong turn (Barnett, 1986). Summarising the debate, Welshman (1998) concludes that the evidence for change is stronger than the evidence for continuity and Glennerster (2000, p 2) finds that, although historical antecedents can be found (and it would be surprising if they could not), the period 1944 to 1948 does constitute "one of the most coherent and long-lasting institutional legacies in modern British history".

The second area of controversy prompted by Titmuss's account surrounds the existence or otherwise of a consensus on social policy at this time. Lowe (1990) identifies three separate questions: at what level of society, if any, was there a consensus; whether the subject of consensus was problems, objectives or remedies; and at what time consensus was at its height. Lowe argues that, during the war itself, there was at all levels a rejection of the fatalism that had predominated during the Depression, but agreement between political parties about objectives and mechanisms for reform was reached from differing ideological perspectives and hence was both fragile and narrow in scope. The civil service remained divided as ever along departmental lines, while the cooperation of organised labour was by no means to be taken for granted. For the population at large, the sense of social solidarity engendered by a common enemy and common hardship – the aspect emphasised by Titmuss - has to be set against heightened awareness of class differences brought about through uncommonly close contact and grievances that sacrifices were *not* falling evenly on all sections of society. Thus there was a broad public consensus that something should and could be done to make Britain a better society, but agreement on policy and implementation was short-lived.

* * * * *

As Titmuss observed, society is never static and the needs which welfare provision is required to meet are transformed as the economic and political environment changes. Nevertheless, there are some constants: the embeddedness of welfare provision in a specific economic and social context; the often-overlooked distributional effects of fiscal policy; and tensions between targeting and universalism. It is the fact that Titmuss identified and discussed so many of these that lends his work such enduring relevance.

The welfare state: Images and realities

The welfare state has evolved as a particular manifestation of Western democratic societies. The Communists disdain it, perhaps because Stalin regarded equality as a bourgeois prejudice. The earliest use of the term in Britain was apparently by William Temple, Archbishop of Canterbury, in *Citizen and churchman* (1941). He developed the notion of a welfare state in place of the conception of the 'power state'. This notion, he argued, held only if the state fulfilled its moral and spiritual functions in promoting human welfare. The concept, if not the phrase itself, is to be found in the wartime debate which led, on the international plane, to the Allied programme agreed upon between Mr Churchill and Mr Roosevelt off Newfoundland in August 1941 and in the Atlantic Charter and the Four Freedoms – freedom of speech, freedom of religion, freedom from want and freedom from fear.

On the national plane in Britain, the phrase came to mean the minimum programme of social reform and reconstruction agreed upon between the three political parties in the wartime Coalition government. The need for radical changes in British society had been recognised earlier by conservative opinion and was reflected in much of the new social legislation for education, medical care and social security developed in the later years of the Second World War and after the Labour government assumed power in 1945. But the phrase 'welfare state' did not become part of the everyday language of social policy until after it had appeared on the American political stage. It was used in 1949 by former President Hoover, who described it as "a disguise for the totalitarian state" and it figured prominently in the congressional campaign of 1950. The British then took it over and it formed one of the major issues around which the general election of 1951 was fought. This election saw the Conservative Party return to office for the longest period in the 20th century to date [1951-64].

The term has apparently come to mean all sorts of things. Some have seen the development of the welfare state in historical perspective as part of a broad, ascending road of social betterment for the working classes, beginning in the 19th century and achieving its goal in our time. This interpretation of change as a process of unilinear progression in collective benevolence for these classes led to the belief that, in the year 1948, the welfare state was finally established in Britain with the introduction of the NHS and other social services. To this body of principally left-wing opinion, 1948 represented the pinnacle of achievement, a state of political compromise to be defended for all time as part of the good society. To others, who also assumed its establishment as one of the facts of life, the welfare state was condemned for its harmful effects on the individual and society.

The critics of the welfare state have been as much at fault as its defenders in failing to define the concept and in confusing ends and means. The former have seen it as a major instrument of redistribution of wealth from rich to poor; as a means of impoverishing the professional and middle classes; as a denial of charity and cultural excellence; as the cause of social decadence among the working population; and as the responsible agent in undermining the virtues of thrift, individual effort and family stability. With qualifications and different shades of emphasis, these views were sincerely held and widely cultivated by many writers and leaders of opinion during the late 1940s and throughout the 1950s. They found expression in such influential books as *The ethics of redistribution* by De Jouvenel (1951) and *The English middle classes* by Lewis and Maude (1949). These were accompanied by a steady stream, at times almost a torrent, of critical pamphlets, articles and newspaper editorials written for a wide audience, from the man in the street to the economic specialist.

This movement of opinion in Britain after the Second World War had the result that, to many people, 'welfare state' became a term of abuse. In some senses, this change can be interpreted as a reaction to the hardships and levelling of the civilians' war; as a dash for unlicensed freedom at all costs after the rigours of nearly ten years of rationing and 'fair shares for all'. In other respects, these views rest on the premise that it is theoretically possible to abstract an undefined welfare, as a self-contained entity, from society as a going concern. The assumption is also made that the promise of social legislation has been translated into concrete fact.

* * * * *

Is the Britain of 1962 a 'welfare state'? The question, as far as it is a helpful one to categorise societies at all, can be answered only on a comparative basis and with the aid of clearly defined values and facts.

Attempts to assess the role of the welfare state in Britain and other countries have broadly adopted two different but associated approaches. One is the historical method, the other a contemporary analysis of government policies, services and expenditures. Gunnar Myrdal (1960, p 45), the eminent Swedish economist and political scientist, writes:

> In the last half-century, the State, in all the rich countries in the Western world, has become a democratic 'Welfare State,' with fairly explicit commitments to the broad goals of

economic development, full employment, equality of opportunity for the young, social security, and protected minimum standards as regards not only income, but nutrition, housing, health, and education for people of all regions and social groups.

If these broad criteria are adopted, it is arguable that economic prosperity and the enactment of universal political rights are the distinguishing marks of a 'welfare state'. Apart from Russia and other communistic countries, ruled out as dictatorships, the world thus divides into the relatively rich welfare states on the one hand, and the poor, underdeveloped countries on the other. According to this view, the prosperity of the democracies largely obliterates differences in political ideologies. Whether they know it or not and whether they like it or not, Democrats and Republicans, Conservatives, Socialists and Liberals in North America and Europe have become welfare-statists.

Like much of Toynbee's interpretation of history, this view is difficult to accept. The sweep is too broad and the view too long to form a basis for comparative judgments about contemporary societies. Of course, if one starts from the age of the Mercantilist or even with the beginning of the 19th century, all countries are now classifiable as welfare states. No Western democracy, whatever its political colour, is today publicly committed to an official policy of more unemployment, less education, no social security provisions for the needy and no tax deductions for the needs of dependents. Whether economic coordination is planning or planning is politely described as coordination, all governments are involved to some degree in the general management of the economy. The natural tendency for older generations to take the backward view and to contrast the economic role of government when they were young with its seemingly pervasive role today, inevitably contributes to that opinion which considers the welfare state an established fact. But the society of their youth, however rosily remembered in tranquillity, was a very different society with different problems and needs. For one thing, it had a much smaller proportion of non-workers aged 60 and over; for another, it did not have to spend a quarter or more of its national income on defence and road programmes; for a third, it was then thought less necessary to emphasise the role of people as consumers of goods and services in order to keep the economy on the move.

The broad historical assessment that isolates and takes account only of material indicators is not, we may conclude, a fruitful approach to the problem of definition. It is dangerous to chain history to contemporary slogans, particularly those that hide more than they proclaim. We have to particularise; we have to examine the causal factors at work in each society; we have to understand the social costs of change, which are continually creating new areas of dependency; and we have to recognise that the aims of welfare include the enlargement of personal freedom and the discovery and maintenance of more and more justice. The criteria of moral progress are to be found in the growing power of altruism over egoism and these are also embedded in the philosophy of welfare as it has developed in Britain since the 19th century.

I now consider the second approach to definition. Here we must specify those activities of government which are broadly accepted in Britain as falling within the concept of the welfare state. The general management or oversight of the economy is not usually thought of as one of its distinctive characteristics. In all Western countries the state intervenes, regulates and directs to a far larger extent than in the past. It does so for many public purposes and uses a variety of methods: budgetary, credit, fiscal and other controls for maintaining the balance and full working of the economy; the promotion of industrial and agricultural development through the use of subsidies to farmers and private enterprise for research, price support and other purposes; the regulation of the balance of overseas payments; defence, law and order; and the provision of an immense variety of public services, ranging from atomic energy development to sanitation, roads and public libraries.

The cost of the common and impersonal public services, which have to be provided collectively if they are to be provided at all, is now responsible for a large part of the public budget in most Western countries. Expenditure in this sector has grown greatly, much of it from the social costs of a more affluent society. Taxpayers little realise that the cost of the whole 'social apparatus of living' in the modern state is a far more important item in the budget than it used to be. In a sense, governmental outlay in this sector, like social welfare expenditures, is redistributive, but with different effects. The rich benefit more than the poor from state provision of a better ordered, more efficient, more civilised social environment. They know how to make better use of this environment for more dignified living. Some elements in this sector may be regarded as welfare-statism; others may not. The growth of the diseconomies of consumption on consumption, which often call for more welfare services, has increasingly blurred the distinction between public services and social welfare services. The car is an example of the consequences of technological change. Many more people have been injured in road accidents and their treatment and aftercare costs have been borne largely by a social welfare service. One of the reasons for the rise in the number of road accidents is the fact of growing urban congestion and the failure of road programmes to meet traffic demands, failure which is in part attributable to a phenomenal increase in land values in London and other cities. More demands for medical care thus result from the growth of the diseconomies or social costs of consumption.

The aim of securing full employment also accounts for an enlargement in the role of the state, but to take measures to avoid the social and economic evil of mass unemployment is not peculiar to Britain or necessarily a distinctive feature of the welfare state. Such measures are now accepted as a commitment of government in most advanced Western countries. A good deal turns, of course, on the rationale and character of government intervention in pursuing policies of full employment. They may be adopted for mainly social reasons, in the interests of economic growth, or for purposes of strengthening the defence of the country. Only in some senses can the aim of full employment be regarded as an integral part of welfare-statism.

We now have to examine the social services or social welfare, the generic name given to a variety of cash benefits and services provided for individuals and their families by public authorities, central and local. These services which are largely responsible for Britain being described as a 'welfare state', fall into four main categories (education, medical care, social security and housing) and a fifth, comprising a number of smaller services concerned with child care, juvenile delinquency, employment bureaux and financial grants to many voluntary bodies. Here I consider only the first three, which are the largest in public outlay.

Of these three, education from the junior school to the university is easily the most costly social service to taxpayers and ratepayers. Government expenditure on education more than doubled, in real terms, during the twenty years up to 1962, partly as a result of a rising birth rate and partly as a result of efforts and to raise standards to make up for the neglect of school-building during six years of war. Nevertheless, much of the promise of a new deal and equal opportunity for all children, written in the wartime 1944 Education Act, has not been fulfilled. In 1962, over 70% of all children in Britain leave school at the age of fifteen or less, and only 6% go to a university. The proportion of young people receiving any form of higher education is 9%. The comparable figures in Canada and the United States are around 20% and 30%.

In Britain, as in some quarters in the United States, public opinion is beginning to realise that our communities have been seriously under-spending on education for many years. Education, we are told, is facing a crisis. Demand for higher education in Britain is outrunning supply and it is probable that a smaller rather than a larger proportion of young people will be admitted to the universities in the future. In 1962, Britain spends about 4.5% of its gross national product on education, compared with a higher proportion in other European countries, about 3.6% in the United States and 5% in the

Soviet Union. There is little here to justify singling out Great Britain as a welfare state because of its investment in education. To meet even this bill, it is now being suggested among some sections of the Conservative Party that fees should be charged for elementary education. To others, who regard free education as a 'nation-building' investment for economic development, this would be considered a retrogressive step.

When similar comparisons are made between the social security systems of different Western countries, it also appears that British standards are below those for a number of other countries. Per capita expenditures for social security are less in Britain than in Sweden, West Germany, France and other European states. American benefits, as a proportion of previous earnings, are about the same as the British in respect to old age and survivors' and disability insurance, and for unemployment insurance in some states. For sickness, maternity and certain other risks, the British insurance scheme is more generous in the sense that practically all workers are covered. The benefits, however, are all flat-rate and, as a proportion of average industrial earnings, are not markedly higher than social security benefits paid before the Second World War. Old age pensions are less than 20% of earnings. Family allowances for second and subsequent children are also universal in Britain, but their value is very small, as few adjustments have been made to bring them into line with changes in the value of money since 1946. By contrast, children's allowances as a deduction from income tax and surtax are worth far more to families paying tax. The cost to the treasury of this form of benefit for taxpayers is much more than twice as large as the bill for family allowances for the whole population.

For those people whose needs are not met by social insurance schemes or fringe benefits from their employers, all Western countries have some type of public assistance. Compared with the unevenness and diversity of provision in the United States, the British system is uniform throughout the country. No relief is given, however, without full inquiry into means and there is still much public aversion to the stigma of the means test.

* * * * *

A report on the first nationwide budget survey for more than 25 years of the economic circumstances of old people in Britain was published by Cole (1962). The findings, relating to the years 1959-60, may be briefly summarised. Of all old people of retirement age, 21% received some help from National Assistance. For the great majority who were receiving the flat-rate state retirement pension (£4 a week for a married couple) approximately 26% were having this pension supplemented by National Assistance. But the survey also found that another 10% of all old people who were entitled to assistance did not apply because of ignorance, because of their dislike of the means test, or because they were determined to 'manage while they could'. Another 11% were barely on the wrong side of the eligibility line. In short, state benefits remain crucial for determining the standard of living of more than half the old people.

For the ten years to 1962, the policy of the government allowed the value of social insurance benefits to fall below its public assistance definition of 'subsistence'. The declared aim was to concentrate help on those whose need was greatest, by successively raising assistance rates after an inquiry into means. Another study (Lynes, 1962) examined the thesis that government policy gave those on National Assistance a share in "increasing national prosperity". This raises the difficult methodological problem of how one measures 'prosperity' and 'subsistence'. If, instead of using official price indices (not properly applicable to low-income groups), one takes changes in average disposable income per head, a different conclusion emerges. From 1948 to 1962, it appears that persons on National Assistance received a smaller share in rising national prosperity and that the gulf between their standard of living and the national average widened substantially.

While opinion naturally varies about the extent to which social security systems as a whole do, or should, help to relieve cases of hardship, the facts show that these schemes do not make the lower-income groups appreciably better off in relative terms. In Britain in 1962, about the same proportion of the national income (5-6%) is spent on social security payments as before the Second World War, despite a substantial increase in the number and proportion of old and widowed people. Developments and changes in the social services during the 1940s and 1950s have not abolished poverty in Britain. The numbers who may be considered, by any criteria, to be in need are undoubtedly smaller than during the depression years of the 1930s. Full employment and a remarkable rise in the paid employment of married women have been the two main causes of higher living standards. Nevertheless, it has been estimated that about 15% of the total population are living precariously close to the margins of poverty. Social security payments have kept them from destitution but, compared with the rising standards of the rest of the population in a much wealthier society, the difference in levels of living between this group and the average worker is larger than it used to be. If it is the task of each generation to define (or redefine) its concept of poverty, it cannot be said that the present system of social security in Britain has gone too far in the direction of giving the old, the sick, the unemployed, widows, war pensioners and other groups a proportionate share in the rising prosperity of the rest of the community.

No attempt to assess the role of social security in the modern state can leave out of account fringe benefits provided by virtue of one's employment. There have been remarkable developments in Britain in the provision of these benefits; by contrast, the directly administered state system has changed very little.

* * * * *

The value of these occupational welfare benefits rises very sharply with income after tax. Considered as a whole, these developments have chiefly affected the salaried classes (as distinct from those paid weekly or manual workers). Within these classes, the value and variety of welfare benefits provided tends to rise proportionately or more than proportionately, with salary, especially when account is taken of the value of benefits which are not subject to tax and death duties.

If these developments are indicative of the spread of the welfare state in Britain, then it has to be recognised that they are coming to represent a different version from the commonly accepted one. There are some who regard this trend toward a corporate form of neo-feudalism as inimical to freedom of movement. If employees change their job, their pension and other benefit rights are usually not transferable. During the four years 1957-60, over one million workers (or about one-third of those covered by such schemes) lost some or all of their pension expectations under occupational schemes carried by insurance companies. Most of these workers were in the lower-income groups. Nevertheless, all these schemes are approved by the state, tacitly or by legislation, and more than half the cost is met by the Treasury through the operation of tax deductions. This means, to take one instance, that the annual cost to the Treasury of employer-provided pension schemes exceeds its contribution to the state pension scheme.

As yet these trends in occupational welfare have not included medical care for employees, except for a very small group of highly paid executives who are helped with their private medical bills. The NHS is by far the most popular and widely accepted branch of social policy evolved in Britain during the twenty years to 1962. It is more comprehensive in scope and more universal in application than any other single section of welfare. To some people, the NHS and the welfare state have become interchangeable terms; to others, there is little doubt that this experiment in the organisation of medical care has been seen as a major part of the ideology of 'welfare-statism'.

When it was conceived by the wartime Coalition government as an extension of the existing Health Insurance Scheme (started by Lloyd George in 1913), the aims for the NHS were said to be "to divorce the care of health from questions of personal means or other factors irrelevant to it" (Titmuss, 1958, pp 70-3). This principle of free access to medical care services by all who wanted to use them – personal freedom for the patient, professional freedom for the doctor – was embodied in the Act which became effective in 1948. Although charges have since been imposed on various parts of the service –

chiefly dental, ophthalmic and drugs – this principle still holds for most of the services provided. In 1962, approximately 70% of the cost was met by the Treasury; 16% by a flat-rate tax on all workers and the remainder by payments by patients and local authorities.

Approximately 95% of the population use the NHS and the vast majority of doctors take part in it, either by capitation fees for each patient, fees for sessions in hospitals or clinics, fees for specific services like maternity care and dental treatment, or salaried employment.

When the NHS was introduced in 1948, a majority of the medical profession were strongly opposed, chiefly because of the question of pay. That they have now come to accept it is partly attributable to the fact that it has appreciably raised their standard of living. Another reason for its popularity is that it has given most doctors more professional freedom – to prescribe drugs, or order surgical and other treatment and to employ the ever increasing battery of diagnostic, therapeutic and ancillary aids in the care of the physically and mentally ill.

Despite the fact that the NHS is very largely a free service, there is little evidence that it has been abused by the vast majority of patients. Measured in terms of general practitioners' consultations and visits per patient per year, all the figures suggest that demand during the 1950s was, if anything, a little lower than before the NHS was established. Nor has it bankrupted the nation, as some observers predicted. The cost of medical care has risen more slowly in Britain than in the United States. In 1959-60 a lower proportion of the national income was spent on the NHS than ten years earlier. The proportion in 1962 is 4.1% of gross national product at factor cost which is lower than that in the United States (over 6% from private and public funds) and other countries.

The problem of how best to organise and distribute the benefits of scientific medicine in the modern age is an extraordinarily difficult and complex one for all Western societies. Essentially, it raises in many disguises the question of reconciling the liberties of patient and doctor with equity in the allocation of scarce medical resources. In the long history of organised medical care in Britain, the issue of liberty was uppermost in the mind of the medical profession when, before 1911, it pleaded for state intervention to release doctors from the bureaucratic controls of the then existing forms of private medical practice.

Here, as in other sectors of social welfare, the influence of history is paramount in working out contemporary moral objectives. Britain's class divisions, its early and deeply felt experience of industrial change, its failure to correct for great inequalities in the distribution of wealth, the impact of three wars in two generations and the defensive attitudes engendered by nearly twenty years of trade depression – all these elements had combined to produce, by 1960, a confused and contradictory pattern of state provision in the fields of medical care, social security and education.

* * * * *

The struggle for justice to counter the imposed inequalities and adversities of social, political and technological change in Britain has contributed in no small measure to the shaping of the confused pattern of today. And, like many of the 18th century philosophers before them, those who argued for justice placed equality at the very centre of things: equality of opportunity in education, equality of access to medical care, equality of treatment in the natural and artificial adversities of life. This was to give emphasis to the common-needs principle rather than to criteria based on productivity or performance. The social ethic was essentially democratic and altruistic; to recognise that 'no man is an island, entire of itself' was to pursue individual freedom.

This was the thought of yesterday. People are not moralised by history despite themselves. The challenge of the second half of the 20th century is to reinterpret the ethics of welfare in a more complex and wealthier society. This challenge is unlikely to be accepted if the democracies cling to a static conception of society embodied in the term 'welfare state'. The notion of a settled equilibrium is, as every student of history must affirm, simple nonsense.

Chapter Two

The social division of welfare: Some reflections on the search for equity

Some students of social policy see the development of the welfare state in historical perspective as part of a broad, ascending road of social betterment provided for the working classes since the 19th century and achieving its goal in our time. This interpretation of change as a process of unilinear progression in collective benevolence for these classes led to the belief that in the year 1948 the 'welfare state' was established. Since then, successive governments have busied themselves with the more effective operation of the various services, with extensions here and adjustments there and all parties, in and out of office, have claimed the maintenance of the welfare state as an article of faith.

On this view it could be supposed that, speaking generally, Britain is approaching the end of the road of social reform; the road down which Eleanor Rathbone and other reformers and rebels laboured with vision and effect. This would seem to be the principal implication of much public comment on the social services and one which has received endorsement in policy statements of the Conservative and Labour parties. Some of the more important writings on the subject since 1948, far from suggesting that social needs have been neglected, argue that the welfare state was 'established' too quickly and on too broad a scale. The consequences, it was argued, have been harmful to the economic health of the nation and its 'moral fibre'.

Against this background, compounded of uneasiness and complacency, criticism has mainly focused on the supposedly egalitarian aims or effects of the social services. It is said that the relief of poverty or the maintenance of a national minimum as an objective of social policy should not mean the pursuit of equality; "a fascinating and modern development" for the social services according to Hagenbuch (1953, p 5). The Beveridge 'revolution' did not, it is argued, imply an egalitarian approach to the solution of social problems. The error of welfare state policies since 1948 has been, according to this diagnosis, to confuse ends and means and to pursue egalitarian aims with the result that the 'burden' of redistribution from rich to poor has been pushed too far and is now excessive. Thus, the upper and middle classes have been impoverished, in part a consequence of providing benefits for those workers who do not really need them. "Why" ask Macleod and Powell (1952, p 5) "should any social service be provided *without* test of need?" Their conclusion, like that of Hagenbuch and other writers, is that there should be a closer relationship between what people pay in and what they take out. Social security should be based on 'more genuine' actuarial principles, while the ultimate objective for other social services should be 'self-liquidation' as more and more people are raised above a minimum standard of living to a position of freedom in which they may purchase whatever medical care, education, training and other services they require. The mass of the people would thus in time come to behave like, if they do not resemble, the middle classes (who are presumed to derive little benefit from the social services). Pursued to its logical conclusion then, the welfare state would eventually be transformed into the 'middle-class state'. Meanwhile, social legislation and its application should recognise much more clearly that (as Macleod and Powell put it) "the social services only exist for a portion of the population", namely, that portion which takes out more than it puts in.

These views were tersely summed up by *The Economist* (5 June 1954, p 783) when it affirmed, as a guiding principle for social policy, that "no one should live on the taxpayer unless he needs to". Already, "the social well-being of the nation had been endangered by the redistribution of wealth" (Conservative Political Centre, 1950) a phrase which, according to a variety of social theorists, embraced more deeply felt anxieties than a simple material concern about economic and fiscal trends. De Jouvenel (1951), for example, drew attention to the "sordid utilitarianism" of redistributionist social services; to a "precipitous decline" in voluntary, unrewarded services upon which culture and civilisation depend, and to a "tremendous growth" in the power of the state as a consequence of the rising cost of the social services. At the same time, Lewis and Maude (1949, 1952) painted a picture of a decaying, overworked and anxious middle class. Finally, we may note the specific counter-proposals of two other critics. Ffrangcon Roberts (1952) entered a vigorous plea for state medicine to return a business profit and for the benefits of the National Health Service to be reserved for economically productive workers. Colin Clark (1954), foreseeing a totalitarian threat in the continued existence of the social services, would 'denationalise' them and entrust some remnant of their functions to the churches, local friendly societies and voluntary organisations.

* * * * *

Whatever their validity in fact or theory, these views have had an important influence in shaping opinions about the future of the social services. They have helped to produce in the public eye something akin to a stereotype or image of an all-pervasive welfare state for the working classes. Such is the tyranny of stereotypes that this idea of a welfare society, born as a reaction against the social discrimination of the poor law may, paradoxically, widen rather than narrow class relationships. As Gerth and Mills (1954, pp 88-9) have pointed out, "if the upper classes monopolize the means of communication and fill the several mass media with the idea that all those at the bottom are there because they are lazy, unintelligent, and in general inferior, then these appraisals may be taken over by the poor and used in the building of an image of their selves". That is one danger in the spread of the welfare state stereotype. A second emanates from the vague but often powerful fears that calamity will follow the relaxation of discipline and the mitigation of hardship which, in the eyes of the beholders, seems implicit in this notion of collective benevolence. Such fears inevitably conjure up a demand for punishment and reprisal.

Having set the stage in this general way, it is now proper to state the main purposes of this chapter: first, to examine certain assumptions underlying these views of social policy; secondly, to outline the development of three major categories of social welfare; and thirdly, to relate these developments to trends in the division of labour and the search for social equity. At the end, in drawing together these different threads, it emerges that much of the criticism and all the complacency about the welfare state is either irrelevant or unbalanced and that we need to re-examine, by returning to first principles, current notions of what constitutes a social service.

First, however, it is necessary to bring into view certain assumptions, seldom made explicit, which run through practically all the recent critical writings on social policy. These are the assumptions:

- The intended or declared aims of social policy since the 1942 Beveridge Report have been wholly or largely achieved in the translation of legislation into action; in other words, that the performance of welfare has more or less fulfilled the promise of welfare.
- The aggregate redistributive effects of social service activity since 1948 have wholly or largely represented a transfer of resources from rich to poor.
- It is possible to define what a 'social service' is and to identify, in each sector of state intervention, who has benefitted and who has paid.
- It is practicable, desirable and meaningful in a complex society undergoing rapid and widespread change to abstract a 'social service world' from the Greater Society and to consider the functions and effects of the part without reference to the life of the whole.

The first and second assumptions call for a detailed study of the 'unintended consequences' of social policy over the past decade. This cannot be attempted here. I must content myself with making explicit the nature of these assumptions. In the following section, however, I examine certain facts relevant to the third and fourth assumptions.

* * * * *

All collectively provided services are deliberately designed to meet certain socially recognised 'needs'; they are manifestations, first, of society's will to survive as an organic whole and, secondly of the expressed wish of all the people to assist the survival of some people. 'Needs' may therefore be thought of as 'social' and 'individual'; as interdependent, mutually related essentials for the continued existence of the parts and the whole. No complete division between the two is conceptually possible; the shading of one into the other changes with time over the life of all societies; it changes with time over the cycle of needs of the individual and the family; it depends on prevailing notions of what constitutes a 'need' and in what circumstances; and to what extent, if at all, such needs, when recognised, should be met in the interests of the individual and/or of society.

I want to consider particularly the period from the end of the 19th century to about 1950, for it is this period, the era of rising expectations, that witnessed the emergence and growth of those forms of state intervention which, by custom and common approval, have come to be called 'the social services'. The development of these services from the welfare revolution of 1905-14 under a reformist Liberal government, through the experience of two world wars and mass unemployment, to the Beveridge 'insurance revolution' and its aftermath has been amply documented in legislative detail. At the same time as the services themselves developed in scope and range, the term 'social service' has come to be applied to more and more areas of collective provision for certain 'needs'. It has indeed acquired a most elastic quality; its expanding frontiers, formerly enclosing little besides poor relief, sanitation and public nuisances, now embrace a multitude of heterogeneous activities. For example, Boer War pensions and disablement benefits were officially classified as social services in 1920; the universities and public museums were added after the Second World War. No consistent principle seems to obtain in the definition of what is a 'social service'.

The following simple examples (CSO, May 1955) give some indication of the area of confusion concealed by the assumptions of the critics of social policy and warn us of the dangers in any conception of a self-contained social service system expressly designed for the transmission of benefits from one income group of the population to another:

- Approved schools and remand homes are social services. The probation service is not.
- Further education and training for ex-members of the defence forces is a social service. The Youth Employment Service is not.
- The training of doctors is a social service. Marriage guidance services are not.
- Pensions and allowances attributable to the Boer War and First World War are social services. Industrial health services are not.
- The family allowance is a social service The child allowance as remission of tax is not.
- The investigation of legal aid applications is a social service. Legal aid grants are not.
- Village halls and playing fields are social services. Cheap tobacco for old age pensioners is not.
- Technological training and further education is a social service. Subsidised housing for miners is not.
- Compensation to doctors for loss of right to sell medical practices is a social service. Non-contributory pensions and superannuation under occupational pension schemes are not.
- University education is a social service. The training of domestic workers is not.

When so much confusion exists (and these examples are but a selection from a large body of data) it is difficult to know precisely what it is that the critics are criticising. Those acts of state intervention which have somehow or other acquired the connotation of 'social' have developed alongside a much broader area of intervention not thought of in such terms but having in common similar objectives. It is this differential development I want to emphasise: the growth in the social division of welfare in response to changing situations and conceptions of 'need'.

Considered as a whole, all collective interventions to meet certain needs of the individual and/or to serve the wider interests of society may now be broadly grouped into three major categories of welfare: social welfare, fiscal welfare and occupational welfare. When we examine them in turn, it emerges that this division is not based on any fundamental difference in the functions of the three systems (if they may be so described) or their declared aims. It arises from an organisational division of method, which, in the main, is related to the division of labour in complex, individuated societies. So far as the ultimate aims of these systems are concerned, it is argued that their similarities are more important than their dissimilarities. The definition, for most purposes, of what is a 'social service' should take its stand on aims, not on the administrative methods and institutional devices employed to achieve them.

The development in the 20th century of our first category of welfare, that which commonly goes by the term 'social service', has already been mentioned. A major factor in this development should now be noted, for it has played a similarly important role in the growth of our two other categories of welfare.

With the gradual break-up of the old Poor Law, more 'states of dependency' have been defined and recognised as collective responsibilities, and more differential provision has been made in respect of them. These 'states of dependency' arise for the vast majority of the population whenever they are not in a position to 'earn life' for themselves and their families; they are then dependent people. In industrialised societies, there are many causes of dependency; they may be 'natural' dependencies as in childhood, extreme old age and child-bearing. They may be caused by physical and psychological ill health and incapacity; in part, these are culturally determined dependencies. Or they may be wholly or predominantly determined by social and cultural factors. These, it may be said, are the 'man-made' dependencies. Apart from injury, disease and innate incapacity, they now constitute the major source of instability in the satisfaction of basic needs. They include unemployment and under-employment, protective and preventive legislation, compulsory retirement from work, the delayed entry of young people into the labour market, and an infinite variety of subtle cultural factors ranging from the 'right' trade union ticket to the possession of an assortment of status symbols. All may involve to some degree the destruction, curtailment, interruption or frustration of earning power in the individual, and more pronounced secondary dependencies when they further involve the wives, children and other relatives.

In general, many of these culturally determined dependencies have grown in range and significance, partly as a result of a process of cumulative survivorship, for those who experience such states of dependency do not now die as others did before the 20th century. Apart, however, from the effects of this process, the dominating operative factor has been the increasing division of labour in society and, simultaneously, a great increase in labour specificity. This is perhaps one of the outstanding social characteristics of the 20th century: the fact that more and more people consciously experience at one or more stages in their lives the process of selection and rejection – for education, for work, for vocational training, for professional status, for promotion, for opportunities of access to pension schemes, for collective social benefits, for symbols of prestige and success, and in undergoing tests of mental and physical fitness, personality, skill and functional performance. In some senses at least, the arbiters of opportunity and of dependency have become, in their effects, more directly personal, more culturally demanding, more psychologically threatening.

We cannot, however, pursue here the deeper psychological

implications of this trend, implied but not described in detail by Durkheim (1933, p 13) when he observed that, as man becomes more individual and more specialised, he becomes more socially dependent. This is of primary importance in understanding the development of systems of welfare; this and the fact that, simultaneously, man becomes more aware of what has caused his dependency, and thus more exposed to uncertainty and conflict about the purposes and roles he himself is expected to fulfil. More self-knowledge of the 'man-made' causes of dependency has been reflected in social policies through the greater recognition accorded to individual dependencies and their social origins and effects. It has also influenced the growth of our other categories of welfare.

I now consider these notions in relation to the development of fiscal welfare and occupational welfare.

* * * * *

Under separately administered social security systems, like family allowances and retirement pensions, direct cash payments are made in discharging collective responsibilities for particular dependencies. In the relevant accounts, these are treated as 'social service' expenditure since they represent flows of payments through the central government account. Allowances and reliefs from income tax, though providing similar benefits and expressing a similar social purpose in the recognition of dependent needs, are not, however, treated as social service expenditure. The first is a cash transaction; the second an accounting convenience. Despite this difference in administrative method, the tax saving that accrues to the individual is, in effect, a transfer payment. As Cartter observed (1953, p 219), "By reducing the tax liability of a person with dependants the State is sharing in the responsibility of caring for each taxpayer's family just as certainly as if it were paying cash allowances in each case". In their primary objectives and their effects on individual purchasing power there are no differences in these two ways by which collective provision is made for dependencies. Pigou (1932, p 98) recognised this when he wrote of tax relief for children as "deliberate and overt bounties" for large families. Both taxes and transfer payments are manifestations of social policies in favour of identified groups in the population and both reflect changes in public opinion in regard to the relationship between the state, the individual and the family.

Since the introduction of progressive taxation in 1907 there has been a remarkable development of social policy operating through the medium of the fiscal system. This has chiefly taken the form of increasing support for the family through the recognition of more types of dependencies and substantial additions to the value of the benefits provided. Another important aspect of this development is that, originally, these dependants' benefits were deliberately restricted to the lowest paid sections of the income tax population; in the course of time these restrictions have disappeared. The Royal Commission on Taxation (1955) proposes that such benefits should be allowed in the calculation of liability to surtax.

A brief historical sketch of the main features of fiscal welfare shows the growth in public concern and responsibility for 'states of dependency', family and kinship relationships, individual 'self-improvement' and standards of 'minimum substance' among income taxpayers. It shows too, as Friedmann (1951, p 262) has pointed out, the extent to which Taxation Acts are now regarded as social purpose Acts; that taxation has more or less ceased to be regarded as an impertinent intrusion into the sacred rights of private property and that, for the purposes of social policy, it can no longer be thought of simply as a means of benefiting the poor at the expense of the rich (Lewis, 1955; Robbins, 1955).

A child allowance of £10 for all children aged under 16 for those whose incomes were under £500 was introduced in 1909, thus ante-dating by thirty-seven years family allowances for second and subsequent children. The income qualification was raised in 1916, 1918 and 1919 and finally extended to all taxpayers in 1920. The allowance has been further developed to include children receiving full-time education at a university or other educational establishment for the reason that, in the words of the Royal Commission, "the child's immediate earning capacity has been foregone in order that he should qualify himself for work on a higher level in the future". Social policy has thus been extended beyond the confines of support for childhood dependency to the support of individual 'self-improvement'. These allowances are given regardless of education and scholarship awards. The Royal Commission proposes a further major development, namely, that the allowance should vary with the size of the taxpayer's income up to a limit of £160 for all income and surtax payers, and that such allowance should continue to the age of 21 for all 'incapacitated' children. The estimated cost of the existing allowances in 1955-56 was £200 million covering broadly about half the child population. We may illustrate these differences in social policy by considering the respective awards to two married men, one earning £2,000 a year and one earning £400 a year. Both have two children aged under 15. The first father now receives an annual net bounty of £97; the second one of £28. Over the lives of the two families the former will receive a total of £1,455 and the latter a total of £422. The fact that already the child bounty rises steeply with increasing income appears to have been overlooked by Robbins (1955, p 12) in his plea that, "to eliminate some of the injustices of progression", these allowances should be provided "in some measure proportionate to the expenses of the income group into which they are born".

Equally fascinating to the sociologist is the story of when and why women were recognised in this system of social welfare (significantly enough in 1918); aged, incapacitated and infirm kinship dependants; housekeepers according to particular situations of family need; widowed mothers; incapacitated wives; unmarried daughters assisting infirm taxpayers; 'unmarried wives' and children of deceased members of the forces; mourning costs (under estate duty); old age; professional 'self-improvement'; divorced wives, unemployed taxpayers (loss of office compensation); married women at work (first introduced in 1920 in recognition of 'extra household expenses'); housekeepers for professional women on full-time work and, as a 'special indulgence' for poorer taxpayers and those with precarious incomes finding it difficult to save for their dependants and for old age, life assurance and superannuation allowances. The latter benefit, though partly attributable to developments in fiscal policy, would seem to be more logically classified under 'occupational welfare'. It is therefore discussed under this heading.

Underlying all these individual stories of the growth in fiscal welfare policies is a continuous search for a reasonable 'subsistence minimum' for income taxpayers. It was needed as a basis for the various benefits, for fixing exemption limits and for determining the extent to which a taxpayer's kinship relationships and particular states of need should be recognised. This problem is, however, part of a much more fundamental one which has plagued the Royal Commissions after both world wars of reconciling, on the one hand, the imperious demands of preferential social policies with, on the other, 'a general equitable principle' of fairness and progression in assessing individual taxable capacity. This duality of roles is the major source of conflict and confusion. The more that the uniqueness of individual needs and dependencies is recognised and relieved in an occupational society based on individual rewards, the more may principles of individual equity fall into disrepute. Since 1921, the concept of individualism in direct taxation has increasingly become more tenuous. For both Royal Commissions, the claims of social policy have overruled the claims of individual equity. As a result, the cost of dependants' benefits has risen from a negligible figure in the early 1920s to over £425 million in 1955. This compares with a total net cost to the Exchequer in 1954–55 of £770 million for all direct cash payments under national insurance, industrial injuries, family allowances, national assistance and non-contributory pensions.

* * * * *

During the period that has witnessed these far-reaching developments in social and fiscal welfare benefits, there has also occurred a great expansion in occupational welfare benefits in cash and in kind. They have reached formidable and widespread proportions as the Final

Report of the Royal Commission recognised. Their ultimate cost falls in large measure on the Exchequer. They include pensions for employees, wives and dependants; child allowances; death benefits; health and welfare services; personal expenses for travel, entertainment, dress and equipment; meal vouchers, motor cars and season tickets; residential accommodation; holiday expenses; children's school fees; sickness benefits; medical expenses; education and training grants; cheap meals; unemployment benefit; medical bills and an incalculable variety of benefits in kind ranging from "obvious forms of realisable goods to the most intangible forms of amenity". The implications of this trend are cautiously noted by the Royal Commission: "Modern improvements in the conditions of employment and the recognition by employers of a wide range of obligations towards the health, comfort and amenities of their staff may well lead to a greater proportion of an employee's true remuneration being expressed in a form that is neither money nor convertible into money."

A substantial part of all these multifarious benefits can be interpreted as the recognition of dependencies: the dependencies of old age, of sickness and incapacity, of childhood, widowhood and so forth. They are in effect, if not in administrative method, 'social services', duplicating and overlapping social and fiscal welfare benefits. The rapidity of their growth has increasingly diminished the value and relevance of salary, wage and income statistics. Occupational pension schemes, to give an example of the present order of provision, may cover one half of the total male labour force (excluding agriculture). Their cost to the Exchequer (including tax-free deferred salaries) already runs to £100 million as year (1955), a figure substantially in excess of the Exchequer cost of national insurance pensions. Contrary to the apparent intentions of the 1920 Royal Commission, which considered tax relief for such schemes appropriate for poorer taxpayers, the benefits have increasingly favoured wealthier taxpayers through the medium of tax-free lump sums and other devices. In this sense, they function as concealed multipliers of occupational success.

Sick pay and other 'social service' benefits have followed a similar upward trend. An official sample inquiry tentatively suggested that about half the claimants for national insurance sickness benefit were also covered by employer's sick pay schemes, the proportion ranging from one-third among manual workers to 90% for administrators (Ministry of Pensions and National Insurance, 1955). Adding these benefits together, sickness is now a better financial proposition for many people than health.

No doubt many of these forms of occupational social services express the desire for 'good human relations' in industry. Their provision is part of the model of the 'good' employer. But as they grow and multiply, they come into conflict with the aims and unity of social policy; for in effect (whatever their aims might be) their whole tendency is to divide loyalties, to nourish privilege and to narrow the social conscience as they have already done in the United States, France and Western Germany. One fundamental question of equity that they raise (which is analogous to that raised by the dual roles of fiscal policy) is whether and to what extent social service dependency benefits should be proportionately related to occupational and income achievement.

* * * * *

Three different systems of 'social services' have been briefly surveyed. Considered as a whole, their development shows how narrowly conceived and unbalanced are the criticisms so frequently levelled at the one system traditionally known as 'the social services' or, more recently and more ambiguously, as the 'welfare state'. The latent assumptions which commonly underlie these criticisms can therefore have little relevance while they remain attached to a stereotype of social welfare which represents only the more visible part of the real world of welfare. The social history of our times inevitably becomes, in the process, sadly distorted.

These three systems are seen to operate as virtually distinct stratified systems. What goes on within and as a result of one system is ignored by the others. They are appraised, criticised or applauded as abstracted, independent, entities. (The 1942 Beveridge Report paid no particular regard to fiscal welfare benefits and the Reports of the Royal Commission on Taxation in discussing social policies virtually ignore the commonly termed 'social services'.) Yet, despite this division, they all in varying degrees signify that man can no longer be regarded simply as a 'unit of labour power'; they all reflect contemporary opinion that man is not wholly responsible for his dependency and they all accept obligations for meeting certain dependent needs of the individual and the family. Nevertheless, despite these common social purposes, the search for equity between taxpayers – that like all cases should be treated in like manner – proceeds regardless of the need for equity between citizens. The drive to 'buy' good human relations in industry widens class and vocational divisions through the provision of differential welfare benefits based on occupational achievement. The lack of any precise thinking about what is and what is not a 'social service' confuses and constrains the social conscience, and allows the development of distinctive social policies based on different principles for arbitrarily differentiated groups in the population.

Behind the facts of this development, we can see the play of powerful economic and political forces: the strength and tenacity of privilege; the continuing search for equity in a rapidly changing society. Conceptions of 'need' and 'dependency' have simultaneously been profoundly affected by technological, industrial and social change, "the gales of creative destruction", to use the striking phrase of Schumpeter (1950, p 84). The problems of equity in social policy have thus become more complex as a result of the accumulation of long-lived 'disservices': the increasing division of labour; higher standards of labour specificity; the lengthening of the 'natural' dependencies of childhood and old age; the diversification, creation and decay of functional skills and roles; and the growth of sectional solidarities which in turn have tended to enlarge the area and significance of social differentiation. More social differentiation – whether by age, class, education, personality, physical standards, intelligence quotient or professional qualification – may result, as Friedmann (1952) observed in more social inequalities. Failure, ineffectiveness and social inferiority thus acquire a deeper significance. External inequalities – those which do not express natural inequalities – become "more insupportable as labour becomes more divided". More insight into the complexities of human stress allied to the tendency of special groups to become more self-conscious leads to the search for sectional equalities. In so far as they are achieved, the interests of society as a whole at one extreme, and of the 'unattached' and dependent individual at the other, are subordinated to the interests of the group or class. The aims of equity, ostensibly set for society as a whole, become sectional aims, invariably rewarding the most favoured in proportion to the distribution of power and occupational success.

At the centre of this process of division based on the specialised content of individual occupational performance, people become more dependent; they also become, in the pursuit of individual life goals, more aware of dependency, more vulnerable to failure, more exposed to pain. The corollary for any society which invests more of its values and virtues in the promotion of the individual is individual failure and individual consciousness of failure.

Within this theoretical framework, it becomes possible to interpret the development of these three systems of social service as separate and distinctive attempts to counter and to compensate for the growth of dependency in modern society. Yet they are simultaneously enlarging and consolidating the area of social inequality. That is the paradox; the new division of equity which is arising from these separate responses to social change. That is the real challenge to social policy and to those who, mistakenly, still look to the past for a solution.

Chapter Three

War and social policy

In an article in _The Listener_ (6 October 1955) Gibbs politely but firmly criticised past historians for bringing their histories to a stop when the guns started firing and in opening a new chapter only with the return of peace and of normal diplomatic and institutional relationships between sovereign states. Gibbs was faced with a lack of balance in the material available to him in reflecting upon the nature of war and society. He could hardly complain, however, about the _quantity_ of historical studies at his disposal. Military and naval documents, regimental histories, the lives of captains and kings, political, diplomatic and even philosophical works jostle each other for a place in the crowded 'war' index and bear witness to the energy and interests of past students of war and to the endemic character of war in the history of man.

By contrast, I am doubly handicapped in discussing the relationship of war and social policy. So far as the story of modern war before 1939 is concerned, little has been recorded in any systematic way about the social and economic effects of war on the population as a whole. Only long and patient research in out of the way documentary places can reveal something of the characteristics and flavour of social life during the experience of wars in the past, and these records are often undisciplined and unreliable. There are, for example, somewhat highly coloured accounts of popular reactions on the south coasts of England to the threat of invasion when Napoleon Bonaparte was master of all western Europe: of the effects of the Crimean and Boer Wars on Poor Law policy in those days; of a remarkable decline in criminal behaviour among civilians in Britain during the First World War and an equally remarkable outbreak of panic among the civilians of London when the first Zeppelins arrived with their primitive bombs, most of which failed to explode (Titmuss, 1950; Trotter, 1916). But even such accounts, unreliable as they may be, are hard to come by and, strangely enough, one often turns away from the novelists in disappointment; it is difficult to believe, for instance, that some of Jane Austen's novels were written during one of the great wars in history, a war which signified for this country, if Greenwood (1942) got his sums right, a proportionately greater loss of life among soldiers and sailors than during the First World War and, consequently, more widespread effects among the families of those who served in the armed forces.

These are some of the reflections which I have recalled, though in a more tranquil mood, from the days when I was engaged on the social policy history of the Second World War. In studying the effects of the evacuation of civilians from London and other cities, I was led to wonder whether there were any recorded accounts of the movement of civilian populations in past years as a calculated element in war strategy. I had to go back to the Greeks, to the great Hellenic wars, before I was rewarded. Here is Plutarch's description in *Vita Themistoclis* (10, 5; North's translation) of the evacuation of the civilian population of Athens as a military necessity during the Persian invasion in 480 BC. The Peloponnesian city of Troezen, on the far side of the Saronic Gulf, became a 'reception area'. According to Plutarch,

> The most part of them [the Athenians] did convey their aged fathers and mothers, their wives and little children, into the city of Troezen, where the Torezenians received them very lovingly and gently. For they gave order that they should be entertained of the common charge, allowing them apiece, two oboloes of their money a day, and suffered the young children to gather fruit wheresoever they found it, and furthermore, did hire schoolmasters at the charge of the commonwealth, to bring them up at school.

From this account it would seem that conscious thought was given by the responsible authorities to the social and psychological needs of the evacuated population. There was a plan: a concerted social policy, a deliberate public attempt to foresee events, to estimate behaviour, to minimise hardships and to control a social situation in the interests of a community at war.

It was this fragment of history, illuminating the way in which war and social policy influence each other, that helped to shape the ideas for this essay. In discussing social policy, I mean those acts of government deliberately designed and taken to improve the welfare of the civil population in time of war. I am not therefore simply concerned with the social and biological consequences of war; my main interest is with the organised attempts of governments to control these consequences. Much of what I have to say will be confined to the experiences of this country since the middle of the 19th century. There is a problem distinguishing between policies related to peacetime needs and policies concerned only with the immediate wartime situation. It is bound up with the assumption that war is an abnormal situation; that peace is, or ought to be, the normal lot of mankind.

In considering, however, the results of deliberate attempts to organise a society for war (either in the military, economic or social spheres), we are confronted with one of the major characteristics of large scale, modern war: the fact that modern war casts its shadow long before it happens and that its social effects are felt for longer and longer periods after armed conflict has ceased. In the timescale of these effects, modern war stretches over a greater span of men's lives, unlike the wars of religion and those wars which Toynbee (1950) called 'the sport of Kings'. Many of them started abruptly, without planning; without any preparatory action to provide for the needs of the civilian population; without any consideration of how war might affect the social and economic life of the country. They were organised military wars; otherwise, and apart from the particular territories over which battles were fought, normal life proceeded, and was assumed to proceed, normally. By contrast, however, as the plans and policies of 20th century governments for war and peace have become more interrelated, it is in consequence increasingly difficult to detach the 'abnormal' from the 'normal', and to attribute precisely the acts of government to one or other of these situations.

* * * * *

I now consider how developments in modern war have affected social policy. It is a commonplace among students of the subject that in Western history, war has been following war in an ascending order of intensity. In scale, in depth and in time, war has been waged more intensively and ferociously. This crescendo in the organisation of war has enveloped a larger proportion of the total population and has left its marks on them for a longer period of time. These developments have affected social policy in a variety of ways. Among these, perhaps the dominating one has been the increasing concern of the state in time of war with the biological characteristics of its people. The growing scale and intensity of war has stimulated a growing concern about the quantity and quality of the population.

We may mark certain well-defined stages in this progression of biological interests. The first stage of organised interest was with quantity; that is, with the number of men available for battle. This developed as the scale upon which war was fought increased and it was no longer safe for the authorities to assume that there were abundant supplies of men available. This growing concern with quantity at different periods and in different societies has been one of the forces which has stimulated the interest of governments in population trends and in the taking of national censuses. As we know from our own history of vital statistics, opposition was raised in the 19th century to census operations because of a fear that they were being carried out for military reasons.

The second stage in this progression is marked by the increasing adoption of qualitative standards applied to military and naval recruits. The standards demanded have risen enormously since the day when Florence Nightingale discovered that the British Army Medical Service was staffed by a few clerks and an odd messenger boy or two. We now have the most complex system of standards comprising a variety of physical, functional, psychological and social attributes. According to Hoffer (1954) it was not love but wartime necessity which made American psychiatry turn towards Freud. He suggests that one of the principal reasons why psychiatry occupies such a commanding position in the American social scene is because of what he calls the 'unforgettable role' that psychiatrists played in the organisation of the war effort.

All this has two important implications for social policy: first, that increasingly higher demands are made upon society for those who are physically and psychologically fit, intellectually bright and socially acceptable on grounds of personal character; second, that, as a result, the proportion of men rejected and invalided from the armed forces tends to rise rather than fall. Many then become the clients of the social services. This is one example which shows that what is done in the name of 'defence' determines, in substantial measure, some of the roles and functions of the social services. The social costs of the Boer War and the First World War, as measured by expenditure on pensions, widows' benefits, medical care, rehabilitation, sickness claims, rent subsidies and national assistance, represent a substantial proportion of the social service budget in the 1950s.

The third stage of interest is reached when public concern about the standard of fitness of men of military age moves out to embrace concern about the health and wellbeing of the whole population and, in particular, of children, the next generation of recruits. This stage was reached in Britain at the beginning of the 20th century and it is worth enquiring a little more closely into events at that time because of their importance for the subsequent development of public health policies.

It was the Boer War, not one of the notable wars in human history to change human affairs, that touched off the personal health movement which led eventually to the NHS in 1948. Public concern was roused at the end of the war by the facts that were published about sickness and mortality among the troops and by a report from the inspector-general of recruiting which spoke of "the gradual deterioration of the physique of the working classes from whom the bulk of the recruits must always be drawn". At a time when many leaders of opinion still held to the 19th century doctrine of the inevitability of social progress, this report from the inspector-general came as a shock. Could it be, at the end of a century of unprecedented material progress, that the health and fitness of the bulk of the population was deteriorating? There followed, in rapid succession, one commission of inquiry after another into these questions of physical deterioration, systems of medical inspection, the causes of high infant mortality and many other matters affecting the wellbeing of the population.

As a consequence of this ferment of inquiry we may trace the establishment in 1906 of the school medical service, the feeding of children in elementary schools, a campaign to reduce infant mortality and many other social measures.

All these elements of social policy stemmed directly from the Boer War and show how our concern for communal fitness has followed closely upon the course of our military fortunes. The story repeats itself in the First World War. In 1917, we note the introduction of the first instalment of a free NHS when facilities were offered, to civilians and soldiers alike, for the treatment and prevention of venereal disease. At the close of the war the phrase 'a C3 nation' crept into contemporary journalism after the report of the Ministry of National Service had told the country that only one man in three of nearly 2.5 million examined was completely fit for military service [also see Part 1, Chapter Three]. It is possible that, among other reasons, the age of retirement for men in the National Insurance Scheme has not been raised because of the long range effects of the First World War.

The ancient Greeks, in attaching some moral significance to the idea of keeping fit, almost as though they had convinced themselves that vigour of body was an absolute good, had sound reasons for keeping fit. Their civilisation involved them in continuous wars and so has our civilisation of the 20th century.

When we consider the effects of the Second World War, a war in Britain which depended on the efforts of virtually all citizens, we reach a fourth stage in our ascending scale of interest. Not only was it necessary for the state to take positive steps in all spheres of the national economy to safeguard the physical health of the people; it was also an imperative for war strategy for the authorities to concern themselves with that elusive concept 'civilian morale'; with what Cyril Falls called, in his Lees Knowles lectures (1941, p 13), 'demostrategy'. By this he meant, in military terms, that the war could not be won unless millions of ordinary people in Britain and overseas were convinced that we had something better to offer than had our enemies, not only during but after the war.

The effect on social policy of these ideas about war strategy was profound. It was increasingly sharpened as the war went on for, not until three years had passed and victory was at last a rational (rather than an emotional) conception, could the enemy claim that he had killed as many British soldiers as women and children.

* * * * *

Much of the story of the war effort in terms of applied social policies is told in the series of volumes in the Official War History by myself [*Problems of social policy*, 1950] and my colleagues. I shall not attempt to recount the story here, except to draw out of it one or two general conclusions.

The social measures that were developed during the war centred on the primary needs of the whole population, irrespective of class, creed or military category. The distinctions and privileges, accorded to those in uniform in previous wars, were greatly diminished. Comprehensive systems of medical care and rehabilitation, for example, had to be organised by the state for those who were injured and disabled. They could not be exclusively reserved for soldiers and sailors, as in the past, but had to be extended to include civilians as well, to those injured in the factories as well as the victims of bombing. The organisation and structure of the Emergency Medical Service, initially designed to cater for a special section of the population, became in the end the prototype of a medical service for the whole population.

In the sphere of food policy, it was no longer thought appropriate for members of the armed forces to receive better diets than the civilian population. The scales of rationing as in many other spheres of need as well had to be kept in balance between civilian and non-civilian.

This wartime trend towards universalising public provision for certain basic needs did not come about as a result of the traffic of ideas in one direction only. It also worked the other way, that is from civilians to non-civilians. Educational facilities in the form of music, drama and the arts, open to civilians in time of war, could not be withheld from men and women in the forces. No longer could it be said that soldiers 'would get above themselves' if, instead of drinking, they read books and papers, and that army discipline would thereby be endangered as was said in May 1855 by the War Office to Florence Nightingale when she opened a reading room for injured soldiers in Scutari (Woodham Smith, 1950, p 239). By the 1940s the military authorities in Britain had taken to heart, no doubt unwittingly, Aristotle's epitaph on the 'Lycurgean' system of Spartan training for war. This was the way he summed it up:

> Peoples ought not to train themselves in the art of war with an eye to subjugating neighbours who do not deserve to be subjugated.... The paramount aim of any social system should be to frame military institutions, like all its other institutions, with an eye to the circumstances of peace-time, when the soldier is off duty; and this proposition is borne out by the facts of experience. For militaristic states are apt to survive only so long as they remain at war, while they go to ruin as soon as they have finished making their conquests. Peace causes their metal to lose its temper; and the fault lies with a social system which does not teach its soldiers what to make of their lives when they are off duty.

To apply this Aristotelian precept to the modern world means, in effect, that a social system must be so organised as to enable all citizens (and not only soldiers) to learn what to make of their lives in peacetime. In this context the 1944 Education Act becomes intelligible; so does the 1942 Beveridge Report, the 1945 Family Allowances, the 1946 National Health Service and the 1951 National Insurance Acts. All these measures of social policy were in part an expression of the needs of wartime strategy to fuse and unify the conditions of life of civilians and non-civilians alike. In practice, this involved the whole community in accepting an enlargement of obligations – an extension of social discipline – to attend to the primary needs of all citizens.

In no sphere of need is the imprint of war on social policy more vividly illustrated than in respect to *dependant* needs: the needs of wives, children and other relatives for income-maintenance allowances when husbands and fathers are serving in the forces. To trace in detail the system of service pay and allowances from the Napoleonic Wars to the Second World War is to see how, as war has followed war in an ascending order of intensity, so the dependant needs of wives and children have been increasingly recognised. The more that the waging of war has come to require a total effort by the nation, the more have the dependant needs of the family been recognised and accepted as a social responsibility.

This trend in the wartime recognition of family dependencies has also profoundly affected social security policies in general. New systems of service pay and allowances threw into sharper prominence the fact that in industrial society money rewards take no account of family responsibilities; nor, until 1939, did many of the payments made under various social services. Thus, one immediate effect was that dependants' allowances were added to workmen's compensation and other schemes. Another was that in many respects war pensions and industrial injury pensions had to be brought into line. This was done because it seemed inappropriate to make distinctions between war and peace, civilians and non-civilians.

* * * * *

Looking back over the various points I have made about the relationship between the war effort of a community and its social policies in peace as well as in war, one general conclusion may be ventured. The waging of modern war presupposes and imposes a great increase in social discipline; moreover, this discipline is only tolerable if, and only if, social inequalities are not intolerable. The need for less inequality is expressed, for example, in the changes that take place in what is socially approved behaviour; marked differences in standards of living, in dress, in luxury entertainment and in indulgencies of many kinds are disapproved.

It follows that the acceptance of these social disciplines (of obligations as well as rights) made necessary by war, by preparations for war and by the long-run consequences of war, must influence the aims and content of social policies not only during the war itself but in peacetime as well. "The discipline of the army", wrote Max Weber (Gerth and Mills, 1946, p 261), "gives birth to all discipline". In some senses he was not far wrong, but it should be remembered that this thesis rested on an analysis of military organisation from the days of Sparta down to the professional European armies at the beginning of the 20th century. Britain's war effort in 1930 did not rest on a professional military base. Nevertheless, it is a tenable proposition that military wars demand a military discipline and that this kind of discipline (or "warrior communism" as Weber described it) demands certain kinds of perfected conduct from a small section of the population. We have some classic examples of this perfection of discipline in the infantry drill of Spartan soldiers and the exquisite movements of Lord Cardigan's cavalry in the Crimean War. Both inevitably required – and this was the point of Max Weber's analysis – an 'aristocratic' structure in military organisation and in society as a whole. Both essays in war came to a bad end. The social disciplines demanded by the civilians' war in Britain of 1939 were very different; they derived their strength from internal sources rather than from external commands and had to rest on a social system which sought to teach all its soldiers what to make of their lives when off duty.

The aims and content of social policy, both in peace and in war, are thus determined, at least to a substantial extent, by how far the cooperation of the masses is essential to the successful prosecution of war. If this cooperation is thought to be essential, then inequalities must be reduced and the pyramid of social stratification must be flattened. This, in part, is the thesis advanced by Andreski (1954) in a sweeping, untidy but brilliant study. In analysing the character of war and its conduct from pastoral and pre-literate societies down to the advent of atomic war, he argues that what he calls the military participation ratio determines the social stratification of a society. Mass war, involving a high proportion of the total population, tends to a levelling in social class differences. On the other hand, professional wars, conducted by military leaders recruited from a social élite and depending on support from only a small proportion of the population, tend to heighten existing social inequalities. This study effectively answers Herbert Spencer's theory that war conduces to greater social inequalities. It may have been true of some wars in some periods and cultures but not of all wars. However, we must fairly admit that Spencer was writing before the advent of the mass wars of the 20th century.

Modern war has had, at least in Britain, a profound influence on social policy and, reciprocally, the direction of social policy has influenced the way in which war is prosecuted. I am confident, more perhaps by faith than by reason, that this is not the whole of the story in the evolution of social policy. Man does not live by war alone. To explain the social life of a community in terms of aggression and struggle is [to borrow a phrase from Edward Fitzgerald's *Rubaiyat of Omar Khayyam*] to explain only part of 'this sorry scheme of things entire'.

Unfinished business

The three themes of evacuation, hospital service and help for the victims of air attack have largely dominated the account of the effects of the war on the ordinary, peacetime social services. In the opening part of this chapter, however, some of the more important developments in the field of social policy are briefly noted; these, set against the background of government policy to protect and sustain the civilian population from air bombardment, serve as an introduction to a tentative analysis of the total effects of the war on the people's health.

It would, in any relative sense, be true to say that by the end of the Second World War the government had, through the agency of newly established or existing services, assumed and developed a measure of direct concern for the health and wellbeing of the population which, by contrast with the role of government in the 1930s, was little short of remarkable. No longer did concern rest on the belief that, in respect to many social needs, it was proper to intervene only to assist the poor and those who were unable to pay for services of one kind and another. Instead, it was increasingly regarded as a proper function or even obligation of government to ward off distress and strain among not only the poor but almost all classes of society. And, because the area of responsibility had so perceptibly widened, it was no longer thought sufficient to provide through various branches of social assistance a standard of service hitherto considered appropriate for those in receipt of poor relief – a standard inflexible in administration and attuned to a philosophy which regarded individual distress as a mark of social incapacity.

That all were engaged in war, whereas only some were afflicted with poverty and disease, had much to do with the less constraining, less discriminating scope and quality of the wartime social services. Damage to homes and injuries to persons were not less likely among the rich than the poor and so, after the worst of the original defects in policy had been corrected – such as the belief that only the poor would need help when their homes were smashed – the assistance provided by the government to counter the hazards of war carried little social discrimination and was offered to all groups in the community. The pooling of national resources and the sharing of risks were not always practicable nor always applied, but they were the guiding principles.

Acceptance of these principles moved forward the goals of welfare. New obligations were shouldered, higher standards were set. The benefits were considerable. The community relinquished, for instance, a ten-year-old practice of not providing cheap school meals unless children were first proved to be both 'necessitous' and 'undernourished'. Better pensions were given to old people as a right and not a concession. Certain groups (such as expectant and nursing mothers and young children) were singled out to receive extra allowances and special aids, not because they were rich or poor or politically vocal, but because common sense, supported by science and pushed along by common humanity, said it was a good thing to do.

These and other developments in the scope and character of the welfare services did not happen in any planned or ordered sequence, nor were they always a matter of deliberate intent. Some were pressed forward because of the needs of the war machine for more labour power. Some took place almost by accident. Some were the result of a recognition of needs hitherto hidden by ignorance of social conditions. Some came about because war "exposed weaknesses ruthlessly and brutally ... which called for revolutionary changes in the economic and social life of the country" (Anthony Eden, MP, 6 December 1939).

* * * * *

Reports in 1939 about the condition of evacuated mothers and children aroused the conscience of the nation in the opening phase of the war; much sooner, indeed, than might have been expected from the country's experience in previous wars of changes in the conception of the nation's responsibilities towards the poor and distressed. It was in 1815, after Waterloo, that Lord Brougham's Committee met to consider "the Education of the Lower Orders". It was after victory in the Boer War that inquests on the physical condition of the people were opened. It was not until the later years of the First World War that plans for reconstruction began to take shape. The evacuation of mothers and children and the bombing of homes during 1939-40, however, stimulated inquiry and proposals for reform long before victory was even thought possible. This was an important experience for it meant that, for five years of war, the pressures for a higher standard of welfare and a deeper comprehension of social justice steadily gained in strength. And, during this period, despite all the handicaps of limited resources in labour and materials, a big expansion took place in the responsibilities accepted by the state for those in need.

The reality of military disaster and the threat of invasion in the summer of 1940 urged on these tendencies in social policy. The mood of the people changed and, in sympathetic response, values changed as well. If dangers were to be shared, then resources should also be shared. Dunkirk, and all that the name evokes, was an important event in the wartime history of the social services. It summoned forth a note of self-criticism, of national introspection, and it set in motion ideas and talk of principles and plans. A remarkable leader in *The Times* (1 July 1940), a few weeks after the evacuation of the British Expeditionary Force from the continent, expressed these views:

> If we speak of democracy, we do not mean a democracy which maintains the right to vote but forgets the right to work and the right to live. If we speak of freedom, we do not mean a rugged individualism which excludes social organisation and economic planning. If we speak of equality, we do not mean a political equality nullified by social and economic privilege. If we speak of economic reconstruction, we think less of maximum production (though this too will be required) than of equitable distribution.

This was a declaration of faith. In a few months, it was to be repeatedly affirmed with the bombing of London, Coventry and many other cities. The long, dispiriting years of hard work that followed these dramatic events on the home front served only to reinforce the war-warmed impulse of people for a more generous society.

* * * * *

These broad generalisations, subject, as they will be, to revision by historians better placed to study this phase of the war, are relevant to the story of welfare. For it was during this period, extending from June 1940 until bombing temporarily ceased in the following year, that certain decisions were taken and certain policies were shaped which not only looked forward to 'social reconstruction' after the war, but were destined also during the war itself to play a vital role in sustaining the health and working capacity of the people. These policies support the proposition that this dangerous period of the war was most fruitful for social policy and action.

The provision of meals at school had been interpreted by most education authorities, until a decisive change in government policy in July 1940, as a relief measure for malnourished children. Dinners of a poor quality were frequently supplied, often by private caterers; a charity outlook combined with the caterers' need to make a profit were reflected in the poverty of the meals and a lack of decency in serving them.

In July 1940 positive steps were taken, with Treasury backing, to broaden the scope of the service and to improve its quality. The number of school meals supplied doubled in twelve months and the provision of school milk rose by about 50%. In September 1941, policy took another big step forward. As part of the national food policy, it was proposed to expand the provision of school meals and milk as quickly as possible. Evidence of unsatisfactory health indices during the first two years of war, such as higher infant death rates and rising tuberculosis rates, had a hand in these proposals. "There is a danger", it was said, "of deficiencies occurring in the quality and quantity of children's diets.... There is no question of capacity to pay: we may find the children of well-to-do parents and the children of the poor suffering alike from an inability to get the food they need". The War Cabinet agreed to these proposals and the campaign, originally launched in July 1940, was pressed forward with renewed vigour to increase the number of children taking meals at school and to provide milk for every child at every school in the country.

Within three years the situation had been completely transformed, both in quantity and quality of service, despite all the very real difficulties caused by the need to provide new dining rooms, school canteens, kitchens and equipment, the rationing of food supplies, inadequate transport facilities in rural areas and shortages of staff. In round figures, one child in three was fed at school in 1945 in place of one child in thirty in 1940.

Between 1940 and 1945 a big advance was also made in the number of children receiving milk at school, although the aim of universal provision was not achieved by the end of the war. In July 1940 the proportion benefiting in primary and secondary schools in England and Wales was around 50%; by February 1945 it had risen to 73%. The Milk-in-Schools Scheme (with its benefit of a reduced price) was also extended to pupils attending private and other non grant-aided schools; thus, children at all types of school in the country were entitled to participate in the scheme.

These developments in the provision of meals and milk at school expressed something very close to a revolution in the attitude of parents, teachers and children to a scheme which, only a few years earlier, had not been regarded with much respect or sympathy. In place of a relief measure, tainted with the poor law, it became a social service, fused into school life and making its own contribution to the physical nurture of the children and to their social education.

The National Milk Scheme, conceived and developed by the Ministry of Health and destined to play an important part in sustaining the health of mothers and young children during the war, was also adopted by the government in the summer of 1940 without dispute or financial argument. Before Dunkirk, the Ministry of Health had been worried by the failure of its scheme of August 1939 for supplying cheap milk to mothers through the maternity and child welfare authorities. What it wanted to do could not, seemingly, be done without a big Exchequer subsidy and no one believed that this would be forthcoming.

In July 1940, however, a new National Milk Scheme provided for every child under five and for all expectant and nursing mothers in Britain a pint of milk daily at 2d instead of the price of 4½d a pint ruling in most districts at the time. If the family income was below 40s a week, the milk was supplied free. The whole cost was borne by the Exchequer.

For over a decade many authorities, vigorously led by Sir John Orr, had demonstrated the need for getting more milk into mothers and children. Consumption per head of the whole population of the United Kingdom was little higher in the 1930s than it had been before the First World War. Among the better-off income groups, however, the quantity drunk each day was about three times in excess of that consumed by the poor. It was in the main a problem of purchasing power. This problem was solved for mothers with young children by a decision of the government five days after the evacuation of the British Expeditionary Force from Dunkirk.

The scheme was an immediate success. Within three months, the response had falsified the estimates of the experts in the Ministries of Food and Health, who appear either to have underestimated the effect of insufficient purchasing power on the consumption of such an essential food as milk, or to have misjudged the extent to which the higher income groups would share in a welfare service of this character.

There are problems affecting the production and supply of milk, including its quality, that cannot be considered here; but it is important to observe at this point that the National Milk and the Milk-in-Schools Schemes led to a more equitable sharing out of what was available and to increased consumption among those groups in the community who most needed milk. As between families of the same size with the same number of children of comparable ages, weekly consumption figures collected by the Ministry of Food during 1941-43 still showed a steady increase, in common with other important foods, from the lowest to the highest income groups. The differences, however, were much less striking than before the war.

Closely associated with the National Milk Scheme, in intention and administration, was the Vitamin Welfare Scheme. This was introduced in December 1941 because of misgivings about a possible shortage of vitamins in the diet of young children resulting from the lack of fruit, particularly oranges, and the shortage of butter and eggs. The scheme began by providing free of charge blackcurrant syrup or purée and cod liver oil for children up to two years of age. Further extensions of the scheme led to all expectant mothers and children aged under five who received cheap or free milk being automatically entitled to cheap or free supplies of orange juice and cod liver oil or vitamin A and D tablets. In January 1944 the proportions entitled to these supplements who actually collected them were orange juice 57%, cod liver oil 30%, vitamin A and D tablets 45%.

* * * * *

What was remarkable about these wartime developments in the provision of school meals, milk and special foods for certain groups in the community was the unanimity underlying policy and the speed at which decisions were acted on. No longer was it argued (as it often was before the war) that the condition of the people did not warrant such measures, or that nothing should be done until unmistakable evidence of a deterioration in the public health had shown itself for some time. No longer were fruit juices for children dismissed as 'exotic', or state aid in such matters as school dinners regarded as an invasion of parents' rights. It was the universal character of these welfare policies which ensured their acceptance and success. They were free of social discrimination and the indignities of the Poor Law.

The same impulse to remove or lessen inequalities was apparent elsewhere: in the higher pensions paid to old people and their removal from the machinery of the Poor Law; in the abolition of the household means test from social service payments; in the transformation after 1941 in the quality of the Assistance Board's work and in the relationship between its officers and its clients (symbolised by the employment of 'friendly visitors' to call on old age pensioners); and in the nationwide character of the scheme for immunising children against diphtheria under which nearly seven million children in Britain were treated during 1940–45. In all these instruments of welfare, there was a conspicuous absence of direct or implied discrimination. Where it was present, as in the ill-fated Ministry of Health scheme for giving special monetary allowances only to tubercular people likely to benefit from treatment, it aroused resentment.

By and large, the experience of those who used the Social Services after 1940 was different from that of the people who had sought social assistance during the 1930s. The spirit in which many of these services were ordered and administered from about 1941 onwards underwent a subtle but noticeable change. To an increasing degree, human needs were considered and dealt with in a humane way. This was a sharp contract with the mass treatment of individual distress during the years of heavy and prolonged unemployment.

Between these two periods with their different conceptions of the meaning of social duty, there was the year of revaluation, the year when needs were made manifest and complacencies shaken. Evacuation, "the most important subject in the social history of the war because it revealed to the whole people the black spots in its social life" (*The Economist*, 1 May 1943), was the first big entry in the balance sheet which war, beginning its great audit, made inevitable. Then came, in the summer of 1940, the "remarkable discovery of secret need" (*The Times*, 19 August 1940) among some 750,000 old people.

From the field of public health there came evidence which called for, and obtained, a new examination of old facts. The standard of fitness of the nation's young men was found in 1940 to fall short of what many believed had been achieved during the 1930s. It had been claimed that the results of the medical examination of men aged 20 and 21 under the 1939 Military Training Act showed a remarkably high standard of fitness. "Only 2.3% of those examined are definitely unfit for military service", said the Minister of Health, "These are striking results".

But, within a year, these views were to be upset. The Comptroller and Auditor General was one of several authorities to put their doubts in writing: "It appears to me that during the early months of the war many men, who were accepted following a cursory preliminary medical examination, were later found on a more thorough examination to be unfit for military service" (Army Appropriation Account 1939).

In many ways it was fortunate for the nation that this revision of ideas and rearrangement of values came so early in the war. They allowed and quickly encouraged great extension and additions to the social services; they helped many of these services to escape from the traditions of the Poor Law and they made them more acceptable to more people. The fact that the area of collective responsibility moved out so soon in a wider circle, drawing in more people and broadening the obligations to protect those in need, was to serve the nation well during the following five years of strain and deprivation. Some of the benefits contributed to a good record of national health during these years. It now remains to consider this record.

* * * * *

An explanation that will satisfy everyone will probably never be given of the causes of the deterioration in certain health indices in 1940 and again in 1941, nor of the reasons why this downward trend was suddenly reversed in 1942, and why improvement continued to the end of the war and beyond. The conjunction of these trends and the new policies of welfare embarked on during the twelve months or so following Dunkirk suggests an easy and simple answer. But cause and effect are seldom demonstrated as fluently as this; the correlation is by no means perfect, the facts fit in some places but not in others; there is always a history of the health of nations as there is of the health of individuals.

During the first year of war there were many expressions of surprise and relief by medical authorities and members of the government that the health of the nation had been maintained at a high standard. So long did this feeling of relief prevail that, even as late as September 1941, the Minister of Food was saying that the nation had "never been in better health for years" (*The Times,* 15 September 1941). Yet, in retrospect, it seems probable that these authorities were still more astonished when, after five years of war, of food shortage, of bombing and other tribulations, many of the important health indices showed improvement, and in some respects astonishing improvement, over the figures for 1938 and 1939.

This relief, so naturally and spontaneously expressed in the first twelve months of war, was, to a limited extent at least, a reaction from previously held fears. It had been thought that, if war was to come, with its new and violent threats to civilian health and life, there might well be more disease in various shapes and forms, and a general deterioration in national stamina. But there were no explosions of disease; no dramatic upsets in standards of health. In some measure, of course, the feelings of relief were psychological descendants of the view of the 1930s that there was not much wrong with the nation's health. According to that view, there was relatively little to gain but a great deal to lose. After a year and more of war, nothing seemed lost.

But, as the winter of 1940 passed, with its strains of bombing and shelter life, and as fresh restrictions were imposed on food supplies, a more cautious note began to colour official views about the health of the people. Signs were accumulating that a deterioration might be setting in; tuberculosis deaths were increasing in number faster than had been the case during 1914-16 (particularly at ages under 20); infant mortality and deaths among young children had risen in 1940 and again in 1941; and reports were reaching the Health Departments of more anaemia among certain groups of women and children.

The trouble was that most of the existing methods of diagnosing the state of the public health relied on instruments which time and progress had blunted. The rate at which people died had lost some of its value to a society with a higher standard of life, but, as yet, little had been put in its place. No comprehensive figures were available before the war concerning the amount of sickness in the community; information on absence from work because of ill-health was fragmentary and unreliable; the statistics of notifications of certain diseases (such as tuberculosis) were unsatisfactory; and the results of the medical inspection of the nutritional state of schoolchildren had proved to be ambiguous and untrustworthy. The lack of sensitive instruments for recording disturbances in public health meant that there was no reliable pre-war baseline from which moderate degrees of change could be measured.

There was only one way to overcome this lack of public health data: to set on foot ad hoc inquiries and surveys to search out and watch for danger signals. At various times during 1941-42 and later in the war many investigations of different kinds were made. Among the more important of these were the Medical Research Council's investigation into anaemia (the haemoglobin survey), the report of the Council's committee on tuberculosis in wartime, and the Ministry of Health's monthly survey of sickness in a small but representative sample of the population aged over 16.

Many of the new investigations had not progressed very far before it began to appear that the signs of deterioration, which had shown themselves during 1940-41, were fading away. The increases in the death rate among infants and young children, and from diseases of poverty like pulmonary tuberculosis, were arrested in 1942. They then began to turn downwards. The improvement in certain of these vital indices continued to the end of the war and beyond.

Among all the changes in health indices between 1941 and 1946, perhaps the most striking were the reductions in the rates of death for infants, young children and mothers in childbirth. The improvements would have been considered by any student of national welfare as a remarkable achievement in peacetime; they were more remarkable for a period of war and doubly so when set in a wider frame of history. In the hundred years or so since national records of infant mortality were first kept for England and Wales, the decline of 28% in the rate between 1941 and 1946 was only once equalled for any similar or shorter period of time: between 1918 and 1923, when the infant mortality rate fell by 29%. In Scotland, the decline of 35% in the rate between 1941 and 1946 was easily the greatest percentage reduction since records were first kept in 1855.

* * * * *

Among young people and adults, wartime vital statistics are even less informative and more difficult to analyse than those for children. Death rates and measures of sickness and absence from work were confused by many special factors, notably the selective recruitment of several million men and women into the armed forces, the changing age and sex composition of the civilian population and the effects of air raids. If the death rates for older men and women are studied, however, it is apparent that substantial gains were achieved after 1941.

Most of the rates for different causes of death which make up the total mortality declined in varying degrees during the war. There was, however, one big exception: tuberculosis. A serious rise took place in 1940 and again in 1941, both in the number of civilian deaths and the number of people notified as suffering from tuberculosis. The drastic ejection of many patients from sanatoria on the outbreak of war and their return home in an infective state probably contributed to these increases. But after 1941 there was in general, except in Scotland, a surprising reversal of these upward trends in mortality.

By the end of the war practically all the tuberculosis death rates for England and Wales had either returned to the level at which they stood in 1938 or had registered some small improvements. Most of the gains were achieved by women over 15 years of age. Scotland, however, fared badly, in that there was an adverse trend in mortality among young people and to a rather less degree, schoolchildren.

Despite the limitations in the use of death rates as an index of tendencies in public health, the conclusions to be drawn from the rates for infants and children are not at variance with the results of the clinical and other studies undertaken in the later years of the war. No evidence was found, for instance, of more undernourishment, more rickets or more anaemia. On the contrary, signs of betterment were detected; one being the improved condition of children's teeth, although the amount of dental treatment given to children under the school medical service was much reduced during the war. Little can be said here about the effects of the war on young men and women because the question of their health is mixed up with their experience of service in the armed forces; the subject is therefore left to the medical historians.

* * * * *

As regards the older men and women who were not recruited into the forces and who made up the bulk of the civilian population, it is not easy to sum up the effects of the war on their health. The trend of the death rate at different ages among men and women considered separately, the different behaviour of the rates for different causes of death, and the varying records for different parts of the country, suggest that the effects were not uniformly borne; some groups and some areas saw more of the adversities of war than others. Conversely, some groups benefited more than others from the social and economic changes wrought by the war. While it is necessary to emphasise these reservations and to remember that averages can hide greater or less internal variation though still presenting much the same sort of face to the world, it is nevertheless clear that, considered as a whole, the trend of the death rate for middle-aged and elderly men and women was far more favourable than might have been expected in 1939. When, however, rates of sickness are examined, the evidence is less favourable. There was, for example, unlike the downward trend during the First World War, a substantial rise in the number of claims for sickness benefit by insured workers under the National Health Insurance Scheme. This was due to an increase in illnesses of short duration and not to any change in the amount of prolonged illness. Many reports from war factories about attendance at work during 1941-44 spoke in similar terms. It is arguable that this increase in the number of short-term illnesses could have been brought about by the great changes which occurred in the composition of the working population, leading to the employment of a much larger proportion of women and unfit and elderly men.

Other factors, which cannot easily be discounted, include the effects of re-employment and long hours of work on people who previously had been unemployed or underemployed, and the consequences of transferring workers away from their homes. Moreover, some increase must be attributed to all the social, psychological and industrial stresses of war, the immediate and after effects of air raids, the evacuation of members of families, the worry and anxiety caused by the absence of menfolk on service and often in danger, the difficulties of getting hospital treatment, greater overcrowding due to the housing shortage and many other factors.

What is known, however, is that in certain parts of the country the number of medical prescriptions given to insured workers increased during the war, particularly for vitamin preparations, nerve sedatives and tonics. Moreover, an astonishingly large proportion of the adult population, perhaps a larger proportion than before the war, dosed themselves with patent medicines, laxatives, aspirins, cold preventives and vitamin preparations (Davies, 1944). One remarkable feature of the economic history of the war was the stability of the patent medicine industry; after four years of war, and despite the shortage of paper, the industry was still spending as much as £2.25 million a year on press advertising alone. While the industries concerned with household equipment, cigarettes, travel, magazines, newspapers, books and other educational items reduced their press advertising expenditure by nearly 90% between 1938 and 1943, that of the patent medicine industry fell by only 28%, although there was no evidence of a fall in demand for its products.

* * * * *

When the whole monotonous array of strains and stresses are assembled in some sort of order and when account is also taken of wartime working conditions – long hours and night shifts, bad ventilation and artificial light because of the 'black-out', the employment of young, inexperienced and elderly people and those excluded from the armed forces, loss of sleep as a result of air raids, and the hardships of queueing for and travelling by crowded buses and trams – it may be thought a remarkable fact that there was not much more sickness and many more absences from work among all adult groups. If doctors could not help, and if aspirins, sedatives, cigarettes and laxatives helped people to stay on the job, then they, and the patent medicine industry, were good things in the short run. And if, in 1945, it meant that health troubles had been stored up for the future, at least there was some satisfaction in knowing that the war was over.

The events that stand out sharply in this brief survey of the public health are three in number. There was the deterioration during 1939-41 and then the arresting change in health trends in 1942. There were the astonishing improvements after 1941 in the health and expectation of life of infants and young children. There was the absence of any sure signs that the health of the workers and the housewives had been undermined despite the burdens they carried for over six years. The war did not lead to any serious recession in the public health or to any dramatic increase in disease. This, in the circumstances, may be regarded as a remarkable and unexpected experience.

It was remarkable, too, when set against the fact that the war deprived the civilian population of a large part of its pre-war medical resources. The difficulties and delays encountered by sick people in getting access to hospital care have already been stated. Similar difficulties, caused by shortages of medical, dental, nursing and other staff hampered the school medical services, the maternity and child welfare clinics and other branches of public health work. By 1943, for example, the number of doctors in all the public health services in Britain had fallen by over 20% from the 1939 strength. In all these services and in all the hospitals, clinics and sanatoria, the medical staff who were left to carry on were generally either very young or elderly or unfit for military service. More important still, the ranks of the general practitioners in Britain were depleted by the end of the war by over one third and, of those who remained, 10% were over 70 years of age.

* * * * *

Why then, was the health of the people, and in particular the health of babies and young children, so well maintained during the war? Why did it start to deteriorate, then stop, then recover? Hardly anyone, medical or lay, expected the British nation to emerge from the rigours of six years of war, bombing, food shortage and incomparably worse housing conditions with some of its vital statistics more favourable than they had ever been in its history.

Full employment doubtless had had much to do with the good record of the British people's health during the Bonapartist wars [1790s to early 19th century]. In the Second World War full employment was not achieved for some time, but, from 1941 onwards, the number of people whose diet was gravely circumscribed by the amount of money in their pockets must have been small. Up to 1941, the rise in the cost of living had been faster than the rise of wage rates, if not earnings, but, in the middle of the year, the government decided to take firm control of the cost of living. Moreover, in 1941 the first benefits were felt of the social policies – chief among them the National Milk Scheme – which were so bravely born in the summer of 1940. The year 1941 was thus a year of many turning points.

A period of time had, of course, to elapse before the effects of these policies were sufficiently powerful to make an impression on the course of vital statistics. An improvement, for instance, in the character of the diet of the poorest third of the population was not likely to be reflected at once in clear-cut signs of better health. But by 1942 the social schemes that had been developed in earlier years were spreading their benefits and the rationing of food was beginning to rest on sounder nutritional principles. These favourable processes were reinforced in 1942 by a general increase in the consumption of milk; by an improvement in supplies of meat, cheese, fresh fruit and vegetables; by a growth in the provision of meals in canteens, schools and British restaurants; by increases in financial aid to members of the armed forces and their families; and by the fact that heavy air raids ceased. Finally, there was the important fact that the nutritive quality of bread was greatly improved by the government's decision, taken in March 1942 because of the shipping situation, to raise the extraction rate of flour from about 70% to 85%, thus leaving in the flour some 15% more of the wheat berry rich in essential nutrients.

All these measures and events, supported by a steady expansion in the application of scientific knowledge of nutrition to the task of providing a good diet in circumstances of shortage, helped to sustain the health and working capacity of a people who were fully employed and who carried more money in their pockets than they had been accustomed to for a very long while.

This powerful combination of influences – full employment, food subsidies, 'fair shares', price control and the welfare foods schemes – which drew their inspiration and bestowed their benefits as a result of government action, and which weighed the scales of national health in favour of less serious disease and fewer deaths, were strongly aided by other forces less directly in the gift of contemporary government. The nation was remarkably fortunate, for instance, in escaping any disastrous epidemics. It may be said that, on the whole, the weather during six winters of war was helpful; certainly there was no long and rigorous spell of cold comparable to that which the country experienced in 1947 when its fuel supplies ran short.

Many authorities had expected that the evacuation of city children to rural areas in 1939 would lead to an increased spread of the infectious diseases of childhood; yet, to the surprise of the medical profession, there was less disease than usual. Many more feared that the overcrowding of shelters, tube stations and rest centres in the winter of 1940, and the constant migration of people to and from bombed areas, would cause outbreaks of respiratory disease; yet, again, nothing exceptional happened.

The achievements of the authorities in protecting the country from a serious outbreak of typhoid during the war were remarkable. Despite the bombing of water mains and sewers and the many consequential opportunities for dangerous pollution to occur, not a single case of typhoid attributable to the water supply was recorded in London throughout the war and no outbreaks of water-borne disease occurred anywhere in the country as a result of enemy action. The benefit of clean water from a public service provides yet one more reason why the nation's vital statistics were better than anyone had expected.

It was not an accident that, with each succeeding year of the Second World War, there was an increasing number of childbearing women who had themselves been born and bred in more favourable circumstances than previous generations of mothers.

Broadly, two reasons may be advanced in support of this proposition. One is represented by the gradual, if uneven, improvement in the conditions of life for the mass of the people since the turn of the 20th century, brought about by a rise in the average level of real wages, better food, better housing and the first effects (mental as well as physical) of developing state education and welfare policies. The full fruits of such policies rarely show themselves at once and never dramatically; a long time may elapse before the nation can assess by scientific method the benefits of universal education, school meals and milk services and social insurance. If Britain continued to gather during the Second World War more of the benefits of past endeavour for social justice, the rewards could not have come at a more propitious time.

The second reason may be sought in the decline of the birth rate, principally in the decline among the families of industrial workers since the census of 1911. This great section of the population, dominating as it does the general level of national birth and death rates, achieved a substantial rise in its standard of life by reducing their size of its families by around one half in less than half a century. Children born into these families thus had a better start in life and were better able to draw benefit from the expanding social and education services. It was not until the late 1930s and especially the 1940s that these children, springing from smaller families, enjoying more parental time and care, and more attention from the state, began themselves, in their turn, to found families.

Such reductions in the number of large families, in conjunction with the pronounced trend towards earlier childbearing, may well have had other consequences beneficial to the nation's vital statistics. For instance, since there were fewer older mothers bearing fifth or subsequent children, the maternal mortality rate may perhaps have profited. There may too have been less sickness and ill health following upon childbearing as a result of these changes in the age of reproduction and size of families. And, because there were fewer large-sized families, there were correspondingly fewer children living in those circumstances of hardship historically associated with big families.

So far as the statistics for mothers and children are concerned, the impressive reductions in death rates which were registered during the war cannot be wholly ascribed to the effects of full employment and all that the government achieved in the field of nutrition and health. Some part of the improvement must, it seems, be credited to the past and some part to the collective decisions of parents both before and during the war to limit the size of their families. The contribution made to the maintenance of health standards by these and all the other inter-related forces discussed in this chapter cannot, of course, be precisely determined. Nevertheless, the deterioration in health indices observed during 1940-41 and the arresting change in trends thereafter, which cannot be fully explained by these favourable social and biological factors, point to the supreme importance of full employment and an adequate diet. The achievements of the government's food and social policies in bringing about an improvement in the diet of poor families may well have been reinforced and backed by the action of other forces, but without these policies there is no evidence that the deterioration would have been arrested.

* * * * *

But just as the advances of one generation may only show their full effects through the lives of succeeding generations so, too, may the retreats. Some of the scars of the First World War may not yet have been wiped away. It has been suggested, for instance, by Stocks (1943) that the unfavourable trend during the 1930s of the death rate among middle-aged men, and particularly that part of it attributable to heart disease, may have been due to the strains and hardships to which they were exposed as younger men during 1914-18. He also pointed out that the arrest in the fall of tuberculosis mortality among young adults after 1926 could possible be traced to the effects on children of the food shortages of 1916-18, resulting in a lowered resistance to active tuberculosis of the lungs as these children reached the sensitive period of young adult life.

These may not be the best illustrations to use, but they suffice to show the character of the legacy that modern war can bequeath to the future. Perhaps all the advances that were made on the social front in 1940 and in subsequent years were sufficient to protect the people from carrying into the future the scars of the Second World War. Perhaps only the children were adequately protected, and here it should be recalled that the nation had two million fewer to nourish than during the First World War. Perhaps more lasting harm was wrought to the minds and to the hearts of men, women and children than to their bodies. The disturbances to family life, the separation of mothers and fathers from their children, of husbands from their wives, of pupils from their schools, of people from their recreation, of society from the pursuits of peace – perhaps all these indignities of war have left wounds which will take time to heal and infinite patience to understand.

Redistribution, universality and inequality

Commentary: John Hills

These three essays from the mid-1960s illustrate Titmuss's thinking on some of the key issues of social policy, now as well as then. Reading them nearly forty years on, it is striking how many of the issues and the questions he addressed then are still of central relevance to policy dilemmas today, even if the context – and hence some of the answers – have changed. Indeed, there are many ways in which the context has changed precisely because of the influence of his ideas and critique of the state of social policy, broadly defined, as it was in the 1950s and 1960s. In other ways, circumstances have changed as a result of some of the social and economic forces he foresaw as of growing importance.

* * * * *

The first chapter, 'The role of redistribution in social policy', picks up and develops some of the ideas Titmuss had discussed in what is included here as Part 2, Chapter Two, 'The social division of welfare', particularly the arbitrariness of what was seen as a 'social service' because it involved public spending, in distinction to other forms of fiscal and occupational welfare.

Titmuss rejects this view of social policy as consisting of public spending in specified areas as both inadequate, because of what it omits, and misleading in implying that welfare provision is unproblematically redistributive from those with more to those with less income. He sees this kind of view as a result of the origins of pre-war British welfare provision in the Poor Law, with its reliance on personal discrimination, dividing the population into "eligible and ineligible citizens", and achieving redistribution *only* by being discriminatory and socially divisive. This first part of the chapter provides a powerful statement of the case against services solely delivered to the poor through a means test.

By contrast, Titmuss stresses that post-war social policy had gradually abandoned the use of "discriminatory and overtly redistributive services for second class citizens". Instead, services like contributory social insurance, universal free secondary education, council housing aimed at all income groups, and the NHS had two aims. One was, to be sure, the redistributive objective, but the second, non-discriminatory objective, was "manifestly [to] encourage social integration". This still often neglected distinction remains of great contemporary relevance. One of the advantages of the emergence of the disputed concepts of social inclusion and exclusion into recent British academic and policy debate has been precisely that they widen the focus beyond the narrow questions of who gains and who loses in cash terms, to include that of how people are treated by public and private systems.

The next part of the chapter develops his comparison of social, fiscal and occupational welfare and their distributional effects, providing further examples of the often more favourable treatment of those with high than those with low incomes. Titmuss relied on hypothetical particular examples in support of his case. More recent analysts can use data for the whole population and their use of services to examine the same questions – for instance, the annual official analysis by the Office for National Statistics of the distribution and redistribution of income using Family Expenditure Survey data; see Lakin (2001) and LeGrand (1982), using General Household Survey data, or Sefton (1997), analysis using both.

This kind of analysis suggests two points of caution in trying to translate Titmuss's conclusions straightforwardly to the present day. The first is that circumstances change. Some of the implicit redistribution he describes within occupational pension schemes from those with shorter-term jobs to those with secure careers has been reduced by 'early leaver' protection provisions of subsequent legislation. Many of the tax reliefs favouring those with high incomes have been reduced or abolished: some of their value was reduced as top rates of income tax were cut in the 1980s; income tax child allowances were subsumed into flat rate universal Child Benefit in the late 1970s; what was the married man's income tax allowance was eventually transmuted by 2001 into a children's tax credit going to all income taxpayers *except* those paying higher rate tax; mortgage interest relief was first extended to non-taxpayers, then restricted to the basic rate of tax, reduced in value, and finally abolished altogether in the late 1990s; occupational pension funds lost a major part of their tax advantages when their dividend incomes were quietly brought into tax in 1997. While the first of these changes under the Thatcher government can hardly be ascribed to Titmuss's influence, the others can in part – illustrating if nothing else the long lag there can be between policy analysis and policy change and the error of judging academic analysis simply by looking at its immediate impact.

The second point of caution is that analysis also develops. In his essays Titmuss stressed the importance of looking at all three forms of welfare together, particularly looking at the tax system as well as public transfers and service provision. But this can be taken further. The tax system is important not just as a source of tax reliefs and allowances (or today, tax credits) but also as the source of funding for public spending. To compare the impact of welfare provision on those in different income or other groups, we really need to look at their *net* gains or losses in a difficult comparison with how the world would look without that provision. At the least, this means examining the question of where the money to pay for things comes from, including the net impact of the taxes people actually pay. If we fail to do this, one might think, for instance, that those with high incomes were losing out as marginal income tax rates were cut in the 1980s and the value of their tax allowances fell. It also means that the universal services which are less overtly redistributive than those provided only with a means-test may none the less be redistributive in impact once we take account of where the money comes from to pay for them.

A final part of this chapter identifies what remains a huge contemporary issue: equality of access to universal services does not guarantee equality of treatment, still less equality of outcome. As when Titmuss was writing, having a national health service and universal secondary education does not mean that the articulate and privileged in terms of where they live receive the same quality of service as those who are less articulate and live in more deprived areas.

* * * * *

These themes are taken up in the second chapter in this part, 'Welfare state and welfare society', originally delivered as a lecture to the British National Conference on Social Welfare in 1967. An early section contains a scathing account of the 'aid' given by poor countries to rich ones, such as the United States, which recruit the skilled medical professionals they have trained at great cost to themselves. In the years since this was written, this has been a recurring issue – and one which has powerful echoes in a Britain at the start of the 21st century, which is supporting its own schools and hospitals in much the same way. As Howard Glennerster discusses in his commentary to Part 6, Titmuss did not see social policy and its impact as confined to national boundaries.

Another point of this lecture was to attack what Titmuss describes as the "public burden model of welfare", the idea that welfare services like the NHS or state education should be seen simply as a drain on the economy, with the cost an impediment to growth. Instead, he points to the positive role that such services can have, even in narrowly measured economic terms. In particular, he highlights the notion of *prevention* as one of the engines behind the move towards social rights and universalism. An aim of extending health and other services was to break the links between poverty, disease, neglect, illiteracy and destitution. But, to achieve this, the services have to be taken up by all and, for this to be done effectively, "they had to be delivered through socially approved channels; that is to say, without loss of respect by the users and their families".

These "socially approved channels" are exemplified for him by the NHS, the 1944 Butler Education Act, National Insurance and family allowances (now developed into Child Benefit). What is notable about this listing from the viewpoint of the start of the next century is the enduring public popularity of these areas, or at least of health, education, pensions and benefits for children as exemplified both by the terms of contemporary political debate and public attitudes (Hills and Lelkes, 1999). But this also suggests two further points, one developed further in this chapter, the other not. The first is that these services have wider functions than simple redistribution, and can be an efficient way of meeting private as well as social aims (Barr, 1998). The second, which Titmuss does not touch on here, is political: the arguments around the "sharp elbows of the middle classes" in defence of services from which they benefit.

Having reinforced the case developed before for universalism, Titmuss goes on to develop an analytical framework which is still useful for examining both the nature and functions of particular services. Their nature can vary in terms of how entitlement is determined, which groups are entitled, and the financial and administrative methods used to implement them. Amongst the seven kinds of function he sets out, what is notable is the stress he puts on the role of social services as *compensation* in whole or in part for dis-services caused by society or the economic system. In other words, receipt of a service can in many cases only be counted as a 'gain' to the recipient if we start with a presumption that the problems caused by other activities should "lie where they fall". As he argues, "it is not just a question of benefit allocation, whose 'welfare state', but also of loss allocation, whose 'diswelfare state'".

With this kind of complex framework in mind, Titmuss rejects as oversimplified the distinction between universalism and selective services. There are many forms of universalism as well as of selection, and many hybrids in between. This leads on to his conclusion, again of contemporary relevance, where he argues that universalism by itself is not enough. The real challenge in his view is to develop an underlying framework of universal services, "within and around which can be developed socially acceptable selective services aiming to discriminate positively". Rather than rejecting the idea of targeted services for groups with particular needs as in opposition to universalism, he sees "universalism as an essential pre-requisite to selective positive discrimination".

His discussion highlights a continuing dilemma for policy: how to structure services so that they generate something for all, but more for those who need them most, and how to tailor that balance without losing political support for the taxes needed to finance them. Exactly that debate rages still from the balance between the Working Families Tax Credit and universal Child Benefit (and hence the value of the Integrated Child Credit to those with different incomes when these strategies are amalgamated in 2003) to that between what is now called the Minimum Income Guarantee for low income pensioners, the promised Pension Credit, and the basic (national insurance) state pension.

* * * * *

The concerns of the third chapter in this part, 'Social welfare and the art of giving', originally published in *Socialist Humanism*, edited by Eric Fromm in 1965 (and in various other forms in 1964 and 1965), are somewhat different. A part of it presages, as the title suggests, some of the arguments developed much more fully in Titmuss's later book, *The gift relationship*. In particular, he quotes a view of modern social welfare as "help given to the stranger". As it becomes harder to identify both those responsible for the harmful side effects of modern societies and economies and the precise levels of private losses resulting from them, he argues that, "altruism by strangers for strangers was and is an attempt to fill a moral void created by applied science".

However, his main concern in this chapter is to attack those, such as Seymour Lipset (1960) or Daniel Bell (1960) who had proclaimed the end of political ideology, as the terms of the "post-war consensus" narrowed debate from major differences in views of the role of the state to minor disputes which made changes of political control of little importance. So far, history is on Titmuss's side. Some of his concerns today seem a little quaint – that synthetic coffee will supplant the need for coffee beans; others seem over-optimistic – that the production of consumption goods will become a subsidiary question for the West. But writing from the other side of Ronald Reagan and Margaret Thatcher, his assault on the idea that political ideology no longer mattered by the early 1960s seems fully justified. Even by early 2001, the idea that there was no real ideological difference between Bill Clinton and Al Gore on the one hand and George W. Bush on the other is being rapidly buried by the early policies of the Bush presidency.

But the chapter also points to other trends which are central to social policy today. First, Titmuss points to growth of inequality in both wealth and incomes in the UK between the late 1940s and mid-1960s. What we know now from more detailed statistics is that, on most measures, wealth inequality was falling in this period and continued to do so until the mid-1970s, since when it has been roughly constant. However, income inequality did indeed grow over the period Titmuss was discussing. This was followed by a significant fall to reach a low point in the late 1970s (Hills, 1996). It was after this – between the late 1970s and early 1990s – that the great reversal of the decline in income inequality took place. Second, one of the engines behind that reversal was indeed the one which Titmuss identifies here: the impact of technical change. Another was precisely the impact of political ideology, reports of whose death, as he argued, had been greatly exaggerated.

Returning to the origins of post-war social welfare, he identifies, the "impulse from below", particularly the friendly societies. They developed from values which underlay "the search for security in an increasingly insecure world [which] are still relevant to an understanding of the role of social welfare in Britain today" and, one might add, to that understanding forty years later.

This leads to Titmuss's concluding identification of what were then and still are unresolved issues: the problem of size, of the tension between universal standards and decentralisation and local control; and the pressures put on welfare systems by the ageing population and the growth in inequality of market incomes. Titmuss looks ahead, like Keynes, to a world where higher levels of production would allow different rules to be lived by in response to these problems, but in truth we have not changed the rules yet.

The role of redistribution in social policy

In the literature of the West, concepts and models of social policy are as diverse as contemporary concepts of poverty. Historically, the two have indeed had much in common. They certainly share diversity. There are those at one end of the political spectrum who see social policy as a transitory minimum activity of minimum government for a minimum number of poor people; as a form of social control for minority groups in a 'natural' society; as a way of resolving the conflict between the religious ethic of compassion and undiluted individualism. In this view, social policy is not good business. Statistical estimates of the national income per capita look healthier if the infant mortality rate rises. At the other end of the political spectrum, there are writers like Macbeath (1957) who has comprehensively stated that, "Social policies are concerned with the right ordering of the network of relationships between men and women who live together in societies, or with the principles which should govern the activities of individuals and groups so far as they affect the lives and interests of other people".

Somewhere between these extreme visionary notions lives a conventional, textbook definition of social policy. [For some discussion on the problems of definition, see Wilensky and Lebeaux, 1958; Myrdal, 1960; Titmuss, 1963.] The social services or social welfare, the labels we have for long attached to describe certain areas of public intervention such as income maintenance and public health, are seen as the main ingredients of social policy. They are obvious, direct and measurable acts of government, undertaken for a variety of political reasons, to provide for a range of needs, material and social, and predominantly dependent needs, which the market does not or cannot satisfy for certain designated sections of the population. Typically, these direct services are functionally organised in separate and specialised ministries, departments or divisions of government, central and local. They are seen as the 'social policy departments'. What they do is thought to be explicitly redistributive; they politically interfere with the pattern of claims set by the market. They assign claims from one set of people who are said to produce or earn the national product to another set of people who may merit compassion and charity but not economic rewards for productive service. In short, they are seen as uncovenanted benefits for the poorer sections of the community. And because these separate functional units of social service are accountable to the public, their activities are, in large measure, quantifiable. We can thus measure the size of the presumed burden (as it is conventionally called) on the economy.

This, I propose to argue, is a very limited and inadequate model of the working of social policy in the second half of the 20th century. In its distance from the realities of today it is about as helpful (or unhelpful) as some models of economic man maximising his acquisitive drives. Later, I attempt to support and illustrate this statement by examining some of the lessons of experience of nearly twenty years [late 1940s–60s] of so-called welfare statism in Britain. First, however, I want briefly to consider one or two of the factors which have contributed to this limited concept of social policy, particularly in relation to its role as a redistributive agent.

Perhaps the most important causative factor in Britain has to do with the heritage of the Poor Law (or public assistance). In the early 20th century, social policy was, in the eyes of the middle and upper classes, Poor Law policy. This model of 'welfare use' was part of a political philosophy which saw society as an adjunct of the market (Dicey, 1905). As Karl Polanyi (1945, p 63) puts it, "instead of economy being embedded in social relations, social relations are embedded in the economic system". The essential, though financially reluctant, role of the Poor Law was to support industrialism and the attempt in the 19th century to support a completely competitive, self-regulating market economy founded on the motive of individual gain. It thus had to create a great many rules of expected behaviour; about work and non-work, property, savings, family relationships, cohabitation, men in the house and so forth. Poverty, as Disraeli once said, was declared a crime by industrialism. Laws about poverty became associated with laws about crime.

This system, which legally survived in Britain until 1948, inevitably involved personal discrimination. The stigmata of the Poor Law test, moral judgments by people about other people and their behaviour, were a condition of redistribution. The requirements of Poor Law and public assistance administration were, we can now see, remarkably attuned to the characteristics of bureaucracy drawn by Weber and others (Gerth and Mills, 1946). It was theoretically a neat and orderly world of eligible and ineligible citizens; of approved and disapproved patterns of dependency; of those who could manage change and those who could not. From its operation for over a century, Britain inherited in 1948 a whole set of administrative attitudes, values and rites; essentially middle class in structure and moralistic in application. The new social service bottles of 1948 had poured into them much of the old wine of discrimination and prejudice. It took nearly two decades of sustained programmes of new recruitment, training and re-training and in-training, and the appointment of social workers to the public services, to eradicate part of this legacy of administrative behaviour.

The history of the Poor Law and public assistance is thus still important to an understanding of social policy concepts today. If one disregards the social costs of industrialism, of allowing a large part of the disservices of technological progress to lie where they fall, then the system (of public assistance) was clearly redistributive. It directly benefited the explicit poor. Those in the greatest need did receive some benefit, but with the limited instruments of policy and administrative techniques to hand in the past, the system could only function by operating punitive tests of discrimination; by strengthening conceptions of approved and disapproved dependencies; and by a damaging assault on the recipients of welfare in terms of their sense of self-respect and self-determination. Within the established pattern of commonly held values, the system could only be redistributive by being discriminatory and socially divisive.

All this is well documented in the archives of social inquiry and is somewhat ancient history. Equally well known is the story of society's response to the challenge of poverty since the 1930s: the discovery that this system of public aid was administratively grossly inefficient; that it could not by its very nature absorb the new dimensions of social and psychological knowledge and that therefore it could not function effectively either as a redistributive agent or as an agent to prevent social breakdown; and that the system was fundamentally inconsistent with the need to grant to all citizens, irrespective of race, religion or colour, full and equal social rights (Beveridge, 1942).

Gradually in Britain, as we tried to learn these lessons, we began to discard the use of discriminatory and overtly redistributive services for those perceived as second class citizens. The social services on minimum standards for all citizens crept apologetically into existence. In common with other countries, we invented contributory National Insurance or Social Security and provided benefits as of right. The actuary was called in to replace the functions of the public assistance relieving officer. Free secondary education for all children, irrespective of the means of their parents, was enacted in 1944 as part of a comprehensive educational system. Public housing authorities were called upon in 1945 to build houses for people and not just for working-class people. A limited and second class health insurance scheme for working men was transformed in 1948 into a comprehensive and free-on-demand health service for the whole population (Hall, 1952).

All these and many other changes in the direct and publicly accountable instruments of social policy led to the notion that, in the year 1948, the 'welfare state' had been established in Britain. While there was general political consensus on this matter there was, on the other hand, much confusion and debate about cause and effect (Titmuss, 1962, ch 9). There were many, for instance, who thought that these policy changes were brought about for deliberately redistributive reasons and that the effects would be significantly egalitarian. This, perhaps, was understandable. Direct welfare in the past had in fact been redistributive, considered apart from the effects of the fiscal system. Therefore it was natural to assume that more welfare in the future would mean more redistribution in favour of the poor. There were others however (among whom I count myself) who believed that the fundamental and dominating historical processes which led to these major changes in social policy were connected with the demand for one society; for non-discriminatory services for all without distinction of class, income or race; for services and relations which would deepen and enlarge self-respect; for services which would manifestly encourage social integration. From some perspectives, these major changes in policy could be regarded as ideological pleas to the middle- and upper-income classes to share in the benefits (as well as the costs) of public welfare.

Built into the public model of social policy in Britain from 1948 there are two major roles or objectives: the redistributive objective and the non-discriminatory objective. To move towards the latter, it was believed that a prerequisite was the legal enactment of universal (or comprehensive) systems of national insurance, education, medical care, housing and other direct services.

What have we learnt about the actual functioning of these services? What has universalism in social welfare achieved? Clearly, I cannot give you a full account of all aspects of this development during a period when, for thirteen of these years [1951-64], the government in power was not, in the early stages at least, entirely committed to the concept of the welfare state. I shall therefore concentrate my conclusions, brief and inadequate though they are, on the theme of redistribution.

Up to this point I have dealt only with what I sometimes call the 'iceberg phenomena of social welfare'. That is, the direct public provision of services in kind (such as education and medical care) and the direct payment of benefits in cash (for example, retirement pensions and family allowances).

I now consider two other major categories of social policy which have been developing and extending their roles in Britain and other countries over much the same period of time as the category we call 'the social services'. Elsewhere, I have described the former as 'fiscal welfare' and 'occupational welfare' [Part 2, Chapter Two, 'Social division of welfare']. These are the indirect or submerged parts of the iceberg of social policy. In both categories, a remarkable expansion has taken place in Britain during the past twenty years [1944-64].

All three categories of social policy have a great deal in common in terms of redistribution. They are all concerned with changing the individual and family pattern of current and future claims on resources set by the market, set by the possession of accumulated past rights, and set by the allocations made by government to provide for national defence and other non-market sectors. Social welfare changes the patterns of claims by, for instance, directly providing in kind education or mental hospital care either free or at less than the market cost. Fiscal welfare changes the pattern of claims by taking less in tax (and thus increasing net disposable income) when a taxpayer's child is born, when its education is prolonged, when men have ex-wives to maintain, when taxpayers reach a specified age, and so on. An individual's pattern of claims on resources is in the mid-1960s greatly varied through fiscal welfare policy by, for example, his or her change in circumstances, family responsibilities and opportunities available (and taken) for prolonged education and home ownership. In Britain, the United States and other countries, the tax system has been regarded as an alternative to the social security system in certain areas; as a policy instrument to be used to provide higher incomes for the aged, for large families, for the blind and other handicapped groups, and for meeting part of the costs of education which may last for up to twenty years or more.

Occupational welfare, provided by virtue of employment status, achievement and record, may take the form of social security provisions in cash or in kind. Such provisions are legally approved by government and, as in the case of fiscal welfare, they may be seen as alternatives to extensions in social welfare. Their costs falls in large measure on the whole population. It is thus, like social welfare and fiscal welfare, a major redistributive mechanism.

In Britain, occupational welfare may include pensions for employees; survivors' benefits; child allowances; death benefits; health and welfare services; severance pay and compensation for loss of office (analogous these days to compensation of loss of property rights); personal expenses for travel, entertainment and dress; meal vouchers; cars and season tickets; residential accommodation; holiday expenses; children's school fees at private schools; sickness benefits; medical expenses; education and training grants and benefits ranging from 'obvious forms of realizable goods to the most intangible forms of amenity' (*Royal Commission on Taxation*, 1955) expressed in a form that is neither money nor convertible into money.

A substantial part of these occupational welfare benefits can be interpreted, like fiscal welfare, as social policy recognition of dependencies; the long dependencies of old age, childhood and widowhood, and such short-term dependencies as sickness and the loss of job rights.

The population to which these three categories of welfare relate differ, but a substantial section of people may be eligible for benefits in respect of all three. In Britain, most of the social welfare services (except national assistance and university education) are universalist and citizen-based; they are open to all without a test of means. Thus, access to them does not depend upon achieved or inherited status. Fiscal welfare relates to a smaller population: that is, only to those who pay direct taxes and not those who pay property taxes and social security contributions. Occupational welfare relates to the employed population and predominantly favours white-collar and middle-class occupations. Benefits are thus related to achievement.

All three categories of welfare are redistributive; they change the pattern of claims on current and future resources. They function redistributively as separate, self-contained systems and they do so also in relation to the whole economy. Here is one example. Many private pension schemes, which include manual and non-manual workers, tend to redistribute claims on resources from lower paid to higher paid employees. This happens because the lower paid workers change jobs more frequently; in doing so, they do not have credited to them the full amount of pension contributions or premiums. It is estimated in Britain that the cost of full preservation of pension rights for all employees in the private sector could add 15-25% to the actuarial costs of private schemes. Moreover, as at present organised, the cost to the Treasury (the whole community) of private pension schemes substantially exceeds the Treasury contribution to social security pensions for the whole population. The pensions of the rich are more heavily subsidised by the community than the pensions of the poor. [See Part 4, Chapter One, 'The irresponsible society'.]

This in part happens because occupational welfare and fiscal welfare benefits are fundamentally based on the principles of achievement, status and need. If there is need, then the higher the income, the higher the welfare benefit. By contrast, social welfare benefits generally take account only of needs: the need for medical care, for education and so on, irrespective of income or status.

I have now described in very general terms three categories of social policy redistribution, with particular reference to their operation in Britain. They are publicly viewed as virtually distinct systems. What goes on within and as a result of one system is ignored by the others. They are appraised, criticised or applauded as abstracted, independent entities. Historically, they have developed different concepts of poverty or subsistence; different criteria for determining approved dependencies; different standards of moral values in determining eligibility for welfare. Some examples will illustrate this point.

The social policy definition for subsistence as developed in the fiscal system for determining exemption from taxation, income needs in old age, and so on, differs markedly from the definition used in public assistance. In some areas of policy, the fiscal definition of poverty is employed as, for instance, in determining grants to university students. In other and similar areas of policy, the public assistance definition is employed as, for instance, in determining aid for poor parents of 16-year-old children at school. It is odd that dependency at age 16 is assessed at a lower standard of assistance than dependency at 18 or even 23 (in the case of medical students and graduates).

We have in fact two standards of poverty for determining aid from the community, both highly subjective and unscientific, and both employed to assist dependent states: a working-class standard and a middle-class standard. The former has been investigated, studied, measured and argued about for long by sociologists, social workers and economists, and made the subject of many books and doctoral theses. By contrast, the latter has been virtually ignored.

One further example of double standards operating in different categories of welfare may be selected from a large field, illustrating the role of moral values in social policy.

In the category of social welfare, cash aid, from public funds for unsupported mothers and their children may be stopped if it is believed that cohabitation is taking place. This is an event, or a relationship, that can rarely be legally proved. It is hardly a scientific fact. We have in Britain a cohabitation regulation; in the United States, there is a man in the house regulation. They amount to the same thing and cannot be spelt out in precise operational terms. Their application in practice depends in large measure therefore on hearsay and moral judgment.

The same problem of to give or not to give arises in the category of fiscal welfare. As an example, I quote from a memorandum by Lord Justice Hodson to the 1952 Royal Commission on Marriage and Divorce. "A super-tax payer may, and quite frequently nowadays does, have a number of wives living at the same time since after divorce his ex-wives are not treated as one with him for tax purposes he can manage quite nicely since he is permitted" (a social policy decision) "to deduct all his wives' maintenance allowances from his gross income for tax purposes leaving his net income comparatively slightly affected."

In both instances, redistribution takes place; the community renders aid in these situations of need and dependency. But while the decision to help the public assistance mother may involve judgments about moral behaviour, in the case of the taxpayer the decision is automatic and impersonal. The logic of the double standard is not apparent. If one is socially acceptable and approved behaviour, then why not the other?

What have been the lessons of experience in Britain about the actual functioning of these three categories of welfare? Obviously, I cannot give you more than a fragment of an answer and even this involves over-simplifying to a dangerous degree. To analyse and measure the redistributive effects of this process of the social division of welfare would be an immensely complex task, even if the essential statistical data were available. All I can offer are a few generalised conclusions.

The major positive achievement which has resulted from the creation of direct, universalist social services in kind has been the erosion of formal discriminatory barriers. One publicly approved standard of service, irrespective of income, class or race, replaced the double standard which invariably meant second class services for second class citizens. This has been most clearly seen in the NHS. Despite strict controls over expenditure on the NHS by Conservative governments for many years, it has maintained the principle of equality of access by all citizens to all branches of medical care. Viewed solely in terms of the welfare objective of non-discriminatory, non-judgmental service, this is the signal achievement of the NHS. In part this is due to the fact that the middle classes, invited to enter the NHS in 1948, did so and largely stayed. They tended not to contract out of socialised medical care as they did in other fields like secondary education and retirement pensions. Their continuing participation, and their more articulate demands for improvements, have been an important factor in a general rise in standards of service, particularly in hospital care (Lindsey, 1962).

But, as some students of social policy in Britain and the United States are beginning to learn, equality of access is not the same thing as equality of outcome. We have to ask statistical and sociological questions about the utilisation of the high-cost quality sectors of social welfare and the low-cost sectors of social welfare. We have to ask similar questions about the ways in which professional people (doctors, teachers, social workers and many others) discharge their roles in diagnosing need and in selecting or rejecting patients, clients and students for this or that service. In the modern world, the professions are increasingly becoming the arbiters of our welfare fate; they are the key-holders to equality of outcome; they help to determine the pattern of redistribution in social policy.

These generalisations apply particularly when services in kind are organised on a universalist, free-on-demand basis. When this is so we substitute, in effect, the professional decision maker for the crude decisions of the economic market place. We also make much more explicit, an important gain in itself, the fact that the poor have great difficulties in manipulating the wider society, in managing change, in choosing between alternatives and in finding their way around a complex world of welfare.

We have learnt from fifteen years' experience of the NHS [1948–63] that the higher income groups know how to make better use of the service; they tend to receive more specialist attention; occupy more of the beds in better equipped and staffed hospitals; receive more elective surgery; have better maternity care and are more likely to get psychiatric help and psychotherapy than low income groups, particularly the unskilled (see Titmuss, 1963, appendix on the NHS).

These are all factors which are essential to an understanding of the redistributive role played by one of the major direct welfare services in kind. They are not arguments against a comprehensive free-on-demand service, but they do serve to underline one conclusion. Universalism in social welfare, though a needed prerequisite towards reducing and removing formal barriers of social and economic discrimination, does not by itself solve the problem of how to reach the more-difficult-to-reach with better medical care, especially preventive medical care.

Much the same kind of general conclusion can be drawn from Britain's experience in the field of education. Despite reforms and expansion during the fifteen years 1948 to 1963, it is a fact that the proportion of male undergraduates who are the sons of manual workers is about 1% lower than it was between 1928 and 1947. Although we have doubled the number of university students, the proportion coming from working-class homes has remained fairly constant at just over a quarter (Robbins Committee, 1964).

The major beneficiaries of the high cost sectors of the educational system in the welfare state have been the higher income groups. They have been helped to so benefit by the continued existence of a prosperous private sector in secondary education (partly subsidised by the state in a variety of ways including tax-deductibles) and by developments after 1948 in provisions for child dependency in the category of fiscal welfare. Take, for example, the case of two fathers each with two children, one earning $60,000 a year, the other $1,500 a year. In combining the effect of direct social welfare expenditures for children and indirect fiscal welfare expenditures for children, the result is that the rich father now gets thirteen times more from the state than the poor father in recognition of the dependent needs of childhood.

Housing is another field of social policy which merits analysis from the point of view of redistribution. Here we have to take account of the complex interlocking effects of local rate payments, public housing subsidies, interest rates, tax-deductibles for mortgage interest and other factors. When we have done so, we find that the subsidy paid by the state to many middle-class families buying their own homes is greater than that received by poor tenants of public housing (local government) schemes (Nevitt, 1964).

These are no more than illustrations of the need to study the redistributive effects of social policy in a wider frame of reference. Hitherto, our techniques of social diagnosis and our conceptual frameworks have been too narrow. We have compartmentalised social welfare as we have compartmentalised the poor. The analytic model of social policy that has been fashioned on only the phenomena that are clearly visible, direct and immediately measurable is an inadequate one. It fails to tell us about the realities of redistribution which are being generated by the process of technological and social change and by the combined effects of social welfare, fiscal welfare and occupational welfare.

How far and to what extent should redistribution on the principle of achieved status, inherited status or need take place through welfare channels? This is the kind of question which, fundamentally, is being asked in Britain today. And it is being directed, in particular, at two major areas of social policy: social security and housing. Both these instruments of change and redistribution have been neglected. We have gone in search of new gods or no gods at all. It is time we returned to consider their roles afresh and with new vision. Perhaps we might then entitle our journey 'Ways of extending the welfare state to the poor'.

Welfare state and welfare society

Generalised slogans, such as 'the welfare state', rarely induce concentration of thought; more often they prevent us from asking significant questions about reality. Morally satisfied and intellectually dulled, we sink back into our presumptive cosy British world of welfare. Meanwhile, outside these islands (as well as inside) there are critics, economic and political, who are misled into confusing ends and means, and who are discouraged from undertaking the painful exercise of distinguishing between philosophical tomorrows and the current truths of reality in a complex British power structure of rationed resources, and great inequalities in incomes and wealth, opportunities and freedom of choice.

From what little is known about the reading habits of international bankers and economists, I think it is reasonable to say that they do not include much in the way of studies on welfare and the condition of the poor. How then are their views shaped about the British 'welfare state'? This we do not know, but at least we can say that, if we mislead ourselves, we shall mislead them. But the matter does not end there. Models of public welfare can assume different forms and contain different assumptions about means and ends. Concepts of welfare can imply very different things to different people.

One particular model is the 'public burden model of welfare'. In general terms, this sees public welfare expenditure, and particularly expenditure which is redistributive in intent, as a burden; that is, an impediment to growth and economic development. Given this model of the British patient, the diagnosis seems simple. We are spending too much on the welfare state. Such explanations are, moreover, encouraged by the concept of private economic man embedded in the techniques of national income accounting. An increase in public retirement pensions is seen (as it was seen internationally during the balance of payments crisis in 1964) as an economic burden. A similar increase in spending power among occupational (publicly subsidised private) pensioners is not so seen. Yet both involve additions to consumption demand.

Take another example: medical care, public and private. It is argued that, by encouraging the growth of private medical care through a voucher system and by allowing people to contract out of taxation, the 'burden' of the NHS would be reduced. The objective it seems is to reduce the assumed 'burden'; thus, those who contract out diminish the burden. Logically, we should extend to them our gratitude and moral respect for contracting out of public commitments. But, if J. Enoch Powell (1966, p 72) may be accepted as an authority, this "voucher scheme resolves itself merely into a method of increasing state expenditure upon medical care". In other words, it is a proposal for redistributing more medical resources in favour of private patients. The case for contracting-out must therefore be justified on grounds other than the 'welfare burden' argument.

* * * * *

If we insist, come what may, on the continued use or misuse and misapplication of the term 'the welfare state' then we must accept the consequences of international misunderstanding. We cannot assume that observers abroad share, or will share, the social or moral criteria we may apply to welfare; to many of our creditors and currency colleagues in Western Germany, France and the United States, the 'welfare state' is equated with national irresponsibility and decadence; an easy way of living off foreign loans. To the political scientist as well as the economist, these opinions are relevant facts in the same way as (according to some sociologists) social class is what men think it is. These opinions do not, moreover, differ markedly from those expressed in the published statements on welfare during the past fifteen years [1952-67] by bankers, insurance directors, financiers and others in the City of London.

Many of these monetary experts abroad appear to place a different valuation on countries which depend heavily on 'borrowing' human capital as distinct from those which borrow financial capital. For such transactions, no payment is made to the lending country; there are no interest charges and there is no intention of repaying the loan.

Since 1949 the United States has absorbed (and to some extent deliberately recruited) the import of 100.000 doctors, scientists and engineers from developed and developing countries. In about eighteen years the United States will have saved some $4,000 million by not having to educate and train, or train fully, this vast quantity of human capital. It has spent more on consumption goods, less on public services. It has taxed itself more lightly while imposing heavier taxation on poorer countries. Estimates have been made that this foreign aid to America is as great or greater than the total of American aid to countries abroad since 1949. Moreover, such estimates leave out of account the social and economic effects in Britain (and much more significantly in the poor countries of the world) of having to train more doctors, scientists and engineers, and of having to pay heavily inflated rewards to prevent American recruitment with all their harmful repercussions on incomes, prices and levels of taxation.

In medicine alone, foreign doctors account for nearly 20% of the annual additions to the American medical profession. The world now [1967] provides as much or more medical aid to the United

States in terms of dollars as the total cost of all American medical aid, private and public, to foreign countries. A study I have made of the columns of the *British Medical Journal* and the *Lancet* from 1951 to 1966 shows that advertisements for British doctors (often accompanied by recruiting campaigns and sometimes actively encouraged by senior British doctors) rose fom a yearly average of 134 in 1951 to over 4,000 in 1966. The total number of newly qualified doctors in Britain in 1966 was around 1,700; each of them cost about £10,000 to train, excluding expenditure on student maintenance.

The United States is not alone in attempting to develop its welfare systems (and Medicare) at the expense of pooorer countries through the discovery that it is much cheaper and less of a public burden to import doctors, scientists and other qualified workers than to educate and train them. Britain is also relying heavily on the skills of doctors from poorer countries, in part due to the belief less than five to ten years ago among Ministers and leaders of the medical profession that we were in danger of training too many doctors. And, we may add, the belief among liberal economists and sections of the medical profession that Britain was spending too much on the Health Service which was in danger of bankrupting the nation. Even as late as 1962, there were influential voices in the British Medical Association who were speaking of the profession's recent experience of a "glut of doctors" and the need to avoid medical unemployment in the late 1960s. Guilty as we have been in our treatment of doctors from overseas, and in our failure in the past to train enough health workers for our own national needs, at least it cannot be said that we are deliberately organising recruitment campaigns in economically poorer countries.

These introductory reflections on some of the international aspects of welfare point to three general conclusions. First, they underline the dangers in the use of the term 'the welfare state'. Second, they remind us that we can no longer consider welfare systems solely within the limited framework of the nation-state; what we do or fail to do in changing systems of welfare affects other countries besides ourselves. Third, to suggest one criterion for the definition of a 'welfare society': namely, a society which openly accepts a policy responsibility for educating and training its own nationals to meet its own needs for doctors, nurses, social workers, scientists, engineers and others. Just as we have recognised the injustices and the waste in the unrestricted free international movement of goods, material and capital, so we must now recognise the need for the richer countries of the world to take action to protect the poorer countries of the world from being denuded of skilled manpower.

To this end, a number of measures could be taken, some unilaterally, some by international agreement. Among the most important would be for the rich countries to decide to spend less on personal consumption goods and more on training young people for the social service professions; to decide to devote more of their resources for genuine international aid to the poorer countries; to decide to ban the deliberate recruitment overseas of skilled manpower; to decide to revise and broaden their immigration policies so that movement between countries is not restricted to the highly educated and trained; and to take other measures too complex to discuss in this paper.

For the rich countries of the world to take action in such ways would represent a few modest steps towards the notion of 'a welfare world'. Those countries assuming leadership with policies of this nature might then with some justification regard themselves as 'welfare societies'.

This principle of community responsibility for the provision of adequate resources to implement the objectives of national legislation is particularly relevant to the whole field of welfare. The quantity, territorial distribution and quality of any country's social services – education, medical care, mental health, welfare, children's and other personal community services – depends enormously on the quantity and quality of professional, technical, auxiliary and administrative staff. To enact legislation designed to create or develop services – yet not to invest adequately in the training of doctors, nurses, social workers, teachers and many other categories of skilled manpower and womanpower – is a denial of this principle of community responsibility. To rely on the private market and autonomous professional bodies to fulfil these training needs is nothing less than a ridiculous illusion. The private national market has failed lamentably in this country and in the United States to produce enough doctors, teachers, social workers and nurses. To resort to the international market to remedy the deficiency of national social policies can only have tragic consequences for the poorer countries of the world.

In considering the international aspects of these welfare manpower issues, it seems the height of collective immorality for the rich countries of the world to preach to the poorer countries about the economic benefits of family planning while, at the same time, making it more difficult for these countries to develop family planning programmes by drawing away the skilled manpower they need for the infrastructure of services required to provide birth control as well as death control services.

I now want to consider certain other questions of principle in systems of welfare.

* * * * *

In any discussion of the future of what is called 'the welfare state', much of the argument revolves round the principles and objectives of universalist social services and selective social services. Time does not seem to have eroded the importance of this issue.

I think it is unnecessary to cover in detail the many complex questions of principles, goals, methods and assumptions involved in this debate. Consider first the nature of the broad principles which helped to shape substantial sections of British welfare legislation in the past and particularly the principle of universalism embodied in such enactments after the Second World War as the 1944 Education Act, the 1945 Family Allowances Act, the 1946 National Health Service Act and the 1951 National Insurance Act.

One fundamental historical reason for the adoption of this principle was the aim of making services available and accessible to the whole population in such ways as would not involve users in any humiliating loss of status, dignity or self-respect. There should be no sense of inferiority, pauperism, shame or stigma in the use of a publicly provided service; no attribution that one was being or becoming a 'public burden'. Hence the emphasis on the social rights of all citizens to use or not to use as responsible people the services made available by the community in respect of certain needs which the private market and the family were unable or unwilling to provide universally. If these services were not provided for everybody by everybody, they would either not be available at all or only for those who could afford them, and for others on such terms as would involve the infliction of a sense of inferiority and stigma.

Avoidance of stigma was not, of course, the only reason for the development of the twin concepts of social rights and universalism. Many other forces – social, political and psychological – during a century and more of turmoil, revolution, wars and change, contributed to the clarification and acceptance of these notions. The novel idea of prevention – novel, at least, to many in the 19th century – was, for example, another powerful engine, driven by the Webbs and many other advocates of change, which reinforced the concepts of social rights and universalism. The idea of prevention – the prevention and breaking of the vicious descending spiral of poverty, disease, neglect, illiteracy and destitution – spelt to the protagonists (and still does) the critical importance of early and easy access to and use of preventive, remedial and rehabilitative services. Slowly and painfully the lesson was learnt that, if such services were to be utilised in time and were to be effective in action in a highly differentiated, unequal and class-saturated society, they had to be delivered through socially approved channels; that is to say, without loss of self-respect by the users and their families.

Prevention was not simply a child of biological and psychological theorists; at least one of the grandparents was a powerful economist with a strongly developed streak of nationalism. As Bentley Gilbert (1966) has shown, national efficiency and welfare were seen as complementary. The sin unforgivable was the waste of human resources; thus, welfare was summoned to prevent waste. Hence the beginnings of four of our social services: retirement pensions, the health service, unemployment insurance and the school meals service.

The whole welfare debate in the days before the First World War was a curious mixture of humanitarianism, egalitarianism, productivity and old-fashioned imperialism. The strident note of the latter is now silenced. The Goddess of Growth has replaced the God of National Fitness, but can we say that the quest for the other objectives is no longer necessary?

Before discussing such a rhetorical question, we need to examine further the principle of universalism. The principle itself may sound simple but the practice, and by that I mean the operational pattern of welfare in Britain, is immensely complex. We can see something of this complexity if we analyse welfare (defined here as all publicly provided and subsidised services, statutory, occupational and fiscal) from a number of different standpoints.

* * * * *

Whatever the nature of the service, activity or function, and whether it be a service in kind, a collective amenity, or a transfer payment in cash or by accountancy, we need to consider (and here I itemise in question form for the sake of brevity) three central issues:

- What is the nature of entitlement to use? Is it a legal, contractual or contributory, financial, discretionary or professionally determined entitlement?
- Who is entitled and on what conditions? Is account taken of individual characteristics, family characteristics, group characteristics, territorial characteristics or sociobiological characteristics? What, in fact, are the rules of entitlement? Are they specific and contractual, like a right based on age, or are they variable, arbitrary or discretionary?
- What methods, financial and administrative, are employed in the determination of access, utilisation, allocation and payment?

Next we have to reflect on the nature of the service or benefit. What functions do benefits (in cash, amenity or in kind) aim to fulfil? They may, for example, fulfil any of the following sets of functions, singly or in combination:

- As partial compensation for identified disservices caused by society (for example, unemployment, some categories of industrial injuries benefits and war pensions) and the disservices caused by international society as exemplified by the oil pollution resulting from the Torrey Canyon oil tanker disaster costing at least £2 million.

- As partial compensation for unidentifiable disservices caused by society (for example, 'benefits' related to programmes of slum clearance, urban blight, smoke pollution control, hospital cross-infection and many other socially created disservices).

- As partial compensation for unmerited handicap (for example, language classes for immigrant children, services for the deprived child and children handicapped from birth).

- As a form of protection for society (for example, the probation service, some parts of the mental health services and services for the control of infectious diseases).

- As an investment for a future personal or collective gain (education – professional, technical and industrial – is an obvious example here; so also are certain types of subsidised occupational benefits).

- As an immediate and/or deferred increment to personal welfare or, in other words, benefits (utilities) which add to personal command-over-resources either immediately and/or in the future (for example, subsidies to owner-occupiers and council tenants, tax-deductibles for interest charges, pensions, supplementary benefits and curative medical care).

- As an element in an integrative objective which is an essential characteristic distinguishing social policy from economic policy. As Kenneth Boulding said "social policy is that which is centred in those institutions that create integration and discourage alienation" (1967, p 7). It is thus profoundly concerned with questions of personal identity, whereas economic policy centres round exchange or bilateral transfer.

This represents little more than an elementary and partial structural map which can assist in the understanding of the welfare complex. Needless to say, a more sophisticated guide is essential for anything approaching a thorough analysis of the actual functioning of welfare benefit systems.

Further study would have to take account of the pattern and operation of means-tested services. It has been estimated by Mike Reddin that in England and Wales local authorities are responsible for administering at least 3,000 means-tests, of which about 1,500 are different from each other. This estimate applies only to services falling within the responsibilities of education, child care, health, housing and welfare departments. It follows that, in these fields alone, there exist some 1,500 different definitions of poverty or financial hardship, ability to pay and rules for charges, which affect the individual and the family. There must be substantial numbers of poor families with multiple needs and multiple handicaps whose perception of the realities of welfare is to see only a means-testing world. Who helps them, I wonder, to fill all those forms?

I mention these social facts, by way of illustration, because they do form part of the operational complex of welfare in 1967. My main purpose, however, in presenting this analytical framework was twofold. First, to underline the difficulties of conceptualising and categorising needs, causes, entitlement or gatekeeper functions, utilisation patterns, benefits and compensations. Second, to suggest that those students of welfare who are seeing the main problem in terms of universalism versus selective services are presenting a naive and over-simplified picture of policy choices.

Some of the reasons for this simple and superficial view are due to the fact that the approach is dominated by the concept or model of welfare as a burden; as a waste of resources in the provision of benefits for those who, it is said, do not need them. The general solution is thus deceptively simple and romantically appealing: abolish all this welfare complexity and concentrate help on those whose needs are greatest.

Quite apart from the theoretical and practical immaturity of this solution, which would restrict the public services to a minority in the population leaving the majority to buy their own education, social security, medical care and other services in a supposedly free market, certain other important questions need to be considered.

As all selective services for this minority would have to apply some test of need-eligibility, on what bases would tests be applied and, even more crucial, when would the lines be drawn for benefits which function as compensation for unidentifiable disservices, compensation for unmerited handicap, as a form of social protection, as an investment, or as an increment to personal welfare? Can rules of entitlement and access be drawn on purely 'ability to pay' criteria without distinction of cause? And if the causal agents of need cannot be identified or are so diffuse as to defy the wit of law, then is not the answer 'no compensation and no redress'? In other words, the case for concentrated selective services resolves itself into an argument for allowing the social costs or diswelfares of the economic system to lie where they fall.

The emphasis on 'welfare' and the 'benefits of welfare' often tends to obscure the fundamental fact that for many consumers the services used are not essentially benefits or increments to welfare at all; they represent partial compensations for disservices, for social costs and social insecurities which are the product of a rapidly changing industrial-urban society. They are part of the price we pay to some people for bearing part of the costs of other people's progress: the obsolescence of skills, redundancies, premature retirements, accidents, many categories of disease and handicap, urban blight and slum clearance, smoke pollution and a hundred and one other socially generated disservices. They are the socially caused diswelfares, the losses involved in aggregate welfare gains.

What is also of major importance is that modern society is finding it increasingly difficult to identify the causal agent or agencies, and thus to allocate the costs of disservices and charge those who are responsible. It is not just a question of benefit allocation (whose 'welfare state') but also of loss allocation (whose 'diswelfare state').

If identification of the agents of diswelfare were possible, if we could legally name and blame the culprits, then, in theory at least, redress could be obtained through the courts by the method of monetary compensations for damages. But multiple causality and the diffusion of disservices (the modern choleras of change) make this solution impossible. We have therefore as societies to make other choices: either to provide social services or to allow the social costs of the system to lie where they fall. The 19th century chose the latter, the laissez-faire solution, because it had neither a germ theory of disease nor a social theory of causality; an answer which can hardly be entertained today by a richer society equipped with more knowledge about the dynamics of change. But knowledge in this context must not, of course, be equated with wisdom.

If this argument can be sustained, we are thus compelled to return to our analytical framework of the functional concepts of benefit and, within this context, to consider the role of universalist and selective social services. Non-discriminating universalist services are in part the consequence of unidentifiable causality. If disservices are wasteful (to use the economists' concept of 'waste'), so welfare has to be 'wasteful'.

The next question that presents itself is this: can we and should we, in providing benefits and compensation (which in practice can rarely be differentially provided), distinguish between 'faults in the individual' (moral, psychological or social) and the 'faults of society'? If all services are provided (irrespective of whether they represent benefits, amenity, social protection or compensation) on a discriminatory, means-test basis, do we not foster both the sense of personal failure and the stigma of a public burden? The fundamental objective of all such tests of eligibility is to keep people out, not to let them in. They must therefore be treated as applicants or supplicants, not beneficiaries or consumers.

It is a regrettable but human fact that money (and the lack of it) is linked to personal and family self-respect. This is one element in what has been called the 'stigma of the means test'. Another element is the historical evidence we have that separate discriminatory services for poor people have always tended to be poor quality services: read the history of the panel system under National Health Insurance; read Beveridge on workmen's compensation; Newsom on secondary modern schools; Plowden on standards of primary schools in slum areas; Townsend on Part III accommodations in *The last refuge* (1964); Titmuss (1950) and so on.

In the past, poor quality selective services for poor people were the product of a society which saw 'welfare' as a residual, as a public burden. The primary purpose of the system and the method of discrimination was therefore deterrence; it was also an effective rationing device. To this end, the most effective instrument was to induce among recipients (children as well as adults) a sense of personal fault, of personal failure, even if the benefit was wholly or partially a compensation for disservices inflicted by society.

* * * * *

With this heritage, we face the positive challenge of providing selective, high quality services for poor people over a large and complex range of welfare; of positively discriminating on a territorial, group or 'rights' basis in favour of the poor, the handicapped, the deprived, the coloured, the homeless and the social casualties of our society. Universalism is not, by itself, enough in medical care, in wage-related social security and in education. This much we have learnt in the 1940s to 1960s from the facts about inequalities in the distribution of incomes and wealth, and in our failure to close many gaps in differential access to and effective utilisation of particular branches of our social services (Nicholson, 1967; Townsend, 1967).

If I am right, Britain is beginning to identify the dimensions of this challenge of positive, selective discrimination in income maintenance, education, housing, medical care and mental health, child welfare, and the tolerant integration of immigrants and citizens from overseas; of preventing especially the second generation from becoming (and of seeing themselves as) second-class citizens. We are seeking ways and means, values, methods and techniques, of positive discrimination without the infliction, actual or imagined, of a sense of personal failure and individual fault.

The challenge that faces us is not the choice between universalist and selective social services. The real challenge resides in the question: what particular infrastructure of universalist services is needed in order to provide a framework of values and opportunity bases within and around which can be developed socially acceptable selective services aiming to discriminate positively, with the minimum risk of stigma, in favour of those whose needs are greatest? [For a more specific formulation of this issue, see *Commitment to welfare*, 1968.]

This is the fundamental challenge. In different ways and in particular areas it confronts the Supplementary Benefits Commission, the Seebohm Committee, the NHS, the Ministry of Housing and Local Government, the National Committee for Commonwealth Immigrants, the policy-making readers of the Newsom Report and the Plowden Report on educational priority areas, the Scottish Report on social work, and thousands of social workers and administrators all over the country wrestling with the problems of needs and priorities. In all the main spheres of need, some structure of universalism is an essential prerequisite to selective positive discrimination; it provides a general system of values and a sense of community, socially approved agencies for clients, patients and consumers, and also for the recruitment, training and deployment of staff at all levels; it sees welfare, not as a burden, but as complementary and as an instrument of change and, finally, it allows positive discriminatory services to be provided as rights for categories of people and for classes of need in terms of priority social areas and other impersonal classifications.

Without this infrastructure of welfare resources and framework of values, we should not be able to identify and discuss the next steps in progress towards a welfare society.

Social welfare and the art of giving

It has been said in the United States that, "modern social welfare has really to be thought of as help given to the stranger, not to the person who by reason of personal bond commands it without asking" (Wilensky and Lebeaux, 1958, p 141). It has therefore to be formally organised, to be administered by strangers and to be paid for collectively by strangers.

Social welfare or the social services, operating though agencies, institutions and programmes outside the private market are becoming more difficult to define with precision in any society. As societies become more complex and specialised, so do systems of social welfare. Functionally, they reflect, and respond to, the larger social structure and its division of labour. This process makes it much harder to identify the causal agents of change, the microbes of social disorganisation and the viruses of impoverishment, and to make them responsible for the costs of 'disservices'. Who should bear the social costs of the thalidomide babies, of urban blight, of smoke pollution, of the obsolescence of skills, of automation, of the impact of synthetic coffee (which will dispense with the need for coffee beans) on the peasants of Brazil? The private benefits are to some extent measurable and attributable, but the private losses are not. Neo-classical economics and the private market cannot make these allocations; they are not organised to estimate social disruption and are unable to provide adequately for the public needs created by social and economic change.

Our growing inability to identify and connect cause and effect in the world of social and technological change is one reason for the historical emergence of social welfare institutions in the West. Altruism by strangers for strangers was and is an attempt to fill a moral void created by applied science. The services and programmes developed in the West to give aid to the stranger have inevitably and necessarily become more specialised and complex.

* * * * *

The 'social services' in Britain are largely the product of the 20th century, a delayed response to the industrialism of the 19th century. The term is generally and loosely interpreted to cover such public (or publicly supported) services as medical care, education, housing, income maintenance in old age and during periods of unemployment, sickness, disability and so forth, child allowances, and a variety of specific services for particular groups of people with special needs:

for example, neglected children, unmarried mothers, the blind, mental defectives, young delinquents, discharged prisoners and others. All these services came apologetically into existence to provide for certain basic needs which the individual, the family and the private market in capitalist societies were unable or unwilling to meet. In the United States and other Western countries, the terms 'social welfare' or 'social policy programmes' are used as alternative generic labels to embrace a similar variety of collectively organised services which may differ widely in scope and structure, methods of administration and finance, and in the fundamental objectives underlying them.

The concept of the welfare state, which entered the arena of political thought in the 1940s, is generally accepted as a wider definition of the role of the state in the field of social and economic policy, embracing more than the provision of social services. Most writers on the subject, whether on the Right or Left politically, take it to mean a more positive and purposeful commitment by government to concern itself with the general welfare of the whole community and with the social costs of change. [This topic is developed in Part 2, Chapter Four, 'The welfare state: Images and realities'.]

The renaissance of private enterprise in North America and Europe, the Keynesian Revolution and the adoption of techniques of economic management, rising standards of living and the achievements of political parties and trade unions on behalf of the underprivileged have led all these culturally different societies along the same road to welfare statism, a road unforeseen by Marx. Whether they know it or not, and whether they like it or not, Democrats and Republicans, Socialists and Liberals in North America have become 'welfare statists'. The Germans and the Swedes may have more 'advanced' pension systems, the British a more comprehensive health service, the French more extensive family allowances, and the Americans may spend more on public education but the generalised welfare commitment is nevertheless viewed as the dominant political fact of modern Western societies. Governments may come and go; the commitment to welfare, economic growth and full employment will remain with minor rather than major changes in scope and objectives.

* * * * *

In historical and comparative terms, these are sweeping conclusions and leave many questions of values and facts unexamined. To what extent are they based on the real facts of income and wealth distribution, property, power and class? Has the welfare state abolished poverty, social deprivation and exploitation? Have people a greater sense of social control and participation in the work and life of their community? What will be the human consequences of further social and technological changes? Will the future resemble the immediate past or are these views a simple projection of a transient phase in the development of large scale and predominantly competitive societies?

A growing number of political commentators, economists and sociologists on both sides of the Atlantic, in proclaiming the end of political ideology in the West, have either ignored such questions or have tended to imply that they are no longer of primary importance for our societies. Their reasons for doing so are explicit in their general thesis. Seymour Lipset in *Political man* (1960) spoke for many when he said (in summarising the discussions of a world congress of intellectuals in 1955) that "the ideological issues dividing left and right [have] been reduced to a little more or a little less government ownership and economic planning"; and there was general agreement that it really makes little difference "which political party controls the domestic policies of individual nations". With minor differences, parties of both the Right and the Left will attempt to alleviate those social injustices that still remain, and will continue to seek improvements in social welfare, education, medical care and other sectors of the economy for the general wellbeing. All will share, rich and poor, in the benefits of growth. By a natural process of market levitation, all classes and groups will stand expectantly on the political Right as the escalator of growth moves them up. Automatism thus substitutes for the social protest.

To quote Lipset again (1960, pp 404-6), although writers in a similar vein such as Bell (1960) or others in England, France and Germany could equally be cited:

> ... the fundamental political problems of the industrial revolution have been solved: the workers have achieved industrial and political citizenship, the conservatives have accepted the welfare state, and the democratic left has recognised that an increase in overall state power carries with it more dangers to freedom than solutions for economic problems. This very triumph of the democratic social revolution in the West ends domestic politics for those intellectuals who must have ideologies or utopias to motivate them to political action.

As a generalisation, it is conceivable that this statement may serve as a summing-up for the 1950s in the history books of the 21st century. But from the perspective of 1960 it is, to say the least, a dubious proposition. However, I would not wish this chapter to take the form of a critique of any one particular writer; to do so would carry with it the obligation to discuss in detail an individual interpretation of recent trends and the many qualifications attached to them. I shall therefore treat these statements as an expression not of the views of Seymour Lipset but of a collective *Weltanschauung* and one that seems to be growing in influence in the West, to judge by the number of its adherents.

I shall speculate about some of its basic assumptions so far as they relate to the future role of a humanist social policy in Britain and the United States.

First, it is unhistorical. Implicit in the thesis is the assumption that the industrial revolution was a once-and-for-all affair. Thus, it ignores the evidence concerning the trend toward monopolistic concentrations of economic power, the role of the corporation as private government with taxing powers, the problems of social disorganisation and cultural deprivation, and the growing impact of automation and new techniques of production and distribution in economically advanced societies. If the first phase of the so-called revolution was to force all men to work, the phase we are now entering may be to force many men not to work. Without a major shift in values, only an impoverishment in social living can result from this new wave of industrialism.

Second, it states that the workers have achieved 'industrial citizenship'. The only comment to make on this is to say that it is a misuse of language to imply that membership of a trade union is synonymous with industrial citizenship. Conceptions of what constitutes citizenship for the worker must be related to what we now know about human potential and basic social and psychological needs; they cannot be compared with conditions of industrial slavery in the 19th century.

Third, the thesis implies that the problem of the distribution of income and wealth has either been solved or is now of insignificant proportions in Western society. In any event, such disparities as do exist are justified on grounds of individual differences and the need for economic incentives, and are considered to present no threat to democratic values.

In the 1950s, 1% of the British population owned 42% of all personal net capital and 5% owned 67.5% (Tawney, 1964). Even those proportions are underestimates, for the figures exclude pension funds and trusts and they do not take account of the increasing tendency for large owners of property to distribute their wealth among their families, to spread it over time, to send it abroad and to transform it in other ways.

This degree of concentration in the holding of wealth in 1960 is nearly twice as great as it was in the United States in 1954 and far higher than in the halcyon days of ruthless American capitalism in the early 1920s. Since 1949, wealth inequality has been growing in the United States, the rate of increase being more than twice as fast as the rate of decline between 1922 and 1949. Measured in terms of increase in the percentage of wealth held by the top 1%, the growth of inequality between 1949 and 1956 was more striking than at any time since 1920. Not unexpectedly, the distribution of income also appears to be becoming more unequal, affecting in particular the one fifth to one quarter of the United States population living below the currently defined 'poverty line' (Keyserling Report, 1961; Harrington, 1962; Lampman, 1962). These are not all blacks; 80% of the American poor are white and only one fifth receive welfare aid. Economic growth in the richest society in the world has not been accompanied by any automatic, built-in equaliser. Crime for the young unemployed acts as a substitute within the prevailing system of values, the modern form of acquisitive social mobility for the lower classes.

There is no evidence to suggest that Britain has not been following in the same path from the end of the 1940s to the 1960s. It is even possible that inequality in the ownership of wealth (particularly in terms of family holdings) has increased more rapidly in Britain than in the United States since 1949. The British system of taxation is almost unique in the Western world in its generous treatment of wealth-holders in respect of settlements, trusts, gifts and other arrangements for redistributing and rearranging income and wealth. This is reflected in the remarkable fact that, in the mid-1950s, it was in the young adult age group that the tendency for wealth to be concentrated in a few hands was most marked.

Such evidence as this is ignored by those who proclaim the end of political ideology. Similar trends are probably in operation in de Gaulle's France and Erhard's Germany. Over a quarter of a century of political upheaval, global war, 'welfare statism', managed economies and economic growth made little impression on the holdings of great fortunes in at least two of the largest industrial nations: the United States and Britain. The institution of concentrated wealth appears to be as tenacious of life as Tawney's intelligent tadpoles. Wealth still bestows political and economic power, more power than income, though it is probably exercised differently and with more respect for public opinion than in the 19th century.

Changes in the distribution of incomes appear to be following a similar pattern in Britain as in the United States. At the end of the 1940s, a wartime movement towards more equality (before and after tax) in both Britain and the United States was reversed. The poorest tenth of the British population were relatively worse off compared with the higher standards of the rest of the nation in 1963 than they were in 1948 (Lynes, 1963).

How can these great disparities in the private ownership of wealth and in the exercise of economic power be viewed as consistent with the thesis that we have reached the end of the political dialogue? No political utopia since Plato has ever envisaged such degrees of economic inequality as permanent and desirable states. Socialists protest at such disparities, not because they want to foster envy; they do so because, as Tawney argued, these disparities are fundamentally immoral. History suggests that human nature is not strong enough to maintain itself in true community where great disparities of income and wealth preside.

Fourth and finally, there is in this thesis an assumption that the establishment of social welfare necessarily and inevitably contributes to the spread of humanism and the resolution of social injustice. The reverse can be true. Welfare, as an institutional means, can serve different masters. A multitude of sins may be committed in its appealing name. Welfare can be used simply as an instrument of economic growth which, by benefiting a minority, indirectly promotes greater inequality. Education is an example. We may educate the young to compete more efficiently as economic men in the private market with one another, or we may educate them because we desire to make them more capable of freedom and more capable of fulfilling their personal differences irrespective of income, class, religion and race.

Welfare may be used to serve military and racial ends, as in Hitler's Germany. More medical care was provided by state and voluntary agencies not because of a belief in human uniqueness, but because of a hatred of a narrowly defined group of people.

Welfare may be used to narrow allegiances and not to diffuse them, as in employers' fringe benefit systems. Individual gain and political quietism, fostered by the new feudalism of the corporation, may substitute for the sense of common humanity nourished by systems of non-discriminatory mutual aid.

What matters then, what indeed is fundamental to the health of welfare, the objective towards which its face is set? To universalise humanistic ethics and the social rights of citizenship, or to divide, discriminate and compete?

* * * * *

In reality, of course, the issues are never as clear cut as this. The historical evolution of social security measures in Britain since the end of the 19th century shows how complex and various were the forces at work. Fear of social revolution, the need for a law-abiding labour force, the struggle for power between political parties and pressure groups, a demand to remove some of the social costs of change (industrial accidents, for example) from the back of the worker, and the social conscience of the rich, all played a part.

But the major impulse came from below, from the working-man's ethic of solidarity and mutual aid. It found expression and grew spontaneously from working-class traditions and institutions to counter the adversities of industrialism. By means of a great network of friendly societies, medical clubs, chapel societies, brotherhoods, cooperatives, trade unions and savings clubs, schemes of mutual insurance were developed as a method of prepayment for services the members could claim when they were in need – in sickness, disablement, unemployment, old age, widowhood and death. The 'good' risks and the 'bad' risks, the young and the old, shared one another's lot. They constituted microscopic welfare states, each struggling to demonstrate that people could still exercise some control over the forces of technology. By the end of the 19th century, some 24,000 different friendly societies were in existence, with a total membership representing about half the adult male population of the country. Aptly and significantly named, during a century of unbridled competition, they were *the* humanistic institution for the artisan and his family, far outdistancing in active membership all trade unions, political parties and religious bodies.

We can now see this great movement as the amateur's compassionate answer to the challenge of the economic and psychological insecurities of industrialism and individualism. It expressed also the ordinary person's revulsion from a class-conscious, discriminating charity and a ruthless, discriminating Poor Law. The Poor Law was hated because it spelled humiliation; it was an assault on the individual's sense of self-respect in an age when 'respectability', the quality of meriting the respect of others, governed the mores of society.

The values and objectives which underlay in the past the search for security in an increasingly insecure world are still relevant to an understanding of the role of social welfare in Britain. The ways in which they shaped its origins and early development permeate the principles on which the systems of medical care and social security operate today – comprehensive in scope, universal in membership. That they have not yet solved the problems of poverty and neglect, and still provide little place for citizen participation, is another story and one that remains as a formidable challenge for socialism. But we cannot retrace our footsteps to the intimate 'friendly societies' of yesterday; we must find imaginative ways and new institutional means of combining humanity in administration with redistributive social justice in the future development of welfare policies.

* * * * *

These are two of the central unresolved issues for humanists: the problem of size and the problem of inequality. They affect every aspect of social policy: education from the primary school to the university and into adult life; social security in unemployment, sickness and old age; the care of the physically and mentally ill; housing and urban planning, leisure and recreation.

The demand for these services will grow in the future as living standards rise among some sections of the population and fall, relatively or absolutely, among others. The consequences of automation and its technological cousins on the one hand, and more dependent needs in childhood and old age on the other, will call for a much greater investment in people and social service than in consumption goods. Science and technology are today beginning to accomplish as thorough a revolution in social and economic theory as they are in the theory of war and international relations. The conventional doctrine that machines make work is losing its validity; machines are now replacing workers. It is already clear from American experience that these victims of technological displacement are no longer 'resting between engagements' (which is the theory of unemployment insurance); they are *permanently* out of work, permanently liberated from work. By the end of 1962 nearly one third of all young blacks between the ages of 16 and 21 who were out of school were also out of work. Relatively speaking, they were also more handicapped educationally than unemployed young blacks twenty years earlier. Between 1939 and 1958 the disadvantage of not having a college diploma grew in the United States.

In an age of abundance of things, the production of consumption goods will become a subsidiary question for the West. The primary question will be just distribution; in particular, the distribution of services according to needs in place of the principle of productivity and performance in a market economy which today powerfully influences access to education and other social services.

In the past, we have distributed resources on the basis of success and failure in economic competition; in the future, we must decide whether it is morally right to do so in an economy of abundance. To distribute services on the basis of needs will help us to discover equality in our neighbours. "Awareness of equality", wrote Daniel Jenkins (1961, p 21), "always arises in personal relationships and nearly always confronts us as a challenge, for it means placing a greater value upon our neighbour than we have previously been disposed to do. We are all ready to love ourselves. The discovery of equality might be defined as the discovery that we have indeed to love our neighbours as ourselves".

And so we have to ask, 'What are we to do with our wealth?' This is a more relevant question to ask today than those that seek to find more effective ways of punishing criminals, enforcing the law against deviants, preventing abuse of public assistance, forcing men to search for work, compelling them to save for old age when they cannot feed their children adequately, shifting them out of subsidised housing, inventing cheap technological substitutes for education and charging them more for access to medical care.

Yet these aims reflect the values which are often applied in the administration of social services. According to Mencher (1963, p 62), "The present United States welfare [public assistance] program is in keeping with the philosophy of 1830", the philosophy of less eligible citizens enshrined in the 1834 Poor Law Act in England. Social workers, teachers, doctors and social administrators find their functions imprisoned by the 'virtues' of hard work and profit, virtues that are rooted in the economics of scarcity. Their role is to police these virtues as, in a more ruthless context, medical certification of fitness for work became one of the central directives under the Stalinist regime. They have no relevance to the economics of abundance.

And, as Gerard Piel (1961, p 9) has emphasised, any

> ... hard work that a machine can do is better done today by a machine; 'hard' these days means mostly boring and repetitive work, whether in the factory or the office. But the instinct for workmanship, the need to feel needed, the will to achieve, are deeply felt in every human heart. They are not universally fulfilled by the kind of employment most people find. Full employment in the kind of employment that is commonly available, whether blue-collar or white-collar, has been plainly outmoded by technology. The liberation of people from tasks unworthy of human capacity should free that capacity for a host of activities now neglected in our civilisation: teaching and learning, fundamental scientific investigation, the performing arts and the graphic arts, letters, the crafts, politics, and social service. Characteristically these activities involve the interaction of people with people rather than with things. They are admittedly not productive activities; nor are they profitable in the strict sense.

Science and technology in alliance with other structural and demographical changes under way in our societies will call for a major shift in values; for new incentives and new forms of reward unrelated to the productivity principle; for new criteria applied to the distribution of resources which are not tied to individual 'success' as a measure; for new forms of socially approved 'dependencies'. They will make the conventional criteria of capitalism largely irrelevant.

Keynes (1930) foresaw that the time would come when these changes would be needed:

> We shall be able to rid ourselves of many of the pseudo-moral principles which have hag-ridden us for two hundred years, by which we have exalted some of the most distasteful of human qualities into the position of the highest virtues.... All kinds of social customs and economic practices, affecting the distribution of wealth and of economic rewards and penalties, which we now maintain at all costs, ... we shall then be free, at last, to discard.

We shall need different rules domestically to live by and more examples of altruism to look up to. Indeed, our societies in Britain and the United States are already in need of them. In no other way in the long run will it be possible for us to prevent the deprived and the unable from becoming more deprived and unable; more cast down in a pool of apathy, frustration, crime, rootlessness and tawdry poverty.

In all this, what we call the 'social services' will have a central role to play. If this role is defined at all, it will have to be defined by socialists in the language of equality. Here it is that ethics will have to be reunited to politics. The answers will not come and indeed logically cannot come from those who now proclaim 'the end of political ideology'; those who would elevate the principle of pecuniary gain and extend it to social service by equating education and medical care with refrigerators and mink coats; and those who advocate that more and more people should contract out of universal social services and create for themselves new areas of privilege and discrimination. They are the utilitarian doctrinaires; prisoners of the economics of scarcity; oblivious to the social consequences of the march of science and technology; and blind to the need for a sense of moral purpose in their own societies as the motive power in the art of giving to our international neighbours.

Power, policy and privilege

Commentary: Adrian Sinfield

These two extracts, first published in 1959 and 1962, illustrate the ways in which Richard Titmuss engaged with central issues of structural social and economic change. He was concerned that the public social services – as he preferred to call 'the welfare state' – should not be studied out of context "as 'things apart'; as phenomena of marginal interest, like looking out of the window on a train journey" (Titmuss, 1958, p 8). Both readings challenge the conventional wisdom of 'the end of ideology' discussed by John Hill in the Commentary to Part 3. The problem of poverty was seen as ended and inequality was being reduced – and by too much, in the view of many.

* * * * *

By the end of the 1950s in the United Kingdom, there was much invocation of what had become known as the 'You've never had it so good' society, the phrase coined from a comment by Prime Minister Macmillan in the run-up to the 1959 election, when the Conservatives retained power. The resulting policy climate was nicely caught by Richard Titmuss in his long introduction to the fifth edition of Tawney's *Equality* in 1964: "We have had our passions; now we can leave to the sophisticated and the academic these matters of 'nicely calculated less or more'. What remains is social engineering; a mixture of art and technique in the manipulation and ordering of an existing 'good' society" (Titmuss, 1964, p 14). These views he challenges in these two chapters (see also Part 3, Chapter Three, 'Social welfare and the art of giving').

In 'The irresponsible society', Titmuss opens with a challenge to "socialists ... to re-define and re-state the inherent illogicalities and contradictions in the managerial capitalist system", Titmuss explores the impact of "the changing concentrations of economic and financial power". He takes the private insurance sector as a prime example "where combination and concentration may threaten the rights and liberties of the subject to choose the values and decide the social priorities that will shape the sort of society we live in" (p 14).

The power of pension funds and insurance companies and their "irresponsible decisions" were issues which Richard Titmuss was particularly well-equipped to understand from his own early work in insurance. It was a theme he frequently returned to in examining what he called the "threatening concentrations of power and privilege" which, whether consciously or not, "increasingly become the arbiters of welfare and amenity for larger sections of the community" (p 147). Over forty years later, these comments have turned out to be truer than even Titmuss might have expected (Minns, 2001). Private pensions play a much greater role today as the value of the basic state pension has been eroded against wages and the State Earnings-Related Pension System (SERPS) has been halved and then halved again. Its replacement, the state second pension, and now stakeholder pensions will result in a larger role for private pension and insurance funds.

In an essay on 'Pension systems and population change' in 1955, Richard Titmuss had drawn attention to the growth of occupational pensions supported by tax reliefs: "the outlines of a dangerous social schism are clear, and they are enlarging.... Already it is possible to see two nations in old age; greater inequalities in living standards after work than in work; two contrasting social services for distinct groups based on different principles, and operating in isolation of each other as separate, autonomous, social instruments of change" (Titmuss, 1958, pp 73-4).

Almost half a century later, the "two nations in old age" are in some ways much clearer as a result of the continued strength of the largest area of occupational welfare. Those with good private pensions are much better protected against poverty in old age than those who only have the state pensions or means-tested benefits to support them. Two fifths of pensioners receive no private pension at all, a disproportionate number of them women, reflecting their weaker position in the labour market and increasing their risk of poverty. The remainder gain an average of £100 a week, with one-fifth receiving over £150 (DSS, 2000). The development of these pensions continues to be assisted by considerable tax reliefs, one of the most generous forms of fiscal or tax welfare to which Richard Titmuss drew frequent attention (Agulnik and LeGrand, 1998; Sinfield, 2000).

However, private pensions do not protect all of their recipients from poverty. One-third of those who get any non-state pension receive less than £30 a week which adds very little, if anything, to their total income but reduces or removes their entitlement to means-tested benefits. Many of these pensioners will have retired early, often as a result of recent high unemployment, when the value of their pensions will have been severely eroded (Atkinson, 1995, ch 5).

Titmuss's reflections on the different worlds of public and private provision and his comments on "the dwindling role for government" and "government retreats" are particularly relevant today as these issues are fought out again. He particularly noted the differing visibility and accountability of public and private action: "the iniquities of public bureaucrats have been repeatedly exposed to the greater glory of private bureaucrats" (p 149). This tendency he saw then, as he probably would today, reinforced by a press teaching its reader "to sneer at public order and public service and to admire cupidity and acquisitiveness" (p 63).

In these and other ways, Richard Titmuss offered no support for the image of the welfare state going through 'a golden age' in the 1950s or 1960s which seems to have gained credence among many commentators in the Thatcher and post-Thatcher years. To the contrary, he believed then that "The present generation has been mesmerised by the language of 'the welfare state'", and he regularly insisted on the quotation marks to indicate his rejection of what he considered an "ambiguous" term. He frequently criticised "the mythology of 'the welfare state'", underlining the need to study public welfare in a broader context and not to focus on public social policy to the exclusion of other developments in society. Chapter Two in this section once again illustrates his concern to examine the impact of the social services in a broader context of structural change.

'The need for a new approach' is the concluding chapter of *Income distribution and social change: A study in criticism*. The main themes were presented in four articles in the *New Statesman* just before the book was published at the end of September 1962. 'Alice in the Board of Inland Revenue' was Titmuss's own nickname for the study, and his innocent, wide-eyed approach to the traditions, mysteries and assumptions of the official statistics still makes fascinating reading.

He took as his main point of departure a comment in the Annual Report of the Board of Inland Revenue for 1948-49. After examining changes in the distribution of income over the previous ten years, the Board concluded that there had been "a very considerable redistribution in incomes" (BIR, 1950, pp 82-6). This comment was particularly significant, Titmuss believed, providing official confirmation of the prevalent assumption of growing equality which was reinforced by economic studies he also criticised. These created a climate for policy discussion in many areas, particularly taxation, and helped set the agenda on a range of issues.

Emphasising "that data are a product, not an uncovering" (Miller, 1987, p 8), Titmuss provided a detailed and unrelenting critique of the use of "routine administrative statistics" to provide the nation's account of patterns and trends in income distribution. Rather than any law tending towards equality, he suggested that inequalities may have begun to widen again since 1949. The book was an exercise in 'social and statistical archaeology' that revealed that these official data were becoming increasingly unreliable indicators of change as the world changed round them. For example, to compare distributions across the official category of 'income units' without taking account of increased rates of both marriage and labour force participation of married women led to an assumption of reduced inequality that took no account of the fact that more households had two earners and fewer only one (Titmuss, 1962, ch 2).

The strength of the book lay in his meticulous documentation of the myriad possibilities for tax planning and tax mitigation to keep income and wealth tucked away within the family and spread over the generations to avoid the attention of 'the taxman'. It took forward Titmuss's analyses in 'The social division of welfare' (Part 2, Chapter Two) of fiscal or tax welfare. The importance of his conception of income as the 'command over resources-in-time' was recognised by many. In the United States, Mike Miller and Pamela Roby explicitly built on his work in their analysis of *The future of inequality*, acknowledging him as the "intellectual progenitor" (Miller and Roby, 1970, p x).

A few months after Titmuss's death in 1973, Tony Atkinson revisited the issues in a lecture to the Social Administration Association (now the Social Policy Association). Atkinson found the same optimism about trends in income inequality as Titmuss had criticised in subsequent Inland Revenue reviews which "succeeded in presenting a highly misleading picture" (Atkinson, 1975, p 67). He concluded by underlining the lack of any real impact from the publication of "a 240 page catalogue of the deficiencies of available statistics" (Atkinson, 1975, p 67) on both official and independent analyses and on attitudes and beliefs. However, Atkinson, who himself has done much to take research into this area forward, did have some gentle rebukes for Titmuss who did "not on occasion distinguish sufficiently between factors which are important and those which are merely exotic" (Atkinson, 1975, p 61). Later he was sharper, including Titmuss's study in the 'nihilistic' approach to dealing with incomplete evidence (Atkinson, 1983, pp 65 and 283). There is some force to this as Titmuss was more concerned to indicate the gaps and patches in the data and often failed to give any indication whether the revealed statistical deficit was likely to be quantitatively important or unimportant.

The establishment by the Wilson government of the Royal Commission on the Distribution of Income and Wealth in 1974 helped to raise the visibility of the issues, even though the initial reports did little to question the official data. It was starting to pursue the issues more rigorously when, not surprisingly, it was among the first bodies to be abolished after Margaret Thatcher came to power in 1979. Challenging successive governments' neglect, if not outright rejection, of these issues, the Joseph Rowntree Foundation (1995) funded its own *Inquiry into income and wealth* with its second volume providing a comprehensive review of the evidence prepared by John Hills.

Given his own work on health and inequality, Richard Titmuss would have particularly appreciated the ways in which the broad issue of inequality was kept alive through the growing work on health inequalities. The report commissioned by the Labour government at the end of the 1970s, *Inequalities in health*, and its successor, *The health divide*, put the issue back firmly on the policy agenda, however much Conservative government ministers insisted on the use of the word 'variations' in place of 'inequalities' (Townsend et al, 1992). With inequalities in health now openly examined, the importance of adequate benefits and a fairer tax system for tackling these has been emphasised by a government-appointed report.

Nearly forty years after the publication of Titmuss's book, "a number of serious problems remain" with the official statistics, although some of Titmuss's criticisms have been addressed by more recent research (Atkinson, 2000, p 364). In particular, undistributed profits are not taken into account in any way and "no adequate allowance is made for capital gains". Many fringe benefits are still partly or fully omitted. In fact, it was not until a decade ago that official statistics recognised that 'company cars' should be taken into account as a benefit, this alone noticeably raising the level of inequality.

We are still dependent on management consultant surveys for some limited insight into occupational welfare for executives and directors, but these provide little indication of the value of benefits and their distribution across management, let alone the rest of the labour force. Only a glimpse of the national picture is provided by the Family Resources and the Labour Costs of Industry Surveys. Academic work has examined the significance and patterns of the range of occupational welfare (for example, Mann, 1992; May and Brunsdon, 1994 and 1999 including 'commercial welfare'; in the United States, Root, 1982; Stevens, 1986; comparatively, Shalev, 1996) and the interaction of the different welfare systems (Bryson, 1992; Sinfield, 1978).

The area of fiscal or tax welfare has received more attention in this country and abroad in recent years. In this country, reductions in the range and value of tax reliefs have cut the 'reverse targeting' or 'upside-down' nature of these 'tax benefits'. However, there has been a revival of what Titmuss described as a "growing use of the fiscal system as a vehicle of government action in the social policy field", but this time as part of the government's commitment to end child poverty in twenty years and to combat social exclusion (see the discussion in the Commentary to Part 3).

The 'hidden welfare state', providing 'tax benefits' from tax expenditures, has been examined in a number of studies influenced by the work of both Richard Titmuss and Stanley Surrey (1973) – for example, in the United States (Howard, 1997) and comparatively (Bryson, 1992; Greve, 1994; Kvist and Sinfield, 1997 on Denmark and the United Kingdom). The different ways in which the income tax and social security systems treat and label those who fail to comply or commit fraud has been explored by Dee Cook (for example, 1989).

Today, inequalities in the United Kingdom are much greater than they were when Titmuss was writing (Atkinson, 2000). Since 1979, inequalities have widened significantly and the latest official analyses indicate that they are widening still (Lakin, 2001). The conventional wisdom has swung right round. Forty years ago, Titmuss was querying the assumptions of growing equality whilst Atkinson has challenged what he calls the 'Transatlantic consensus' of inexorable increases in inequality. "Rising inequality is not inevitable ... [and] at least in part socially generated.... Differences in national redistributive policies" are a key part of the explanation for the "differing experience across OECD countries with regard to inequality in disposable household income" (Atkinson, 1999, pp 23, 24). Similarly, Jonathan Bradshaw's analysis of changes in the level of child poverty across different societies has demonstrated "that it cannot be argued that child poverty is the inevitable consequence of economic restructuring, globalisation, demographic transitions or whatever.... It is the result of political choices" (Bradshaw, 2000, pp 239, 241). Once again, policy matters, as Titmuss was always concerned to emphasise.

Richard Titmuss called the last chapter of *Income distribution and social change* (1962) 'The need for a new approach' and ended (p 199): "Ancient inequalities have assumed new and more subtle forms; conventional categories are no longer adequate for the task of measuring them". The question which he posed forty years ago still stands as a challenge to social scientists today: "To what extent ... are we becoming prisoners of the statistical houses we built in the past to accommodate the social data of that age?"

The irresponsible society

One of the most important tasks of socialists in the 1960s is to redefine and restate the inherent illogicalities and contradictions in the managerial capitalist system as it is developing within the social structure of contemporary Britain. Much of the doctrine of Victorian Marxism is no longer applicable to a different set of fundamental illogicalities in a different age. The future roles and functions of public ownership and social policy will be more clearly seen if they are analysed in terms of the problems of today and tomorrow.

Not least in importance in this approach to the future will be the study of the changing concentrations of economic and financial power. In R.H. Tawney's phrase (1934), who behind the "decorous drapery of political democracy" has power, who really governs, who is and will be making the critical decisions that will influence the design and texture of social and economic life in the 1960s? It is part of the purpose here to indicate something of the nature of these problems in one sector of the economy. As an illustration, the private insurance sector is examined in a limited fashion. Similar and more far-reaching questions need to be asked in other sectors where combination and concentration may threaten the rights and liberties of the subject to choose the values and decide the social priorities that will shape his society.

* * * * *

Richard Crossman, in a notable Fabian pamphlet (1955), examined the problem of monopolistic privilege and restated the need to expose the growth of irresponsible power, private and public. Since then, rising standards of living, the accumulation of the great tax-free fortunes of the 1950s, the growth of monopoly and other factors, have all served to endorse the need to scrutinise these threatening concentrations of power and privilege.

As the power of the insurance interests (in combination with other financial and commercial interests) continues to grow, they will, whether they consciously welcome it or not, increasingly become the arbiters of welfare and amenity for larger sections of the community. Their directors, managers and professionally trained advisers will be making, in their own eyes and in the eyes of many other people, sober, profitable and responsible decisions. But ultimately and in the aggregate they will not lead to a more rational and balanced disposition of social resources in relation to the needs of the nation and the problems of social organisation in a new age. These office-holders of power will not see that one of the most important problems of the future will centre round the socially effective use of rising national incomes and not the technical running of this or that part of the economic system. A wrong sense of proportion in attitudes to the 'economic surplus', to the savings of the community, for example, may well be one of the more serious dangers to public morality in the 1960s.

Nevertheless, these people will be driven, not as wicked people but as sober, responsible decision-makers, to intensify the contradictions which are distorting the economy and blurring the moral values of society. Social policies will be imposed without democratic discussion, without consideration of the moral consequences which may result from them. In this sense, they will be irresponsible decisions.

I attempt to illustrate the nature of some of these contradictions which are developing in contemporary Britain. Some concern the welfare of the politically obscure minorities: the powerless groups; the dependent poor, the disabled, the deprived and the rejected. There is, I suggest, a direct relationship between the shifting concentration of economic power in a more prosperous society and the future of the public services whose avowed purpose is to assist, without discrimination, these powerless groups. There is little evidence from the history of the 1950s that society is any nearer to the solution of these problems of dependent poverty, inequality and lack of freedom. By any objective criteria of wealth and opportunity, it is in some respects further away.

* * * * *

Expenditure by local authorities on welfare services for the aged, the handicapped and the homeless, for example, recognised as one of the most understaffed and impoverished services in 1949, has risen at a slower rate than almost all categories of private and public expenditure. Nor is there much hope for a better future for these minority groups from the enhanced power of insurance and financial interests. By their nature, by their own rules of selection and rejection without right of appeal, they cannot help those they reject. Insurance and other interests providing private medical care benefits (developing with some rapidity in the United Kingdom) generally exclude 'non-white nationalities', the elderly and other specified classes from certain group schemes. This is but one example from a long catalogue of discriminatory private policies exercised by insurance companies, building societies, property owners, hire-purchase firms, banks and other commercial institutions against those with 'handicaps' (legal, physical, psychological, racial and so forth).

Though not taken on any grounds of intolerance, these decisions can nevertheless easily be interpreted as intended discrimination. Thus, they deepen the sense of powerlessness and rejection among these minorities struggling to make something of their lives in a more affluent and seemingly arrogant society. Social manifestations of frustration are more likely to flourish in Britain (as they have and are doing in the United States) as these forces develop. More prosperity and more violence may be one of the contradictions in a system of unfettered private enterprise and financial power oblivious to moral values and social objectives.

* * * * *

The subject of power has not been fashionable either in the world of political action or in those places where questions of freedom and justice are reputedly discussed. Sociologists have left it to economists who, in turn, have left it to philosophers and they are not interested, so we are told by Ernest Gellner (1959). Perhaps it is that rising standards of living have hidden from sight the less obvious manifestations of arbitrary power. The iniquities of public bureaucrats have been repeatedly exposed to the greater glory of private bureaucrats. The makers of public policies have been decried to the advantage of the makers of private fortunes. A national press which, as a whole, has steadily taught the public to sneer at public order and public service and to admire cupidity and acquisitiveness has no doubt had some effect. Facts themselves matter less; all that matters is how the thing is put. Values matter less; what does matter is the kind of show that people put on. The Minister of Transport may now plead for more social discipline, order and collective planning to overcome the problems of urban congestion and road chaos, but the tide is running against him (*Hansard*, 10 December 1959, vol 615). He and other ministers concerned with social amenity, town planning and a civilised design for living are now the prisoners of their own propaganda.

* * * * *

The 1950s also witnessed a demonstration of the effectiveness of the myth as a motive force in British political beliefs and behaviour. Chief among these has been the myth of the 'welfare state for the working classes'. This has had a number of consequences. Reinforced by the ideologies of enterprise and opportunity, it has led to the assumption that most, if not all, of our social problems have been, or soon will be, solved. Those few that remain will, it is thought, be automatically remedied by rising incomes and minor adjustments of one kind or another. In short, it is coming to be assumed that there is little to divide the nation on home affairs except the dreary minutiae of social reform, the patronage of the arts, the parking of cars and the effectiveness of corporal punishment.

I want to examine some of the implications which flow from these assumptions. To do so may throw a little light on the context in which monopolistic power is likely to operate in the future; my purpose in stating these general propositions is to show a little more clearly the real nature of the choices in the 1960s.

* * * * *

In highly complex and wealthy societies like our own, almost all social forces tend to encourage the growth of conformism unless checked by strong, continuing and effective movements of protest and crticism. If these do not come from socialists and if they are not stated in terms of power, they will not come at all. To assume that there is now little to remedy in the social affairs of the nation further strengthens this trend towards conformism and political consensus. It makes political atheism and professional neutralism more respectable, especially among the young. It avoids the raising of new questions about the changing concentrations of economic and social power. It accepts, with growing affluence, the legitimation of a class structure. It implies not just a truce about equality, but virtually a permanent settlement in the struggle for social justice.

This movement of opinion constitutes a threat to the democratic process. If it is thought that less divides us, there is less to argue about. That is the point of view of many university students today. The Keynesian revolution, the acceptance of the 'welfare state', the upsurge and growth of professional power and the doctrine of Rostow (1960) all combine to provide a justification for the absence of social protest in our society. Material success and the pursuit of professional and class symbols of success are taken to be the basis of all success.

This seems a long way from the 1930s, but can it really be true that within two decades [1940s and 1950s] – so short a period in the struggle to make democracy a cultural and social reality – we have made so much moral progress?

When I was young, what some of us argued about was the democratic process. We wanted to know in our academically illiterate way whether more dialogue, more democracy, was possible. We thought it a dreadful crime to prevent other people from speaking up. We realised that the poor (whether they numbered 2 million or 10 million), the mentally ill, the disabled and other casualties or failures in our society were penalised, not only by their poverty, but because they were denied the social rights of protest and full membership of society. We believed in the possibility of an alternative government. We did not understand that government by the people could mean that power in government, the Cabinet and the City, could lie almost permanently in the hands of those educated at Eton and other public schools.

Thinking then that we could change our representatives and helped by a popular press that was radical and outspoken compared with the acquisitiveness of Fleet Street, we rebelled against the impersonal

agents of injustice and inequality. We rebelled too against the personal
ones: the bureaucratic despotism of large scale private as well as public
agencies; the social discrimination that operated in all the processes
of selection and rejection for education, work, professional and trade
union associations, welfare benefits, pension rights, medical care, tax
concessions and so forth. We began to see, in terms of the individual,
the demoralising effects of cumulative social rejection. But in those
days there was some safety in numbers for the rejected; some
compensation in the company of many others in similar situations of
unemployment and poverty, and with similar life experiences. The
social system could still be blamed for its failure to give people the
rights to *any* sort of work. Now it cannot.

* * * * *

Today, rebellion among the young seems to express itself in different
forms. It is less concerned with political and democratic ideas. Yet if
we are honest, we must admit that the fault is not entirely theirs.
Consider the state of political philosophy in Britain today. Or
economics. Or sociology. Or law. Consider the growing substitution
of specialisation for general education. What education for democracy
is there in much of the professionalised, sectionalised diet served up
to students in most universities, colleges and other places of
instruction? Are we not, indeed, witnessing a triumph of technique
over purpose? What, in fact, are we offering to a majority of the
young beside material success, the social graces, vocational techniques
and, in particular, professional salvation? And what are we offering
to women who, as voters in 1959, outnumber men by more than 2
million?

Changes in the family, in the roles and relationships of husbands
and wives, younger marriage and more marriage, and the contribution
of women to family income are matters of great political significance.
We must not and should not expect women to vote as their husbands
do or their fathers did. Their great and abiding loyalty is not to their
fellow workers, to associations of workers, to concepts of justice in
systems of social security, to abstract ideas about democracy, but to
the material advancement of their families.

Social and economic changes of a far-reaching character in these
and other spheres now face us with a new set of democratic problems.
They represent a challenge to our whole educational system. Yet the
current obsession which sees education as capital investment for the
purpose of 'keeping up in the economic race' suggests that our values
are being distorted. "The fact that politics are controversial – that
honest men disagree – makes preparation for citizenship a difficult
matter for schools … but it ought to be tackled, and not least for the
ordinary boys and girls who now leave school at 15 and often do not

find it easy to see any argument except in personal terms" (Crowther Report, 1959, p 114).

The essential point is that we are now, as a nation, better able to teach our young people about democracy. More of us, as individuals, can now afford to be moral in our attitudes to the great problems of world inequality and racial intolerance. But for this to happen, it surely means that those who hold positions of power and influence in our society should set examples for the younger generation in moral leadership and higher standards of social responsibility. If we cannot put our own moral houses in order, it is difficult to see how we can give disinterested help to the poorer nations. To give, to be taxed, has never been a simple matter in human history; for our neighbours, fellow workers, the poor, the sick, the ignorant and the feckless. In the decades ahead, we shall need all the social inventiveness, democratic skills and sense of responsibility which we can mobilise if we are to begin to close the gap of national inequalities.

The record of the 1950s does not, however, yield much evidence of moral progress in these respects. Economic growth, rising standards of living and a great outburst of scientific, technical and professional training all over the Western world has, along with other forces, installed and strengthened governments wedded to inequality, secretiveness in administration, monopolistic privilege and intolerance of non-conformity. More ominous still is the fact that these trends have been accompanied by a disenchantment with democracy which, as Robert Hutchins (1959) puts it, has little or nothing to do with the seductions of the Kremlin.

It is not only the Labour Party which should be thinking about these issues. To advance and widen democracy through education, by breaking down the barriers of social discrimination in all our public services and by civilising not only government but the great private bureaucracies and professional associations whose decisions so vitally affect our lives, is also a responsibility of government.

What may we expect? Are we likely to see these anti-democratic trends arrested and reversed in the 1960s? Consider what Lord Hailsham has to say in his measured statement of *The Conservative case* (1959):

> Conservatives do not believe that political struggle is the most important thing in life. In this they differ from Communists, Socialists, Nazis, Fascists, Social Creditors, and most members of the British Labour Party. The simplest among them prefer fox-hunting – the wisest religion.

Such a statement would have been unthinkable in the context of 1940 or 1945. Yet its author was elected rector of Glasgow University by its 6,000 students with a great majority.

These are social facts of importance; there are lessons here for all political parties. During the 1959 general election, one of the popular daily newspapers, the *Daily Sketch* (8 October 1959), warned its readers not to vote for the Labour Party because that party, if returned to office, would stop tax evasion and all those practices which go by the name of 'fiddling' in one income group and 'fixing' in another.

Facts such as these cannot be ignored. Along with other evidence, they suggest the growth of irresponsibility in public affairs and in the formation, by precept and example, of public opinion.

This is the context in which I now want to consider, firstly, the position of the dependent poor and other minority groups in relation to the future role of social policy and, secondly, the social control of economic and financial power, taking as an example the power of the private insurance market. Different aspects of social responsibility, of altruism in public affairs, are expressed and reflected in both these spheres. It is necessary, however, to be very selective, particularly as I want to offer some facts in place of generalities. It will not therefore be possible to discuss other important aspects of monopolistic power or each branch of social policy.

* * * * *

I have written elsewhere about what I called 'the social division of welfare' [see Part 2, Chapter Two]. Instead of thinking about the 'welfare state' as an abstraction, I suggested that we should consider the development of social rights and benefits in three categories or systems: occupational benefits, fiscal benefits and social service benefits. All are concerned in some measure and in different ways with increasing or decreasing inequalities in the distribution of income and wealth. All attempt in some degree, and for different sections of the population, to resolve or alleviate the inequalities of dependency; the economically dependent states of old age, widowhood, childhood, sickness and infirmity.

While it seems that we have to a large extent reduced the more serious problems of economic dependency arising from unemployment, far less progress has been made in removing other causes of poverty, inequality and chronic ill health. As Peter Townsend (1958) has shown, there may be some seven to eight million people living precariously close to the margins of poverty. Many are old, disabled and handicapped. Britain is not alone among the more prosperous societies in finding this problem of the poverty of dependency an intractable one. In a United States Senate Sub-Committee on the Aged and Aging, it was asked: "Why is it that despite the substantial liberalization of our old-age income maintenance programs ... we still find that the average income of elderly people is so low?" (US Senate, 86 Congress, 1959, p 167). In 1957 more than a sixth of all persons aged 65 and over in the United

States had no income of their own and about three fifths had incomes of less than the equivalent of about £4 a week.

However unsuccessful they may be in solving this great moral contradiction, at least it can be said that in the United States some attempt is made to find out the hard facts of poverty and dependency. In Britain, we simply do not know. No effort has been made by government to discover the real incidence of poverty and levels of living among the old and other dependent groups. This to me is one of the more striking signs of irresponsibility of the 1950s. In so far as a society fails to identify, by fact and not by inference, its contemporary and changing social problems, it must expect its social conscience and its democratic values to languish.

All one can say with assurance is that, in terms of the relationship of National Insurance benefits and allowances to average industrial earnings, most beneficiaries are relatively worse off in 1959 than they would have been in 1948. The fall in standards for them is a greater fall into poverty. The objective of social policy during the 1950s, it has been said repeatedly, is to concentrate resources on those who most need help. But what are the facts? The new National Insurance Scheme of graded pensions, which adds a few shillings to 50 shillings in ten years' time, omits everyone earning less than £9 a week, yet the Minister has stated quite emphatically in the House, "We do not want to encourage more people to rely on assistance" (*Hansard*, 1 November 1954, vol 532). This policy has been made effective substantially through the operation of 'disregards' in the means test (capital assets, war savings, sick pay, voluntary gifts from relatives and friends and charitable payments). In important respects, these tests are relatively harsher than in the middle of the Second World War when the Determination of Needs Act was insisted on by Ernest Bevin; harsher in some respects than at the height of the slump in 1932; and even harsher in allowing relatively smaller payments for sick pay than in 1904 under the poor law. Yet they were attacked by *The Economist* (January 1951, p 118) as "too generous for a nation which, in one way or another, is going to be forced to curtail its social services".

The improvements which were hurriedly made before the 1959 election to the scales of National Assistance are of no help to those who are discouraged or deterred from applying. In any case, an administrative agency, like the Assistance Board, which finds it necessary to be severe in its handling of the feckless, the 'work-shy', and the coloured immigrant is not likely to be attractive to the 'respectable poor'. And for those who are on assistance, nearly 2.5 million people, these belated improvements have to be weighed against a host of incalculables: the removal of food and general housing subsidies, the loss of tobacco coupons, higher prescription charges, a more expensive and poorer transport system, and the fact that many old people, relative to the standards of the rest of the population, are probably worse off in 1959 than they were in 1951 in terms of housing conditions and domestic equipment.

"No one whom I marry", said the vicar of St George's, Camberwell (*The Times*, 30 November 1959), "now has a chance of getting their own place through the housing list for at least four and a half years". If this is the situation for young married couples in such areas, it is likely to be far worse for the elderly and those on National Assistance. Yet *The Economist* (6 June 1959, p 925) could suggest after the Notting Hill 'race riots' in 1958 that coloured immigrants should be given 'special privileges' on council waiting lists. Coloured workers, it was argued, were "definitely a net gain to the British economy"; they are more "mobile" and more likely to provide a pool of unemployed to keep "the economy functioning smoothly" (*The Economist*, 6 September 1958, p 724). A 'liberal' immigration policy was therefore necessary to provide a pool of unemployed. Any housing difficulties could be met by giving coloured immigrants 'special privileges' on waiting lists. Meanwhile, public housing activities should be ruthlessly pruned. It is sad to see such arguments advanced in the name of liberalism. They are unlikely to appeal to many Commonwealth citizens looking to Britain for moral leadership.

* * * * *

There is little here to suggest that much progress has been made during the 1950s, in which great fortunes have been accumulated, to concentrate help through the public services on those whose need is greatest. For all we know, this conclusion may hold for other branches of the social services, such as medical care, education, housing and other welfare provisions. In terms of the quality and effectiveness of medical care (for the physically and mentally ill), who are the major beneficiaries of the National Health Service? We do not know; no official attempt has been made to find out who utilises the NHS, how often, in what sectors of cost and quality, and with what results. In the field of housing, social workers could quite hopefully put their more serious cases of hardship on council waiting lists. At this time, it is quite hopeless in many areas; waiting lists have either been abolished or remain as a polite administrative fiction. And many people believe that, without a revolution in local government and its financial resources, the 1959 Mental Health provisions for community care will remain virtually a dead letter.

These illustrations of the retreat from government in the field of the traditional social services are indicative of what we may expect in the 1960s. Secretiveness in administration, an appalling lack of facts, the decline in quality of Royal Commissions and committees of inquiry have all combined to maintain much of the mythology of the 'welfare state'. Many of us must also now admit that we put too much faith in the 1940s in the concept of universality as applied to social security. Mistakenly, it was linked with economic egalitarianism. Those who have benefited most are those who have needed it least. We are only just beginning to see that the problems of raising the level of living, the quality of education, housing and medical care of the poorest third of the nation calls for an immense amount of social inventiveness; for new institutional devices, new forms of cooperation, social control, ownership and administration, and new ways of relating citizens and consumers to services that intimately concern them. Social ideas may well be as important in Britain in the future as technological innovation.

These problems will not and cannot be solved by the private insurance market, by property speculators, by forcing land values to insanely prohibitive levels, or by any criteria of profits and tax-free gains. In 1959, private enterprise is only building about 1,000 new dwellings a year in London, for example, and most of these are luxury flats for the rich (*The Economist*, 21 November 1959). Nor will they be solved by the growth of the 'social welfare firm' and the provision of more occupational and fiscal benefits. Such developments have nearly all been concentrated on the better off third of the population, particularly in regard to pensions, tax-free lump sums, compensation for loss of office, life assurance, sick pay, school fees, higher education, housing, free clothing, travel and an immense variety of benefits and amenity in kind. Fringe welfare, as it is so charmingly called, rises very steeply with income. The cost per employee for staff pension schemes, for example, exceeds that for works pension schemes by about 700% (Durham, 1958, Table 9). Tax-free lump sums of £60,000 to £100,000 as compensation for loss of office (following takeover bids which may or may not have been 'arranged') are not uncommon. One typical case reported in *The Times* (22 June 1959) was for £60,000 plus a pension of approximately £4,000 a year. No comprehensive information on these benefits can be obtained from the Board of Inland Revenue or any government source.

Tax-free lump sums on retirement run from £100 at the bottom to £40,000 or more at the top. Such ratios would seem high in the USSR. What is now developing rapidly is the provision of private medical care and sickness insurance as a fringe benefit, aided by tax concessions and other devices.

The annual value of fringe welfare, including cheap stock options, may well exceed, if spread over working life, the salaries paid to the managerial, executive and other classes. Their standard of living is doubled or more than doubled. But it is mostly contingent welfare, the undivided loyalty tranquillizer of the corporation, the basis of a new monolithic society which, as Theodore Levitt (1958) has said of the American corporation, is on the way to becoming "a twentieth century equivalent of the medieval church".

To encourage this development, and to bind employers and employees more closely together, the Macmillan government has insisted on the unilateral right of the employer to contract his employees out of the new National Insurance Scheme. More fringe welfare for the better off will then provide the argument that Britain should lead the world in abolishing a state system of social security.

We have indeed almost reached a stage when it would be more appropriate in this world of fringe welfare to speak of 'the pressure group state', expressing a shift from contract to status; from open social rights to concealed professional syndicalism; from a multiplicity of allegiances to an undivided loyalty.

Much of this was foreseen in America by Roscoe Pound (1930, p 14) when he likened the distribution of stock and company welfare to how "the great feudal lords distributed estates in the Middle Ages". Whatever their wider implications for the future in terms of liberty and justice we can see here the connections between social policy, fiscal policy and the distribution of economic and social power in society. Here it is that inequality has a dynamic of its own.

These propositions about trends in our society now lead me into another area even less charted with facts, but we have to enter it if only to understand some of the problems of economic freedom in relation to the growth of irresponsible power.

$$* \quad * \quad * \quad * \quad *$$

It was no fortuitous event or sudden fever in crowd behaviour which led the London Stock Exchange, in the words of *The Times*, to "blaze into glory" on 9 October 1959. Coats were torn and millions were made to signal, in the affairs of the nation, a further extension in the almost unfettered reign of the City – of what Sir Roy Harrod described as "the wonderful recipe of the market mechanism" (*Observer*, 20 September 1959). It is not surprising therefore that certain codes of behaviour, presumably to protect the powerful guilds, are now to be drawn up, not by Parliament, but by the Institute of Directors, the banks and the Investment Protection Committee of the British Insurance Association.

As government retreats and the management of our economic affairs is increasingly delegated to the anonymous authority of the City, we must expect that other of our institutions will also be affected in a variety of ways. At the universities, as we attempt to 'declassify' students in terms of their social origins and then 'reclassify' them in professional ways with professional values (Selvin and Hagstrom, 1960), we must expect that more professors and teachers will become directors of commercial concerns. There will be other teachers too who will increasingly share their values with market consultants, persuaders, the pharmaceutical industry and promotional personnel. Some will get caught up in the process described by Hutchins (1959, p 7) as our "new way of getting rich which is to buy things from one another that we do not want at prices we cannot pay on terms we cannot meet because of advertising we do not believe".

* * * * *

The great insurance corporations and pension funds, taking up securities in public companies at a rate which exceeds in value the total capital issue in the year by those same companies, will recruit to their interlocking directorates and consultant ranks able men from the universities, the civil service and other walks of life. Already, since 1946, of four retiring permanent secretaries of the Ministries of Pensions and National Insurance two have entered the private insurance world; one as director of one of the large conglomerates; the other as executive chairman of the Society of Pension Consultants which was formed in 1958 to represent the views of brokers and pension consultants to the government about unnecessary developments in social insurance schemes. Other staff have been recruited from the Board of Inland Revenue and various departments to senior posts as 'taxation controllers', directors and consultants.

The 1950s witnessed something of an explosion in the accumulation of immense funds in the hands of private insurance companies and pension trusts. The rate of growth in this control over the 'economic surplus' may be even more dramatic in the future. Although there are many causes, it is the relatively sudden impact and union of two major forces in Western society which has led to this explosion: demographic change and economic growth. No one who attempts to foresee the future of the public social services (to say nothing of economic freedom) in Britain, the United States and other countries can now ignore this development.

Although only meagre information has been published, it would seem, comparing New York and London Stock Exchange lists, that the percentage holding of equities by British insurance companies and pension funds was in 1957 already more than double the percentage holding of common stock by their opposite numbers in the United States. In other words, these institutions are twice as powerful in Britain as in America in terms of the ownership of industrial assets.

More significant still is the rate of growth of these funds as a source of new capital. In an important report published by Robert Tilove (1959) for the American foundation, the Fund for the Republic, the author (as well as the 1955 Senate Committee on Banking and Currency) is concerned about the implications of the fact that pension funds (considered alone) are 'the most rapidly growing sector'. It is said that they may soon become "the biggest of the institutional investors in equities" (Tilove, 1959, p 39; US Senate, 1955, Report 376).

This position appears to have been reached years earlier in Britain in respect of insurance companies. According to the Radcliffe Report, the insurance companies and pension funds "constitute by far the largest single source of new capital, the net rate of accumulation of the funds of the two groups of institutions being now some £600 million per annum" (p 290). As investors, they dominate the City.

The significance of the 1956 Finance Act, which gave substantial tax concessions for pensions for the better off self-employed, now falls into place. Equally significant in this context are the five great insurance mergers which took place in 1959 to reduce still further what little competition remains between these large scale bureaucracies. So also is the 1959 National Insurance Act which was deliberately framed to encourage the further growth of private insurance power, according to the joint parliamentary secretary to the Ministry of Pensions and National Insurance (*The Policy-Holder*, 1959).

Among Tilove's conclusions (1959, pp 85-6), he declares "In terms of sheer total of common-stock holdings, there is a vast potential for these institutions to exercise corporate control and influence".

This *potential* for control and influence is greater in Britain. Yet we know nothing about how this responsibility is exercised. The insurance companies even refused to disclose to the Royal Commission on Taxation the market value of their assets (1955, p 285). They publish practically nothing about their purchases and sales of financial assets; they are allowed to maintain hidden reserves which are allocated among the different classes of assets as the directors think fit (*The Economist*, Supplement on British Insurance, 19 September 1959, p 4); their balance sheets "materially under-state the current value of equity assets"; no precise and comprehensive statistics have ever been published for the insurance market's foreign income and expenditure; it is not known whether the funds accumulated by the companies from income from colonial and underdeveloped areas are invested there; they never report the number of people who lose their pension expectations through unemployment, change of job and other reasons.

Nothing is known as to the number of individual 'top hat' pension policies issued with a capital value exceeding £100,000, or of the total cost to the taxpayer of non-contributory back service pension rights for directors and executives. "No comprehensive statistics are published of total business in force on a single date according to types of policy, nor is any breakdown available of endowment assurances into those connected with staff schemes, 'top hat' and other, and those which are 'individual'" (*The Economist*, Supplement on British Insurance, 16 July 1955). In addition, it should be noted that no statistics have ever been published showing breakdowns by age, sex, occupation, type of contribution, distribution of back-service, lump sum and pension benefits and vesting provisions.

Nor do the insurance companies or pension consultants tell us anything about the psychological and social harm they do to people in rejecting them or rating them sub-standard for life and pension purposes. We do not even know who is responsible for making some of the important decisions in the shaping and administration of private pension plans – employers, insurance companies or pension consultants. What we do know is that there is no appeal machinery in this complex and costly bureaucratic system; no opportunity to speak up as there is in the National Insurance system.

* * * * *

What American studies have to say about freedom to change one's work, about the difficulties of middle-aged and elderly men and women in getting work and continuing in work after certain ages, is relevant to the many similar problems we face in the United Kingdom. It is clear from American experience (the British insurance companies having published no facts) that these problems are gravely accentuated by the growth of private insurance plans. In 1958, it should be noted, the British government disbanded its National Advisory Committee on the Employment of Older Men and Women. It was beginning to ask awkward questions about freedom to work in old age and about the growth of unregistered unemployment among the elderly.

In addressing the International Congress of Actuaries in New York in 1957, one of the vice presidents of the Prudential Insurance Company of America estimated that within ten to twenty years at the most all forms of welfare benefits would be paid for by employers – with the continued help of tax concessions. This means not only provisions for pensions, widows and dependants, but also for medical care for the family, sickness insurance, professional training, higher education and other forms of 'fringe welfare'. Ever since the Prudential and other companies entered this field they have done everything, so Vice President Whittaker claimed (1957, p 155) "to make national health insurance unnecessary" in the United States.

That their invasion of the field of welfare has already been extensive is something of a feat because American insurance companies are subject to a far greater degree of public supervision, control over equity investment, inspection and statistical study than their opposite numbers in Britain (Tilove, 1959). Similarly, in Sweden and other countries, public control is wider and deeper (Hansson, 1958). Under the regime of a 'welfare state' in Britain, bitterly attacked on numerous occasions at the annual meetings of insurance companies since 1945, their directors and investment managers, like the medical profession in another context, have enjoyed more freedom to do as they like than in most countries of the Western world. They are, it was remarked at the 1957 Actuarial Congress, "the envy of insurers in the stronghold of private enterprise".

A future historian, interested in the relationships between professional power and financial power, will have to take note of the several thousand statements made since 1945 attacking "the immense and corrupting burden" of the 'welfare state' by insurance companies, banks, investment and hire-purchase firms, the *British Medical Journal*, the Institute of Chartered Accountants, the British Employers' Confederation, the Association of British Chambers of Commerce, the Institute of Directors, actuaries, judges, doctors and other professional men. Even as late as January 1960, the chairman of Barclays Bank could say that the 'welfare state' had "removed financial anxiety about illness and old age and had diminished in the ordinary man the sense of personal responsibility for his own future and that of his family" (address by the chairman to the stockholders).

* * * * *

I have devoted space to these matters because they constitute a major shift in economic power in our society. It is a power, a potential power, to affect many important aspects of our economic life and our social values in the 1960s. It is power concentrated in relatively few hands, working at the apex of a handful of giant bureaucracies, technically supported by a group of professional experts, and accountable, in practice, to virtually no one.

From other points of view, it is a force making for greater centralisation of decision-making power, reminding us again of Disraeli's warning that "centralisation is the death-blow of public freedom".

We do not know how this power is being used in terms of social welfare priorities or how far these massive investment funds are being or will be used to restore the outworn, mid-Victorian social capital of Britain. What we can only call 'social policy decisions' are however continually being made, without any proper awareness or public discussion of what is involved in terms of the common good and what consequences may flow from the choices made. It all goes on in what Weber (Gerth and Mills, 1946, pp 233-5) described as "the secret sessions" of private bureaucratic power. "The 'secret' as a means of power, is, after all, more safely hidden in the books of an enterprise than it is in the files of public authorities".

The insurance companies claim that the financial resources they control are used only for 'pure' investment in profitable enterprises. This is the general view and it was accepted by the Royal Commission on Taxation (1955, pp 87, 285, 290). At the same time, however, it seems somewhat inconsistent to demand, as the insurance companies do, the abolition of what is called "the anachronism of the non-voting share" (letter to *The Times*, 9 November 1959). Moreover, is it so certain that this position will continue to hold good in the future as the funds continue to increase in size?

In any event, there are no published facts apart from what one can learn from an examination of the interlocking characteristics of insurance directorates. Of 126 directors of 10 leading British companies in 1956, one half went to Eton and six other public schools; most of them belong to a small circle of clubs among which the Carlton is the most popular; a high proportion are titled; and most have extensive connections with industry, finance and commerce. Democratic pleas from such quarters on behalf of voteless shareholders remind one of La Rochefoucauld's maxim that "hypocrisy is the tribute which vice pays to virtue".

Looking to the future, there can be little doubt that what is needed is the direction of an increasing flow of savings into the British domestic areas of public squalor. They are easily identified: the slums of Lancashire and the North; the dying coalfields of south Wales and Scotland; and the ugly and ancient hospitals, schools and other public institutions which Brian Abel-Smith so vividly described in his essay in *Conviction* (1958). But if recent experience and the concept of profitability is any guide, this will not happen. Insurance companies have become increasingly interested in the London and South-East property market, Britain's area of private opulence. They have preferred to finance large blocks of office buildings and luxury flats, London's new architectural indignities. One company, Town and City Properties, announced in November 1959, that it had entered into an understanding with the Prudential "to facilitate the provision for finance for such property development as may be approved by the Prudential" (*The Times*, 24 November 1959). Other insurance companies are playing a major role in changing the face of London and the South-East, not least in Piccadilly Circus.

To raise the quality of environment for all our people should be at the very centre of social policy. Yet, over the same period of time in which we have remarked this shift in economic power, there has been a steady retreat from town planning and redevelopment. All the impulse and ideals of the 1940s to recreate, re-build and re-plan have now collapsed. At the level of central government planning, as Matthew said, "all is silence" (*The Listener*, 6 August 1959, p 204). The drift south continues. Without planned redevelopment "on a really heroic scale in the next few years, obsolescence and traffic volume alone between them will kill the quality of urban living upon which we, above all people, depend". This is retreat from government, a retreat into irresponsibility.

* * * * *

Underlying the notions of continued economic growth is the assumption of a dwindling role for government. The public services are increasingly seen, according to Galbraith (1958, pp 104-6), as an incubus; an unnecessary, doctrinaire burden on private enterprise.

The act of affirmation, the positive political decision about equality and its correlate freedom, becomes harder to make as the majority of voters (and not just the top 10%) grow richer. Negatively, they assume, in so far as they are helped to think about these matters at all, that the unseen mechanisms of a more prosperous market will automatically solve the problems of the poverty of dependency, the slums of obsolescence, the growth of irresponsible power and all the contradictions that flow from undirected or misdirected social policies.

As society grows in scale and complexity, new social needs are created; they overlap with and often accentuate the more classical forms of dependent needs. Many of these new needs are born of the disservices of technological and scientific change which, in turn, give rise to new concentrations of self-interested professional and economic power. These needs call for services and social amenities; things which, in Galbraith's analysis, do not easily lend themselves to private production, purchase and sale. If inequalities, individual and territorial, are not to grow and if public meanness is not to become public squalor, these things should be provided for everyone if they are provided for anyone.

The growth of a 'pressure group state', generated by more massive concentrations of interlocking economic, managerial and self-regarding professional power, points in other directions: towards more inequality; towards the restriction of social rights and liberties and the muffling of social protest among a large section of the population. The growing conservatism of professionalism and of the imposed inequalities resulting from the decisions of congeries of social power, were remarked upon, with extraordinary foresight, by Graham Wallas in his chapter on 'Professionalism' in *Our social heritage* (1921). He was concerned, as I have been (although in a much more limited context), with the fundamental problem of reinterpreting social equality and personal liberty in the conditions of a new age and a changed society. Wallas was also one of the first to see the importance of the transferability of pension rights as an element in personal freedom.

* * * * *

Those aspects of economically determined power with which I have been chiefly concerned function as accelerators of inequality, if they are not socially controlled; inequalities in the distribution of income and wealth, educational opportunity, vocational choice, pension expectations and in the right to change one's job, to work in old age and in other spheres of individual and family need. Some part of this process is expressed through the multiplication and division of occupational and fiscal benefits. Some part is traceable to the separation of 'ownership' from the rights of stockholding and the organised concentration of control over the 'economic surplus' which represents a primary source of power in our society. The answers lie in many fields and forms of public ownership, public responsibility and public accountability. The expansion and reshaping of social policy is but one.

To grow in affluence then does not mean that we should abandon the quest for equality. In some senses at least the quest becomes harder to undertake as the cruder injustices of yesterday are reduced and blurred, but new forms and manifestations of social injustice take their place. To substitute the professional protest for the social protest and the arbitrary power of the City for the accountable power of the House of Commons is no answer – no answer for ourselves; no prescription for a participating democracy; no example for Africa and the poverty stricken peoples of the world. It is simply the mark of an irresponsible society.

The need for a new approach

To study the rich and the sources of power in society is not the kind of activity which comes easily to social workers attempting to understand the human condition. Traditionally, they have been concerned with the poor and the consequences of poverty and physical handicap. They have thus tended to take, and perhaps were compelled to take, a limited view of what constituted poverty. It was a view circumscribed by the immediate, the obvious and the material; a conception of need shaped by the urgencies of life daily confronting those they were seeking to help. In so far as they looked at relativities and inequalities in society, which they seldom did, they restricted their studies to the day-to-day differences in levels of expenditure on the more obvious or more blatant necessities of life. Daily subsistence was both the yardstick and the objective.

Far-reaching changes affecting the structure and functions of social institutions; general improvements in material standards of living; and the growth of knowledge about the causes and consequences of social ills in the modern community are now forcing on us the task of redefining poverty. Subsistence is no longer thought to be a scientifically meaningful or politically constructive notion (Lynes, 1962). We are thus having to place the concept of poverty in the context of social change and interpret it in relation to the growth of more complex and specialised institutions of power, authority and privilege. We cannot, in other words, delineate the new frontiers of poverty unless we take account of the changing agents and characteristics of inequality. How then is poverty to be measured and on what criteria, secular, social and psychological?

Each generation has to undertake anew this task of reinterpretation if it wishes to uphold its claim to share in the constant renewal of civilised values. Yet the present generation, it must be conceded, has been somewhat tardy in accepting this obligation. It has been too content to use the tools which were forged in the past for measuring poverty and inequality.

These tools are now too blunt, insensitive and inadequate. They do not go deep enough. These also are the lessons thrown up by study of the primary sources of knowledge about the distribution of incomes. They yield a surface view of society which is increasingly at variance with other facts and with the evidence of one's eyes.

What, it may be asked, has prevented us from sharpening these tools of inquiry and applying them with more precision to contemporary Britain? Three by no means inclusive reasons may be provocatively advanced.

Firstly, it may be said that modern societies with a strongly rooted and relatively rigid class structure do not take kindly to self-examination. The major stimulus to social inquest in Britain during the 20th century has come from the experience of war. On each occasion this experience was sufficiently mortifying to weaken temporarily the forces of inertia and resistance to change. In the absence of such stimuli in the future, we may have quite consciously to invent and nourish new ways and means of national self-examination. This task may be harder to discharge in the face of rising standards of living and the growing influence of the mass media of complacency. Perhaps the most powerful challenge of all will come from the notion that economic growth will solve all our social problems involving choice, distribution and priorities.

Secondly, it becomes clearer as we learn to distinguish between the promise of social legislation and its performance that the present generation has been mesmerised by the language of the 'welfare state'. It was assumed too readily after 1948 that all the answers had been found to the problems of health, education, social welfare and housing, and that what was little more than an administrative tidying-up of social security provisions represented a social revolution. The origins and strength of this climate of opinion will no doubt continue to puzzle historians for a long time to come.

Thirdly, and concomitantly, the 1950s saw the spread of the idea that some natural built-in 'law' was steadily leading to a greater equality of incomes and standards of living. It followed implicitly from this theory that further economic growth would hasten the operation of the natural law of equalisation. This was not a new thesis; Marshall had stated it hopefully many years earlier in *Principles of economics* (1949 [first published 1892], p 712): "the social and economic forces already at work are changing the distribution of (income) for the better; ... they are persistent and increasing in strength; and ... their influence is for the greater part cumulative".

This thesis received powerful support from government and independent statisticians in the 1950s, notably in the studies made by the Board of Inland Revenue (BIR) and by Lydall and Paish. These essays in income distribution were the active agents in encouraging examination of the basic statistics.

* * * * *

Many of the processes of rearranging, transforming and spreading income-wealth were no simple manifestations of high taxation from the 1940s onwards. They were not ephemeral mutations, to be eradicated by such acts as raising the surtax level, but evidence of deeply-rooted trends in the economic structure of a changing society. There emerged what seemed to be highly significant connections between apparently unrelated social and economic institutions: the law on the alienation of income reflecting long-run changes in family relationships, the points at which the private education sector connected with the shifting concept of charity, and the rise of new institutions for storing and redistributing income and property rights. The growth of new social mechanisms for exercising and extending command over resources-in-time was seen as one of the links between these different institutions.

These observations are as relevant to the real world of income-wealth in the 1960s as they are to the 1950s. They have a bearing on the fundamental problem of what constitutes inequality and what poverty means in the second half of the 20th century. Little is known about some of the measurable characteristics in the changing equation of inequality but we cannot begin to learn until we consciously admit to our own ignorance.

* * * * *

One must recognise that those who attempt the task of estimating from the official statistics changes in the distribution of personal incomes are sometimes placed in positions in the real world of action of making the best of imperfect statistical materials. They are confronted with the data; they know that the BIR has sought to make improvements by undertaking sample surveys and they may note the absence for many years of any serious criticism of this body of knowledge. Pressed for answers and often pressed for time, they develop such techniques as are available to guard against erroneous conclusions.

But the imperfections accumulate. They stem from changes taking place in society at large; from more different and complex ways of getting, spending, spreading and storing income; from social and demographic forces which change the characteristics of income units, families and economic classes; from a process of fission affecting the nucleus of rights which we call property resulting in larger concentrations of corporate wealth and power without ownership; from new forms of social benefit and privileged consumption for the family as well as the individual that flow from achieved and inherited status rather than contract; and from the growth of fiscal legislation providing special concessions and distinctive privileges in favour of certain groups or classes in the interests of economic efficiency, saving and investment, professional self-advancement and other socially approved objectives.

Due to these complex factors at work in society, there is clearly a need for a new approach to the problem of measuring inequalities in the distribution of income and wealth. The present mould into which statistics are cast is increasingly delusive as a frame for knowledge. We are in fact expecting too much from the crumbs that fall from the conventional tables. We cannot so easily reduce the complex to the simple. By attempting to do so, we ignore age, sex, kinship occupation, civil status and other critical variables, and we lose sight of the importance of defining clearly the unit of income, the unit of time and the concept of income.

Some of the criticisms made about the statistics of income are also applicable to the statistics of wealth. For example, Campion (1939, p 110) suggested that the distribution of property ought to be measured by families. He drew attention to the tendency for property and the benefits arising therefrom to be shared with wives, children and other relatives. This trend, he considered, could account in part for the reduced inequality of the distribution of property since before 1914. More recent studies emphasise the importance of this factor, commenting on the "growing tendency for owners of large properties to distribute their assets amongst the members of their families well in advance of death" (Lydall and Tipping, 1961, p 85).

The causes of this change in the pattern of economic relationships within the family are probably associated in some measure with changes in family life and in the status accorded to wives, children and other kin relations among the wealthier classes – a subject little examined by sociologists because of the difficulties of access to the primary data. Studies of the distribution of income and wealth which show a gentle decline in inequality in Britain in terms of persons or income units may therefore be concealing a significant growth in inequality between families. Lampman's investigation (1959) into the changes in the share of wealth held by the top wealth-holders in the United States concluded that the decline in inequality between 1922 and 1956 had been overstated on an individual compared with a family basis.

To what extent then, it may be asked, are we becoming prisoners of the statistical houses we built in the past to accommodate the social data of that age? The appeal of continuity in the analysis and presentation of large masses of data must always be strong in a historically conscious society and statisticians, like other people, have their own particular reasons for not wishing to change. Their preferences for stability and order are reinforced when those who use the results of their work fail to appraise its relevance to a different social structure and to changes in economic and institutional relationships.

Though we may now be collecting more information in the field of income distribution than we were years ago, it does not follow that we are better informed about the essential constituents; when or how they may be added together, arranged and presented, and what conclusions are valid. In many respects, the standard of critical thought brought to bear by the users of these statistics has not kept pace with either the volume and complexity of the facts themselves or with the development of methods of statistical analysis. Supported intellectually with more sophisticated aids, we seem to have been entering for races before we are able to walk.

Much of this running in the field of income distribution has been over ground heavily sown with 'routine administrative statistics'. It is not necessarily a criticism of the BIR to say that its annual reports are largely a record of 'work done'. Consequently, its definitions, in so far as they are needed for reporting on the discharge of responsibilities, tend to be administrative definitions. The BIR may justly reply in such terms to the comments we have made; it is not the fault of the BIR if its statistics or 'work done' are misused or misinterpreted by others. All this is undeniable. On the other hand, it should be pointed out that the BIR does not reprove those who mishandle its statistics. Every year, on the occasion of the publication of the BIR's report, the national press is filled with accounts of how inequality is diminishing and how the rich are disappearing as a distinctive class. It is seldom, if ever, announced that, in most years, these accounts are based on the collection and tabulation of administrative statistics. In time we come to believe them as these results are purveyed without qualification, and more and more textbooks on public finance and allied subjects report them as established, indisputable facts.

Nor is the BIR entirely free from criticism in other respects. In response, no doubt, to demands from income statisticians, the Central Statistical Office and other quarters, the BIR has attempted to convert or adapt its administrative statistics for use as indicators of change in the distribution of incomes. These attempts have been pursued since 1938 without any adequate discussion of the fundamental problems of defining the units that are tabulated. In its 1949 Report, the BIR presented an analysis of its administrative statistics, accompanied by two charts, which purported to show that 'there has been a very considerable redistribution in incomes since pre-war'. There was no suggestion here that it was simply reporting on 'work done', on incomes assessed and taxes collected under various schedules. The data were presented in 1950 as a contribution to the study of income distribution. As the BIR must have expected, they were widely and uncritically consumed in this sense.

Their general acceptance is perhaps but one of many symptoms of the intellectual narrowness of writers on public finance and related subjects. They seem to be oblivious of the work being done in neighbouring fields by demographers, sociologists, lawyers, accountants and others. Since 1945, for instance, there has been a veritable spate of literature on what is described as 'tax planning', to say nothing of the rise of new 'professional' groups of tax consultants, pension consultants, death duty consultants and 'one-man company' experts. These phenomena suggest that the conventional models of economic man and income units may be wearing a little thin in terms of fiscal statistics. It is a defensible thesis to advance, against the background of the social changes we have sketched in, that 'yearly income' (in the traditional sense of disposable cash) is now less important among the top income-wealth groups in society. Long-run developments in family relationships and fiscal law; the shifting alignment of forces controlling access to a power system as distinct from individual property rights; the transformation of individual benefits in cash into family benefits in kind; the changing individual age cycle of earning and non-earning; the spreading and splitting of 'income' over life and over the lives of several generations; the metamorphosis of income into capital; the growth of rewards in the form of tax-free payments and the use of credit facilities; all these make 'cash in hand' less necessary for the business of daily life for certain classes and living on overdrafts, trusts and other forms of command-over-resources more fiscally rewarding if, at times, perhaps a little irksome.

While it is easy, of course, to make fun of any specialist group for their unalloyed absorption in a special branch of knowledge, it must be admitted that they are not suffering from a particular occupational disease but from a general epidemic of intellectual short-sightedness. We are all, in some senses, victims and offenders, confronted as we are with the problem of the growth of knowledge in complex societies and the division of intellectual labour into smaller and smaller segments.

Some of these handicaps might be reduced if the statistics of income and wealth were presented in a broader and more analytical framework. Not only do we need to know much more about what is being measured, but alternative ways of presenting the results are required as a corrective to the conventional 'snapshot' view of statutory income. Much too could be learnt if these different analyses were tabulated in terms of age, sex, civil status, family relationships, occupation, types of income, categories of expenditure on certain forms of goods and services, and allocations to savings of various kinds. Some of this information could be cross-checked and amplified by the use of national sample budget surveys of expenditure, saving and the ownership of property. A national census of all discretionary trusts, family settlements and covenants would be essential for the purposes of both income and wealth distributions, and the government would have to take a number of steps to compel insurance companies, charities and corporate bodies in general to furnish much more information than they do at present.

Given the will to be a less secretive society, there is nothing impracticable about these suggestions. They would, of course, take time and resources to implement but the gain in terms of public enlightenment about the constituents of equity could be impressive. It would no longer be possible for pronouncements to be made of such a general character as the 1950s endured. We may consider, as a conclusion, a few of the statements made in recent years about changes in the distribution of income and wealth.

* * * * *

The BIR's report on its 1949 statistics was the text for many writers in the early 1950s. It provided, for example, part of the factual basis for de Jouvenel's influential study *The ethics of redistribution* (1951). *The Economist* (4 February 1950), in a series of articles on personal incomes, went further than the BIR in claiming that its figures indicated "a vast redistribution of incomes" since 1938. Two books by Lewis and Maude, which came in for a great deal of attention at this time, were clearly stimulated by official statistics depicting a considerable decline in inequality. The first, which the authors thought of calling 'The decline and fall of the middle classes', appeared as *The English middle classes* (1949). The second was *Professional people* (1952), in which the conclusion was reached that "the professions have tended to come off worse than any other section of the community except retired pensioners". Colin Clark's *Welfare and taxation* (1954) accepted the BIR's statistics of incomes without qualification.

These and similar studies contributed to the shaping of public opinion and furthered the acceptance of the BIR's statistics. In more specific ways, they were significant in the formation of policies. Thus we find, in 1952 and again in 1954, the BIR's comparison of changes in the distribution of incomes between 1937-38 and 1949-50 being submitted, "as adequate data", to Mr Justice Danckwerts as adjudicator on the remuneration of general practitioners and to the 1954 Royal Commission on the Civil Service. Those responsible for making recommendations to the government must have found it difficult, guided as they were by little expertise on these fiscal matters, to refute or qualify official statistics of this order of complexity.

By the mid-1950s these conclusions had become part of the history of our times. Lionel Robbins (1955, p 18), reflecting on trends in the distribution of incomes and wealth, wrote of a tax structure which "relentlessly, year by year, is pushing us towards collectivism and propertyless uniformity". In much the same strain, Brendon Sewill (1958, p 27) and the Bow Group interpreted the BIR's statistics as depicting "the virtual extinction of the pre-war 'surtax class'". They were also employed by Enoch Powell (1960) in his book on saving to show that the trend towards equality, apparent from the official data for 1938 to 1949, continued to operate for the later years to 1958.

All these writers who attempted comparisons over time in the distribution of income and wealth took as their baseline the official statistics for 1936-38. Whatever their defects, the pattern of inequalities which they disclosed was the one which Keynes (1936, p 374), despite his belief in the value of a significant range of inequality, attacked as socially unjust for its magnitude. Jewkes (1939, p xi), also voicing his disquiet at this time, asked the question: "Must we be prepared to tolerate, so long as we had a system of private enterprise, the apparent paradox that, although men were equal politically, they must inevitably remain as unequal economically as they now are?" Twenty years later, and after one of the greatest wars in British history which might have been expected to exert a profound influence on the distribution of wealth, these measures of inequality in the 1930s were being regarded as acceptable criteria for determining the degree of inequality that might be socially justified.

These views were strengthened by the effects on the tax structure of all the complex forces we have analysed which cumulatively were enlarging the dustbowl of taxable capacity. "We have travelled far down the vicious path of decadent tax systems", said Kaldor at the end of his book, *An expenditure tax* (1955, p 242), "the path of charging more and more on less and less". This journey has moreover been hastened by the growth of social welfare provisions in fiscal law: dependency benefits for children and other family members, allowances for those undertaking higher education and 'self-improvement', relief and exemption in old age, and deductions and discriminatory reliefs for particular categories of saving for retirement and other purposes by certain sections of the population. While it is outside the scope of this study to examine the problems of equity raised by the growing use of the fiscal system as a vehicle of government action in the social policy field [see Part 2, Chapter Two]; it should be pointed out that this development contributes to the further erosion of the tax base. "A programme of tax allowances which costs the State in the neighbourhood of £450m in lost revenues deserves to be recognized", said Cartter (1953, p 227) in referring to dependants' allowances in 1952, "as a major element in the programme of social welfare".

Taken together, all these factors tend to give the standard rates of taxation a spurious role in public life. They involve, as these rates become increasingly ineffective for some groups but not for others, a subtle kind of moral dishonesty. We are thus led to claim, with varying degrees of pride or shame, that Britain is the most highly taxed nation in the world (Peacock, 1960), or that progression in the tax structure is steeper than it has ever been, or that this nominal structure justifies great increases in salaries and tax-free rewards for certain sections of the population – an argument put into effect increasingly in the 1950s. The best of both worlds is thus achieved by some at the expense of others as our tax systems move further away from the notion of equitable neutrality in relation to the dependency burdens of kinship, the costs of higher education and self-advancement, the saving and spreading of income and its transformation into capital, the consumption of particular categories of goods and services and so forth.

Future historians with access to the public archives may find a fascinating theme to unravel in studying the connections between erosion of the tax base brought about by the many forces discussed here, changes in redistributive social policies, reductions in the 'burden' of income tax and surtax that took place after 1951, and the search by governments for new and more effective fiscal systems. They will note the decline in favour of the progressive tax system along with the principle that ability to pay is the right democratic criterion. They will no doubt also analyse the attempts to give greater weight to regressive systems and taxes on consumption and, in particular, the shifting of Exchequer burdens to local rates. Above all, they will be led to study the fashioning of a new and massive fiscal system in the shape of national insurance and health service contributions. By 1961–62 these two regressive poll taxes were yielding close on £1,200m a year, or six times as much as the yield from surtax before the surtax level was raised to £5,000. 'Contributions' levied without regard to personal circumstances were by then the most important form of direct taxation experienced by something like half the working population. For the Treasury in particular, they had the advantage of simplicity in administration, the prospect of a steadily growing yield and a way of redistributing part of the costs and consequences of tax avoidance and erosion.

The implications of this policy could, however, be quite profound. The ease with which this new system can be deployed, and its comparative freedom from avoidance devices, may mean in the long run a gradual abandonment of the search for equity. A situation is created in which it becomes psychologically harder to press for reforms in the older form of direct taxation. Action appears to be less urgent if revenue can be effectively raised in other ways. For many years now, *The Economist* and other commentators have argued that the only solution to the problem of avoidance and erosion – perhaps democracy's hardest domestic problem – is greatly to reduce 'the burden' of the progressive tax (*The Economist*, 13 April 1960). In other words, the only answer to the challenge of moral behaviour is, in the ultimate analysis, to abolish the need to be moral.

* * * * *

These general reflections on the lessons of our study have led us far from its point of departure. That was to examine the statistics on the distribution of incomes before tax and to inquire into the validity of the conclusions reached by others who had studied these data. Whatever else may be said about the criticisms we have made about the sources of information and about those who have interpreted the material, there can be little dispute with the conclusion that we know less about the economic and social structure of our society than we thought we did.

It follows from this that we should be much more hesitant in suggesting that any equalising forces at work in Britain since 1938 can be promoted to the status of a 'natural law' and projected into the future. There are other forces, deeply rooted in the social structure and fed by many complex institutional facts inherent in large-scale economies, operating in reverse directions. Some of the more critical of these factors, closely linked with the distribution of power, and containing within themselves the seeds of long-lasting effects (for instance, in the case of settlements and trusts) function as concealed multipliers of inequality. They are not measured by the statistics of income and only marginally by the statistics of wealth. Even so, there is more than a hint from a number of studies that income inequality has been increasing since 1949 whilst the ownership of wealth, which is far more highly concentrated in the United Kingdom than in the United States, has probably become still more unequal and, in terms of family ownership, possibly strikingly more unequal, in recent years (Jay, 1962, pp 191-215).

It has not, however, been our purpose to estimate the total effect of all the forces which determine the class distribution of incomes and wealth. We have simply attempted to show that fact and economic theory are at variance, and that no conclusion which takes account of an ageless individual and forgets the family, which measures 'income' and omits 'wealth', which disregards the unit of time in command-over-resources, which fails to inquire into the meaning of power, which avoids investigating the interlocking connections between social and economic institutions, and which is oblivious of the key role now played by the educational system in the social distribution of 'life chances', can be relied upon in the context of the social changes we have depicted. Ancient inequalities have assumed new and more subtle forms; conventional categories are no longer adequate for the task of measuring them.

International and comparative dimensions

Commentary: Howard Glennerster

As these extracts from his last writings in this section of the book show, Richard Titmuss was not just an international figure; he also made the academic subject of social policy international. The issues of equity and social justice it posed were truly global in their implications. How could human need be confined to national boundaries? This comes out clearly in the first extract. For students at the London School of Economics and Political Science (LSE), it was their first taste of the subject, the first lecture in the core course all had to attend. There was no dreary attempt to define social policy, no beginning with the English Poor Law; instead, Titmuss jumped right into the dilemma of clashing priorities between good ends and a world stage for the subject. Nor was the world the comfortable world of advanced industrial societies.

* * * * *

To be international, for Titmuss, meant being as concerned with the developing world as with the developed rich north, indeed more so. He was a friend and admirer of Julius Nyerere, the independence leader of Tanzania whose work he mentions in this piece. He urged developing countries to balance economic development with social development long before the idea ever entered the heads of those in the World Bank or other international agencies. Ever practical in his follow through, he launched an MSc at the LSE in Social Planning in Developing Counties to train those from the third world in *social* planning.

In 1957 Titmuss and James Meade, later to win a Nobel Prize for Economics, were asked to help the small island of Mauritius in the Indian Ocean draw up an economic *and* a social plan for their country. Their parallel volumes (Meade et al, 1960; Titmuss and Abel-Smith, 1961) form an exemplar of that approach. Unlike so many economic plans of that period that lie forgotten in some dusty archive, they provided a foundation for a remarkably successful economy: following Meade's advice, it developed a diversified economy; following Titmuss's advice, it adopted a politically difficult policy of population control which in combination has supported an infrastructure of basic health, education and social security.

In late 1996 I visited and toured the little island giving numerous lectures and small impromptu seminars. Everywhere I went, the Meade–Titmuss–Abel-Smith Plan was remembered and held up as the guiding principle of balanced development.

The inclusion of the third world in the social policy literature that most undergraduates read has, however, been slow in coming (Midgeley 1997). So too has a discussion of the impact on poor people throughout the world of the global economy, international investment by global pension funds and powerful international agencies. Now that is changing. For a long time, there were few accessible texts or good comparative research on these issues; now there are a growing number. One of the early pioneers was UNICEF which began tracking the impact on vulnerable groups in the third world of the global recession and economic adjustment programmes, in this case children (Jolly and Cornea, 1984). Now students are deeply interested in these issues. It has taken many academic institutions thirty years to catch up with Richard Titmuss.

* * * * *

As his lecture on conditions of rapid change shows, Titmuss was advanced in his thinking on environmental issues and anticipated the global implications of human pollution. He saw social and environmental policy as merely part of the same debate. Just as in the 19th century the threat of epidemics forced the Victorians to see that public health was a public good that required public collective action so world environmental threats might force us to understand the need for global collective action. It might lead us to recognise the limitations of free markets and selfish private actions. Just to read these extracts is to see how far ahead of his time he was and how painfully contemporary are his strictures.

* * * * *

Before Titmuss, social policy as an academic subject had been grounded in United Kingdom experience. Students of social policy in the 1940s could be forgiven for thinking that Britain had invented the welfare state. Marshall's (1950) account took the development of citizen's rights as they had evolved in the UK as his exemplar. Social policy, students were taught, reached its zenith in the post-war legislation of 1944 to 1948. The 'post war settlement' in Britain produced what later writers called 'the classic welfare state'. Titmuss broke with this narrow Anglo-centrism. He had friends and colleagues abroad: Gunnar Myrdal in Sweden, Eve Burns and a string of American scholars who came to study at the LSE. They included Robert Ball and Ida Merriam, one of those powerful American women civil servants who ran the largest and most professional social security research departments anywhere in the world dating from the Roosevelt era. The US national universal and wage-related pension scheme

Titmuss learned about in detail, as he did the Swedish and German schemes. He thus became acutely aware of the failings of Britain's flat rate pension scheme. When asked by Peter Shore and Richard Crossman to advise the Labour Party on an alternative pension policy, he and his colleagues drew heavily on these international examples in preparing papers for the Labour Party's study group on old age. They were to form the basis of the Labour Party's National Superannuation or the State Earnings Related Pension Scheme (SERPS) as it became nearly twenty years later – too late, as it turned out, to reverse the disastrous turn pensions policy had taken after the Second World War. The low flat rate pension financed by low flat contributions not only kept many poor pensioners still reliant on means tests but left ordinary workers facing a sharp fall in living standards on retirement. For a decent pension, they had to turn to private occupational schemes that trade unions negotiated for the fortunate. By the time a universal all-encompassing national pension scheme was on offer, middle England wanted to be outside it.

* * * * *

So international experience formed an important element in Titmuss's policy analysis and his policy recommendations. It also formed part of his analytical approach. He thought that students would understand their own institutions better if they had the chance to compare them with those of other countries. However, the mass of institutional differences between countries was so confusing and difficult to grasp that there had to be some simplifying and coherent way to compare them. A political scientist would have naturally turned to such unifying concepts as federalism or unitary state constitutions, or to Right versus Left political control in order to group countries for comparative purposes. An economist would have chosen the level of economic development a country has reached. A sociologist would have turned to differences in family and kinship or other social structural differences for a yardstick. Titmuss focused on underlying value systems and the redistributive capacity of the systems in question. This was absolutely in character. It was to set social policy off on a completely different route to other, perfectly valid, approaches to comparative study. The three international models he sets out (see Part 5, Chapter One) became very influential.

Titmuss's 'residual welfare model' was one that assumed that the family and the market were the 'natural' means of providing care and insurance. The state should only step in when these forms of welfare provision could not work. That usually meant, in those days, when families were too poor or incapable of providing for themselves. The state had a residual role – that of an 'ambulance wagon'. The wording was taken more or less directly from an American social work text book (Willensky and Lebeaux, 1958). It summed up American ideals, those authors argued, though increasingly even America had had to accept, reluctantly, that markets and families did not work that well in a range of situations.

However, it was Titmuss's twofold distinction between other kinds of welfare state that was to prove so influential. His 'industrial achievement performance model' was one that saw social protection linked largely to the workplace, whether through public or private provision. Benefits were earned by participation in the labour force. Pensions and other benefits depended on the length of service and the level of wages earned. Membership of a health scheme or social insurance scheme was earned though paid work. The schemes were often organised within the industry of which the worker was a member. Some risks are pooled in such a model but not those that attach to a life of paid work. Women do particularly badly in such a model. Many continental schemes conformed much more closely to that model than the United Kingdom. The 'institutional redistributive model' was, of course, nearest to Titmuss's own ideals. The Scandinavian welfare states came much nearer Titmuss's own ideals than the British, but so did the American social security pension and the British National Health Service.

* * * * *

This basic idea of creating a typology of welfare states or social policies based on their types of entitlement criteria was a breakthrough and set the pattern for comparative social policy studies right up to the present day. It was adopted and essentially elaborated by Esping-Andersen in what was to become his classic piece of theoretical and empirical work, *The three worlds of welfare capitalism* (1990). Esping-Andersen adds the important Marxist derivative notion of 'de-commodification' with which he attempts to measure differences between welfare regimes – the extent to which they depart from market distributions of resources – in simple terms. Titmuss had no measuring rod with which to test his models nor any theoretical justification for their existence. This Esping-Andersen added.

Esping-Adersen's models are:

- a residual Anglo-Saxon model where benefits arise from 'demonstrable and abject need';
- a 'corporatist' middle European pattern where entitlements are based on work performance and the state shares the administration of the system with employers and employee organisations;
- a Scandinavian social democratic model where rights derive from the principle of the universal rights of citizenship.

Esping-Andersen does acknowledge his debt to Titmuss: "To an extent the three system types mirror Titmuss's well-known trichotomy of residual, industrial-achievement, and institutional welfare states" (p 49). However, Esping-Andersen wrongly cites Titmuss's *Essays on 'The welfare state'* as the source for these models, confusing them, I think, with Titmuss's social division of welfare distinctions.

Though Titmuss was comparing principles that underlay social programmes Esping-Andersen is trying to compare whole welfare states. At least, much of his writing sounds as if it is. In practice, his measure of commodificaction covers only some cash benefit systems: pensions, sickness and unemployment benefits. It is this that leads him to categorise Britain, with the United States, as an Anglo-Saxon regime characterised by means testing and access to welfare only in dire emergency. It is not a description that fits health care or indeed education. I think Titmuss would have vigorously contested lumping the United Kingdom with America as an equivalent welfare state!

Titmuss's categories are, however, subject to the same kinds of criticism as Esping-Andersen's have been. They miss out the dimension of gender, unpaid work and the role of the family (Lewis, 1992). This is a criticism Esping-Andersen (1999) has responded to in his later work. As the first extract in this international section shows, Titmuss did draw distinctions between society's welfare regimes in their treatment of women, even if they were not structurally part of his models.

Despite his innovative contribution both to comparative social policy and international awareness, there is still an Anglo-centric element to his thinking. It is perhaps most evident in Titmuss's *The gift relationship* but it pervades much of his writing. Comparisons are usually made that end up suggesting that somehow the British way is better than the American way of doing things or the Russians' or the Germans'. There is a powerful dose of this in the extracts in Part 5. In the first, for example, the Americans are hard on welfare mothers (what is new!); the Soviet Union was not so equalising as it pretended – it was hard on women; the Germans treated their guest workers abominably. The United Kingdom was the only country to be sensible and morally pure about the distribution of blood.

Few would be so proud today. If anything, Britain is now turning to other countries for social policy models to follow. Whereas in the early part of the 20th century the United States looked to Europe for its social policy ideas, the United States has now become a model for many. This is not just because of political shifts but because the United States has experienced first many of the big economic and social changes that are affecting our post modern societies and economies. American social science has become dominant in a way that was only beginning in Titmuss's period. Social policy is powerfully affected by the increased interest of American social scientists in poverty, income distribution, changes in family life, social security and education, and the care of older people. It is increasingly contemptuous of the 'European way'. British and European social policy has an important part to play in the growing international debate about the best balance between economic and social development.

The international perspective

> One belief, more than any others, is responsible for the
> slaughter of individuals on the altars of the great historical
> ideals – justice or progress or the happiness of future
> generations, or the sacred mission or emancipation of a
> nation or race or class, or even liberty itself, which demands
> the sacrifice of individuals for the freedom of society. This
> is the belief that somewhere, in the past or in the future, in
> divine revelation or in the mind of an individual thinker, in
> the pronouncements of history or science, or in the simple
> heart of an uncorrupted good man, there is a final solution.
> This ancient faith rests on the conviction that all the positive
> values in which men have believed must, in the end, be
> compatible, and perhaps even entail one another. (Berlin,
> 1969, p 167)

Not all good things are compatible, still less are all the ideals of
mankind. This is as true in the realm of social policy as in other areas
of human life. What is social policy? Can a distinction be made
between social policy and economic policy?

We live in an age of 'the great simplifiers' brought into being, in
part, by the mass consumption society. The simplifiers are dominated
by the mass media of the press and particularly of television. They
must see everything in terms of black versus white and present
polarised conflict as entertainment: the universalists versus the
selectivists, the spoon-fed versus the independent, or individual choice
versus the rationing state.

Many reasons can be given for the simplification, trivialisation and
denigration of political and moral issues. How far do editors lose
control of their star reporters after they have built them up? How far
do the promotion and rewards of journalists (no longer anonymous)
depend more than ever on the presentation of scandal and violence,
such as student violence. How far does audience rating encourage
the presentation of serious issues as trivial entertainment? How far
does the fear of loss of advertising revenue limit criticism of the
private market? Is this why scandal about government is so much
more newsworthy than scandal about the private sector?

It is fashionable to believe that all power and authority and all
politicians are evil. Just as academic freedom can justify anything
(what Tawney once called "creating a darkness and calling it research")
and clinical freedom justifies private practice and profit-making

175

hospitals in the United States, so the freedom of the press can justify mass entertainment, the commercialisation of sex and the commercialisation of privacy. As these unlimited freedoms become more pervasive, society – and particularly at this point in history, American society – becomes harder and harder to govern. It is not widely known that during the first six months of 1971 more people were murdered in New York alone than all the American soldiers killed in Vietnam during the same six months. Violence and theft have reached such a scale that public assistance officers are armed. In 1971, even in the School of Social Work, New York University, all typewriters, adding machines, tape recorders and other equipment are chained and bolted to the floor.

Poor people in blighted ghetto areas of the United States are no longer able to purchase insurance for their homes and contents against the risks of fire, burglary, theft and vandalism. The insurance industry, with assets totalling over $208 billion, declared the inner core, the blighted centres of cities, as uninsurable risks. All the inhabitants therefore, black and white, are 'bad risks', uninsurable against the risks of violence, vandalism, riots, fire and death.

In *Meeting the insurance crisis of our cities*, a report by the President's Advisory Panel (1968), the main recommendation was that government must come to the rescue; government must take over the 'bad risks' of the richest society the world has ever known. This, in effect, was a social policy directive and also an example of the problem of defining the boundaries of social policy in theory and practice.

There are lessons in all this, lessons to be learnt from history, when we try to understand the issues of freedom and licence, law and discretion, justice and punishment, poverty and stigma, equity and equality. Where does social policy begin and where does it end? How is it possible to describe its scope, meaning, content, formation, execution, principles and theory?

At best it is clear that the study of social policy cannot be isolated from the study of society as a whole in all its varied social, economic and political aspects. An essential background for the study of social policy is a knowledge of population changes, past and present and predicted for the future; the family as an institution and the position of women; social stratification and the concepts of class, caste, status and mobility; social change and the effects of industrialisation, urbanisation and social conditions; the political structure; the work ethic and the sociology of industrial relations; minority groups and racial prejudice; social control, conformity, deviance and the uses of sociology to maintain the political status quo.

Policy, any policy, to be effective must choose an objective and must face dilemmas of choice. But to understand policy, to distinguish between ends (what we want or think we want) and means (how we get there), we have to see it in the context of a particular set of circumstances, a given society and culture, and a more or less specified period of historical time. In other words, social policy cannot be discussed or even conceptualised in a social vacuum, unlike the Robinson Crusoe idea of economic man.

* * * * *

The British are not alone or in any sense unique in devising systems of 'welfare'. There is now a very extensive international literature relating to systems of welfare in developed and developing countries.

The more one attempts to study the international literature about different national social policy institutions, the more one becomes aware of the diversity and complexity. The more one understands this complexity, the more difficult does it become to generalise (to simplify pragmatically) about the different roles that social services are supposed to play, and do actually play, in different countries.

Soviet Russia, for example, has fashioned a model of social welfare based, in large measure, on the principles of work-performance, achievement and meritocratic selection. Wage and salary differentials between the top and bottom of the Russian Civil Service (which includes few black Russians from the East and the South because no Muslims from Central Asia and the Caucasus are allowed to become members of the Communist Party) are larger than wage-salary differentials in the British Civil Service. The social security system tends to legitimate and even enhance these differentials. This is especially so for working-class women who do much of the unskilled, dirty work in the Soviet Union. Lenin's belief that Communism would liberate women has not yet been fulfilled. In the Russian system of public assistance, as in Germany and France, grandchildren and grandparents are responsible for relatives. Their financial resources are assessed to see whether they can be expected to support the claimant. In Britain, only the resources "for husband and wife in the same household, together with those of any dependent children living with them, are each added and treated as the husband's" (*Supplementary Benefit Handbook*, November 1972).

Other Soviet social services, like the mental health services, are in part social control mechanisms, performing a police function in respect of dissenters, non-conformers, deviants and underachievers. In part, they also function to sustain and glorify the work ethic as do the boarding schools in Russia which are preoccupied with character-building and the value of hard physical labour.

When, however, all social services expenditures are aggregated and expressed as a percentage of personal money income for Russia and the United Kingdom, Wiles and Markowski (1971) argue that the Russian expenditures were in the late 1950s more redistributive than in the UK. What is not known, however (and that is the trouble with

Wiles's statistics), is whether redistribution favours the higher or lower income groups. The effects of the social security system, taken alone, do indicate that the higher income groups receive proportionately higher rewards. In short, the objective and the results are based on work performance and achieved work earnings.

In the area of social security, West Germany has a not dissimilar model for its pension programme from that operating in the Soviet Union. Again it is fundamentally based on work rewards, productivity, achievement and merit. There is virtually no element of redistribution built into the system. Its model, geared to dynamism, is based on the private insurance market.

Underpinning and supporting this work-reward system is the presence of 2.25 million guest workers or *Gastarbeiters* medically examined by German doctors in the country of origin and recruited from Turkey, Greece, North Africa, southern Italy, Yugoslavia, Spain and Portugal. The great majority of these two million or so workers do not have their families with them; about 75% are men and nearly all are engaged in the unskilled dirty, menial and domestic tasks of the modern economy. They are all on one-year permits to one employer, renewable on good conduct and (subject to fluctuations in the employment situation) by the authority of that employer.

In the event of serious illness, disability, injury, mental breakdown, alcoholism, homelessness, drug addiction or of offences against the civil or criminal codes, these workers are put on trains or planes and sent home. Similarly, single women workers who become pregnant or produce illegitimate children are returned to their families. They have no voting rights, no welfare rights, no rights to public assistance which in Germany, as in all the Common Market countries as well as Scandinavia, is a municipal responsibility with rights varying between different local authorities, as it was in Britain before the 1930s. Even if they were eligible, the levels of social assistance (or social aid) from the municipal authorities are so low (as they are in the Irish Republic) that the system acts as a deterrent.

The situation of the million or so Irish immigrants in Britain (including their wives and large families) is different. Levels of supplementary benefits and allowances for these families plus family allowances are far higher than earnings for unskilled workers in the Irish Republic and thus act as a magnet for poor Irish families dependent either on parish relief or charity from the church. Irish immigrants – temporary, pseudo-temporary and permanent – represent one of the major factors in the rising number of claimants and recipients of supplementary allowances and thus complicate any estimates of the number of adults and children 'in poverty' or on the margins of poverty in Britain.

We have a situation in which the Irish Republic, partly because of a lack of any national organised system of public assistance, exports a proportion of its public assistance or potential public assistance cases to Britain. West Germany, for very different reasons and with a far higher standard of living than Eire, also exports a major part of its public assistance problem, but to much poorer countries. It is not simply a question of the provision of means-tested cash assistance for people with social handicaps, the newly disabled and chronic sick, ex-prisoners and their families, alcoholics, deserted wives, unmarried mothers and so forth. Many of these people (among the 'under-class' as certain American sociologists would describe them) also need child care and welfare services, provision for homelessness, social work support and a more generous input of educational provision.

It is indeed arguable that a country, which at one and the same time can maintain a flexible pool of some two million unskilled workers and relatively smaller public assistance and welfare programmes, is economically in a better position to sustain a higher rate of economic growth. Nor is it likely to lead to the same degree to pressures from unskilled temporary workers to narrow wage differentials through trade union action. Consequently, the dangers of inflation in the economy become less.

In all the debates about international differences in the rate of growth of gross national product, economists have generally neglected these issues. This is partly because economists make a sharp distinction, at least in theory, between what constitutes economic policy and what constitutes social policy. It can also, of course, be said that many writers on social policy or the social services suffer from the same tendency to compartmentalise their subjects. Few social services textbooks, for example, have much to say about the social costs of unemployment, about regional economic policies (though such policies may be critically important in reducing social and educational inequalities between regions) or about the examples given earlier on the inter-connections between the unskilled market in labour and the role of public assistance programmes. One major exception, among economists and social policy writers, is Kenneth Boulding. Both in *Principles of economic policy* (1968) and in an article, 'The boundaries of social policy' (1967), he attempted to draw together and analyse comprehensively both the social and the economic components of policy and its application in practice.

* * * * *

These illustrations from the Soviet Union, Ireland and West Germany are intended simply to show the difficulties of generalising in any universal sense about social policy and the many conflicting and different roles that such policies (or particular programmes) play in different societies. Many more examples could be given and questions asked about the wider implications of social programmes. What are the objectives of changes in the family allowance system in Israel which discriminate against Arabs and against those Jews who have not served in the Israeli armed forces? What are the objectives of pension arrangements in France which provide higher old–age pensions for those who have had three or more children? Can public assistance programmes in the United States and other countries be regarded as elements of social policy when they compel unmarried mothers and deserted wives with children over the age of three to register for work and to accept *any* work offered to them by the Department of Labour? Should they not, on the other hand, be classified as labour control mechanisms and as part of a work-ethic value system not dissimilar from the provisions of the Poor Law in England? Finally, and by way of contrast, can one regard the Tanzanian Arusha Declaration of 1967, which emphasised the values of self–reliance, work and collective village development, as representing a social or an economic policy for that country (Nyerere, 1968).

The United Nations has brought together much of this worldwide literature under such labels as 'social welfare programmes', 'the world social situation', 'the administration of social services', 'social planning and social development'. The word 'social' (not to be confused with 'sociological') is one word which all these titles have in common. This suggests that the central political issues of ends and means for the governments of all countries, rich and poor, cannot be thought of wholly in economic terms.

'Social policy' must therefore be analysed in a broad political and geographical framework. The perspective gained from comparative studies helps in the understanding of the social policies of one's own country. There is now a larger and increasing body of knowledge about social policy and welfare programmes in many different countries which cannot be ignored. When we study welfare systems in other countries, we see that they reflect the dominant cultural and political characteristics of their societies. But we have, nevertheless, to recognise that they are all concerned fundamentally with certain common human needs and problems.

* * * * *

As an aid to our inquiries, it is helpful to examine three contrasting models or functions of social policy. The purpose of model-building is not to admire the architecture of the building, but to help us to see some order in all the disorder and confusion of facts, systems and choices concerning certain areas of our economic and social life. Tentatively, the three models can be described as follows:

Model A: The residual welfare model of social policy

This formulation is based on the premise that there are two 'natural' (or socially given) channels through which an individual's needs are properly met: the private market and the family. Only when these break down should social welfare institutions come into play and then only temporarily. As Peacock (1960, p 11) puts it: "The true object of the Welfare State is to teach people how to do without it". The theoretical basis of this model can be traced back to the early days of the English Poor Law and finds support in organic-mechanistic-biological constructs of society advanced by sociologists like Spencer and Radcliffe-Brown, and economists like Friedman, Hayek and the founders and followers of the Institute of Economic Affairs in London.

Model B: The industrial achievement-performance model of social policy

This incorporates a significant role for social welfare institutions as adjuncts of the economy. It holds that social needs should be met on the basis of merit, work performance and productivity. It is derived from various economic and psychological theories concerned with incentives, effort and reward, and the formation of class and group loyalties. It has been described as the 'handmaiden model'.

Model C: The institutional redistributive model of social policy

This model sees social welfare as a major integrated institution in society, providing universalist services outside the market on the principle of need. It is in part based on theories about the multiple effects of social change and the economic system, and in part on the principle of social equality. It is basically a model incorporating systems of redistribution in command-over-resources-through-time.

These three models are, of course, only very broad approximations to the theories and ideas of economists, philosophers, political scientists and sociologists. Many variants could be developed of a more sophisticated kind. However, these approximations do serve to indicate the major differences – the ends of the value spectrum – in the views held about the means and ends of social policy. All three models involve consideration of the work ethic and the institution of the family in modern society.

* * * * *

In the first two models (A and B), a dominant role is played by private market institutions as well as by the law – particularly in the fields of income maintenance, housing and medical care in old age, widowhood, sickness, industrial injury, unemployment, childhood and other situations of dependency. In model A, the residual welfare model, only a marginal role is allotted to government – to collective social policies – and then only in respect of an assumed small proportion of the population (the very poor or public assistance sector). There is, therefore, some element of redistribution or transfer payments built into this model – a relatively small flow from the generality of the population to the public assistance sector after a test of means.

For the rest of the population, the model assumes that their income maintenance needs in situations of dependency will be met, on market principles, through various private institutional channels. These channels will, in effect, operate redistributive systems – on the 'worth' and 'work' maxims of distributive justice – but the assumption is made only in terms of the individual. Each individual in the system is thus assumed to take out only what he puts in – the individualistic ethic of private social policies. The Keynesian concept of 'waiting' as an economic sacrifice underlies these assumptions. Those who 'wait', who resist the animal temptations to consume in present gratifications and save (for old age, for home ownership, for unborn grandchildren and so on), must, at the very least, take out what they themselves put in. There must be, therefore, in these private social policies and institutions no element of unmerited subsidy for other individuals. Otherwise, there would be no incentive to 'wait' and defer gratification into future social time.

Another assumption which has crept into this model, alongside the one that there should be no unmerited subsidy for others, is that those who 'wait' should be given, so to speak, a special bonus from the state – from government and the generality of the population – as a reward for 'waiting' and 'saving'. In Britain as in other countries, there is an extensive system of bonuses (or subsidies) of this kind – generally operated through the fiscal system as tax-deductibles – for home ownership, life assurance and other forms of saving, occupational pension schemes and so forth. At this stage, however, the particular point to note is that redistribution does actually take place in part of the private market sector as a direct result of government intervention to provide incentives to save, to acquire property and to work harder among the tax-paying population.

In both our first two models, therefore, the residual welfare (or public assistance) model and the achievement-performance (reward) model, governments do intervene – they do influence and change the pattern of distribution set by market forces. One particular field in which all governments in modern society intervene – or are to an increasing extent expected to intervene and to devote a large proportion of their budgets – is the provision of an immense range of what are conventionally called 'public amenity services'. These have both positive and negative aspects: for example, town and country planning, public transport, car parks and meters, roads, recreation facilities and parks, sewage, sanitation, water, anti-air pollution subsidies, anti-noise subsidies, anti-violence measures (such as damage-proof phone boxes and more police to control football crowds, pop festivals), public libraries, art galleries, museums, even Covent Garden Opera and Ballet (heavily subsidised) – an endless list indeed of social, environmental, aesthetic and amenity provisions which are paid for or subsidised by the whole community. It must not, however, be assumed that the actual provision of more of these so-called public services necessarily leads to an improvement in the social and physical environment. They may simply be a brake on increasing deterioration.

Developing social policy in conditions of rapid change: The role of social welfare

The difficulties or impossibilities of defining and measuring indicators of social growth in many areas of social policy is one among many reasons for current disenchantments and discontents. They have resulted in two consequences which I wish to discuss later: (i) the dominance of the economic and the technocratic over the social in the approach to the problems of change and (ii) trends towards the depersonalisation of access to and the use of social welfare services. Both can lead to the abstraction of people from their social context, a theoretical attempt to isolate what cannot be isolated.

During the United Nations First Development Decade, which was a period of rapid political, economic and social change and of escalating wars, violence, expenditures on arms, and catastrophe, the world's total gross national product increased by $1,100 billion (Society for International Development, 1972). Something like 80% of this increase went to countries where per capita yearly incomes already average over $1,000 and where only one-quarter of the world's population resides. By contrast, only 6% of the increase went to countries where per capita incomes average $200 or less but they contain 60% of the world's people. While the average income in the developed countries stands in 1972 at approximately $2,400 the comparable figure for the developing countries is $180. A severe and growing maldistribution of the world's wealth and income is thus in evidence. Moreover, among many of the developing nations in which significant economic growth has occurred there is evidence that inequalities in their societies have increased; the poorest sectors of these nations may actually have grown poorer while élite groups have prospered during the First Development Decade. The price paid by the more affluent nations for, for example, coffee and sisal dropped by more than a half between 1950 and 1970. This fall had more effect on the standard of living of poor producers in Tanzania, South America and other areas than any increase in social welfare expenditures or international aid (*The Internationalist*, May-June 1972).

In 1972, children under 5 account for only 20% of the population, but for more than 60% of all deaths; two thirds of the children who have escaped death will live on restricted in their growth by malnutrition, a malnutrition that stunts both bodies and minds alike;

there are 100 million more adult illiterates than there were in the 1950s; and a population explosion is adding every five days another million people to the human race. This is a world, in short, in which death and disease are rampant, education scarce, squalor and stagnation common, and opportunities for the realisation of personal development tragically limited. Among all the limiting factors, the growth in unemployment (itself the product of many changes) is the most challenging. While rates of unemployment in developed countries of around 5%-8% are deplored, the level of unemployment (and disregarding low productivity employment and marginal producers) in developing countries in 1972 has been estimated at 25% or so. Moreover, a study of fourteen developing countries showed that unemployment is increasing at the rate of 8.5% per annum (Singer, 1971). These are a few facts describing the conditions of more than 95 developing countries comprising some two billion people.

Underlying the Stockholm Conference on the Human Environment in June 1972 a call went out for international environmental collaboration. Industrial systems in the more affluent societies do not include in the cost of what they produce such diswelfares and diseconomies of production and distribution as the spewing out of effluents into the air, the overloading of the land with solid waste, water and food pollution, industrial and transport hazards or the lack of any charge for the eventual disposal of used-up goods. So they pass on a hidden and heavy cost to the community in the destruction of an amenity. This discovery of pollution, a discovery which has occurred with more remarkable rapidity in historical time among the more affluent sectors of the more affluent nations than the rediscovery of poverty, has led to a questioning of the benefits of increased economic growth and an epidemic of self-interested fear not dissimilar from the fears aroused by the spread of cholera and other infectious diseases in the 19th century. These fears in Britain among the higher income groups represented one of the causal factors in what was called 'the sanitary revolution', a revolution that demanded more governmental intervention; fewer corrupt ministers and civil servants; more public and personal accountability; and more specific roles for social welfare, particularly in the fields of housing, education and public health.

What remains conjectural is whether this concern for the quality of the human environment at Stockholm and elsewhere is leading (or will lead to) a reappraisal and a rethinking of the role of social welfare in our societies. Action by government and people to mitigate and prevent environmental pollution could have far-reaching effects on public policies for housing, education, medical care, family planning and the general welfare of dependent groups in the population: children, the sick and disabled, and the elderly. It could also have in the views of many developing countries severe and deleterious effects on their economies if anti-pollution measures taken by affluent nations lead to a worsening of trade patterns, restrictions on commodities and less concern about international aid.

But less conjectural, however, are a number of conclusions which can usefully be drawn from the discovery of the pollution issue. In summarising them briefly, I would not wish to give the impression that I have joined the jeremiahs of science, the doom computer programmers, in predicting the extinction of the human race. I am optimistic enough to believe that people can control their environment and that, given a far more determined will, the greater and more threatening problems of world poverty, unemployment and race relations can be mitigated and reduced by national and international action. There are alternatives to despair, to opting out, and to policies of apartheid. One that is of special relevance is the future role of social welfare.

The first conclusion I draw from the environmental debate concerns the rapidity of industrial, technological, scientific and demographic change. Equally important as an established and measurable fact is that the sum of human knowledge about the consequences of change, in the form of diseconomies and diswelfares affecting the individual, the family and the group, has been greatly enlarged and deepened in recent years. We now know that the speed of change is increasing; that its effects are becoming more widespread, more subtly non-neutral and potentially more long-run; and that increasingly more people are involved in most countries of the world. Knowledge, once gained, cannot be thrown away, so long as we continue to believe that people can act rationally and that nation states are in some respects governable. Complexity, once understood, can only be disregarded at the risk of tyranny.

What we have also learned about increasing social costs and diswelfares, in part a corollary of increasing private affluence, is that these costs are heavily borne by poorer people, disadvantaged people, non-white as well as white people. Think only, for example, of urban obsolescence and decay in the West or the growth of shanty towns, the rising numbers of landless farm workers and the breakdown of kinship and cultural ties in the third world. Read, for illustration, books like Caplovitz's *The poor pay more* (1963) or *Development in a divided world* (1971) edited by Dudley Seers and Leonard Joy. These and many other books about poverty and race relations which, in effect, challenge neo-classical value theory which has held that social costs are 'marginal nuisances' (so described in some economic textbooks) show something of the social, economic, psychological and educational effects of exposure to the diswelfares of change. Poverty in the broadest sense is implicated; the poverty of command over resources, whether financial or in the form of food crops, land and cattle; the poverty of living from day to day; the poverty of feeling; the poverty of the senses; the poverty of language and communication; the poverty of listening and learning; the poverty of social relations and untouchability. All these poverties may become socially (not genetically) inherited poverties and, according to some students of the human condition, psychologically self-perpetuating poverties.

Those exposed to these consequences of change are at the mercy of events (and often feel that they are) in a world of rising expectations; the expectations of economic growth, which in the 1960s was promising (or so it was thought by many people) that poverty would graciously succumb to growth in the West and that economic growth in developing countries would automatically lead to social progress; the expectations of increasing international aid and the growth of expectations aroused in many parts of the third world by new national independence from colonial power.

Given the knowledge we now have about the creative and destructive consequences of many categories of change in all economic and social systems (from China to Peru) and given that medieval fatalism and the saintliness of poverty are far less acceptable to people today, how and in what ways does or should society respond?

Obviously, there are basic political, ideological and value issues raised by this question. But here I wish to concentrate the debate around the past, present and future role of social welfare. In doing so I would, however, point out that social welfare programmes and social policies (however defined and determined) perform functionally and operate differently (and often under quite different labels and principles) in different types of societies and diverse cultural, economic and value systems. Nevertheless, however their roles may differ, the ends as well as the means of social welfare must be discussed, for social policy is all about conflicting choices in political goals as well as means. We may thus have to consider in different cultural contexts concepts of justice as fairness; the definition of goodness as rationality; the justification of disobedience and compliance; the rule of law and toleration of the intolerant; rights based on needs, capacity, productivity or deserts; duty and obligation; envy and equality; distributive justice, and other fundamental political and philosophical issues without which the discussion of social policy can deteriorate into sterility. To know one's chains or one's limitations is often the first step to freedom, but, as the grand inquisitor said in Dostoevsky's *Brothers Karamazov*, what people dreaded most was freedom of choice and to be left alone to grope their way in the dark. Social welfare and social and community work, as I understand the situation in Britain and may other countries, is based on different principles: that people should be helped to perceive and to make choices; and that it is one of the goals of social policy to provide alternatives to poverty and darkness.

All these issues of cultural diversity and conflicting choices make it much more difficult to generalise theoretically on an international or comparative basis about social policy than about economic policy. Social man, like the social structure of a society, is much more complex in many respects than economic man, if it is permissible to make such a distinction. Moreover, as Pusic (1971) pointed out, basically different cultural and functional societies co-exist or adjoin each other within a nation state and he instanced, as one example, black 'ghettos' and university residential quarters adjoining each other in the United States.

He provided this example in an article which argued that, in order to understand what welfare is, we must come to a better understanding of the nature of social development, and that, in doing so, it would help us to develop theoretical models in analysing the field of social welfare. One of the difficulties that confronts us, however, is the problem of how we distinguish between social welfare, occupational welfare and fiscal welfare and the further problem of the concept of welfare as betterment or as compensation for the diswelfares of change and the external effects of economic growth in different types of society.

In the past, two of the criticisms that can be levelled against students and writers in the field of social welfare and social policy are, first, that they have tended to ignore the role played by fiscal welfare in taxation systems. Simultaneously, they have also neglected to study the role played by occupational welfare in meeting a variety of needs in cash or in kind through the mechanisms of occupational status and length of service in private and public employments.

These writers have failed to recognise that the increasing division of specialisation of labour (one significant factor in the processes of industrial and technological change) has been generally accompanied by an increasing division of welfare, much of it subsidised or paid for in the ultimate analysis by the public at large. Both fiscal and occupational welfare can thus have major redistributive effects in terms of command over resources through time by certain groups in the population. These effects may be quantitatively as significant, or even more so, in developing countries as in developed countries where, as public and private employees benefit from occupational and fiscal welfare, they can also lead to furthering the neglect of social policy for the mass of the population.

One of the consequences of analytically leaving out of account these categories of welfare is to constrict and limit the role of social welfare or social policy. The role thus becomes a marginal one; social welfare is wholly or mainly for poor people and certain dependent groups. They therefore come to be seen as 'problems' for society; problems to be solved or neglected or categorised as social pathology. One effect of isolating or selectively conceptualising poor people as problems is to generate the social processes of stigmatisation; we create what we fear or we create for others what we want to create or need to create to support self-esteem and differential status systems.

Another effect of these limited and narrow approaches to social welfare is to ignore the consequences of change. In this way, an impression is sustained that poor people are a distinctly separate and permanent sector of the population, a class or a race or a caste apart. From these impressions or images or conceptualised 'problems' it seems to follow in some logical sequence that the role of social welfare is to provide benefits or betterment for poor people or only for poor people in urban areas. Where the political ideology of a society is dominated by individualistic values of personal independence, personal autonomy, self-reliance and self-mobility (as it was expressed in Britain's 1834 Poor Law Act), then the general attitude to social welfare becomes, in Pusic's phrase, 'a marginalist attitude'. Those who then make up the marginal group may be considered 'abnormal'. From all this can flow the view that the role of social welfare is a marginal role. An analysis of the contemporary world social situation could supply examples of marginal roles for social welfare in developing as well as developed nations.

Viewed from either an historical or a contemporary angle, these values may be expressed in broad and general terms as the residual welfare model of social policy.

* * * * *

I now want to present another model of social welfare. This I describe, in shorthand, as the institutional-redistributive model of social welfare. It sees social welfare as a basic integrated institution in society providing both universal and selective services outside the market on the principle of need. Universal services, available without distinction of class, colour, sex or religion, can perform functions which foster and promote attitudes and behaviour directed towards the values of social solidarity, altruism, toleration and accountability. To use Kenneth Boulding's (1967, p 3) words:

> If there is one common thread that unites all aspects of social policy and distinguishes them from merely economic policy, it is the thread of what has elsewhere been called the 'integrative system'. This includes those aspects of social life that are characterised not so much by exchange in which a quid is got for a quo as by unilateral transfers that are justified by some kind of appeal to a status or legitimacy, identity, or community.... By and large it is an objective of social policy to build the identity of a person around some community with which he is associated.

Territorially then, social policy (or social welfare) in its universalist role recognises no human boundaries or man-made laws of residence and race. The frontiers of social growth are open. As a model, it is in part based on theories about the multiplier diswelfare and disrupting effects of change, industrial, technological, social and economic, and in part on a conception of social justice which sees people not only as individuals but as members of groups and associations.

It follows therefore that this model not only incorporates and embodies the effects of past and present change but envisages a variety of roles for social welfare to play as a positive and dynamic agent of change: to promote integrative values; to prevent future diswelfares; to penetrate economic policies with social welfare objectives, and in all these ways to bring about a redistribution in command over resources through time. It challenges different societies at different stages of development and within different cultural contexts to determine a particular infrastructure of universalist services within and around which to develop selective or positively discriminating services provided, as social rights, on criteria of the needs of specific disadvantaged categories, groups and territorial areas. The fundamental problem which this model sets for government is to find the 'right' balance between the integrative role of universalist services and the social equality role of selective (or priority) developments. They are inter-dependent roles, subject to continuing adaptation and change, but often in conflict because of limited resources and the values determining priorities and choices which are set by a society at different times in different circumstances.

One of the assumptions underlying this model is that social welfare is not simply an adjunct of the economy or an ameliorative system providing services for poor people. It acknowledges the fact that not all services or grants or exchanges represent 'benefits' for individuals. Some constitute compensation for the 'diswelfares' of change experienced by the individual and the community at large because we cannot identify and legally charge the causal agents of change. But, while accepting a compensatory role (for example, by providing unemployment benefits as of right to those exposed to the forces of change), it also accepts a positive role through the development of social manpower policies, corrective regional and area economic policies, retraining and further education services and other strategies designed to bring about an improvement in the standard and quality of life of the individuals concerned.

There are in our societies today few satisfactions in work for millions of men and women. It could be one of the future roles of social welfare to develop programmes of meaningful activity and to shift more people from the ranks of the unemployed and the underemployed to manpower-intensive social service sectors; to education in the broadest sense, to welfare activities for the old, the young, the sick and disabled, to family planning, neighbourhood projects and to all those areas sometimes described as 'community care'. Social welfare would thus be more labour-intensive and less influenced by management experts advocating forms and computers in place of personal contacts.

In such ways as these, social welfare can function as an enabling agent of change and social integration and not play either a residual role or passively accept the role of an acquiescent adjunct to the economy-market, non-market or mixed. In doing so, the distinction between economic development and social development will become increasingly blurred. "The separation between the social and the economic is often an artefact of academic analysis and government departmentalization" (United Nations, 1961, p 23).

The subject of social policy

Commentary: Pete Alcock

When Richard Titmuss was appointed to the first Chair of Social Administration to be created in the UK at the London School of Economics and Political Science (LSE) in 1950 he took his responsibility as a pioneer for the new subject seriously. As the earlier sections of this book have demonstrated, Titmuss's work both before and after his appointment provided examples of much of what could, and should, be the focus of social policy analysis and action; and, as a result of this, his name is always the first to be associated with the subject in this country, and throughout much of the rest of the world. Titmuss's work therefore provides a guide to the subject of social policy through leading by example and, as we have discussed earlier, many have followed the leads which he provided for us. However, Titmuss was also concerned to address more directly the nature of the subject which, through his appointment, he had been formally placed in a position to shape; and the extracts included in this final section provide the most important examples of this definitional work.

* * * * *

The Chair to which Titmuss was appointed was described as 'social administration' and, as we shall discuss shortly, the professional association which he later co-sponsored was also initially called the Social Administration Association. This has now become the Social Policy Association (SPA), however, and more generally today the subject is referred to as 'social policy' rather than 'social administration'. The change of name has an important symbolic status (most changes of name do). For some, it signified a shift away from an administrative focus upon the organisation and delivery of welfare and wellbeing within the context of post-war state welfare to a broader policy focus upon the theoretical and political contexts within which welfare was debated and developed: from a concern with 'what' and 'how' to a concern with 'why' and 'whether'. The issue was taken up briefly in a debate in the *Journal of Social Policy* between Glennerster (1988), who argued against any abandoning of a concern for the administration and delivery of services, and Smith (1988), who argued for the embracement of political and theoretical debates (see also the commentary by Donnison, 1994).

However, in practice the distinction is largely a false, or a forced, one; and it is significant that it is an issue which did not much detain Titmuss himself. He writes more or less interchangeably about social administration and social policy, as the titles to the extracts here reveal. In his lecture to the new association (Part 6, Chapter One), he dismissed an interpretation of administration as the narrow concern with management and technical planning; and his own work encompasses concern with theory and politics as well as organisation and process. 'Social policy' is the term in current usage and it is the one most widely employed by Titmuss, so we will use it here. It should be taken to cover social policy and administration, which was clearly what he intended his own brief to be.

Another current controversy is the extent to which social policy constitutes an academic *discipline* rather than (merely) a *field* of study. For some, a discipline may be seen to have more status than a field, although this is of course debatable. In an exchange in the *Student's companion to social policy*, Alcock (1998) suggested that social policy did enjoy disciplinary status with its own distinctive departments and degree programmes, whereas Erskine (1998) argued that, in practice, social policy scholarship continued to be based upon interdisciplinary enterprise and academic innovation, although both agreed on its academic importance and substantive content. It is a distinction that does not appear to have affected the growth and development of social policy within academic circles in the UK, however, and it is also an issue to which Titmuss also gave little time. In his extensive analysis of Titmuss's work, Reisman (1977, p 11) refers to his focus on "the discipline called Social Policy and Administration". Titmuss himself, however, more generally referred to his work as the study of the *subject* of social policy, as in Part 6, Chapter One; and it is this more generic term which we have adopted here.

* * * * *

Titmuss gave his inaugural lecture as Professor of Social Administration at the LSE on 10 May 1951 and it was later published as 'Social administration in a changing society' in Chapter 1 of his *Essays on 'The welfare state'* (1958). Here he reviews the development of work in the subject over the first half of the 20th century, in particular within the Department of Social Science at the LSE which then, as now, provided the leading academic base for research and teaching. Here he also 'defined' the subject as "the study of the social services whose object ... is the improvement of the conditions of life of the individual in the setting of family and group relations" (p 14), and went on to point out that this included study of both the machinery of administration and the lives, needs and relations of the communities that these served. This was an early recognition of the importance of the 'consumer', as well as the 'producer', dimension of welfare services;

and, although it did not penetrate deeply into the work of Titmuss or his contemporaries, was evidence of his ability to grasp conceptually those perspectives which would later become key features of academic study and policy debate within the subject.

Titmuss did not focus much on definition in his inaugural lecture, preferring to use the opportunity to range more widely over the history and scope of the study of social policy. He did return to definitional issues later, however, as the three extracts included here reveal. The first, and perhaps the most important, was the address he gave at the first conference of the Social Administration Association at the University of Nottingham on 14 July 1967. By the mid 1960s Titmuss had been at the LSE for around fifteen years. During that time, the subject of social policy had grown in scale and in scope. It was by then studied in most of the established provincial universities and in the newer 'campus' universities established at around that time; and Titmuss and his colleagues at the LSE were publishing research which was profoundly influencing political debate about the future direction of policy planning (notably Abel-Smith and Townsend, 1965).

The case for some forum for debate and for the promotion of scholarship was thus gaining momentum; and Titmuss joined with a number of other prominent figures in the field (including Baroness Wootton and Lord Robbins) to sponsor the establishment of the new association. In its brief statement of aims, the Association promised to provide a meeting ground, to promote exchange of ideas on teaching and research, and to act as a point of contact with government. Since that first conference, the Association which Titmuss sponsored has gone from strength to strength. In 1987, it changed its name to the Social Policy Association, in 1971 it launched the *Journal of Social Policy* and in 2001 it launched a second journal, *Social Policy and Society*. It has remained the professional association for UK social policy academics with over 600 members, including many now from overseas. His founding lecture was thus a key milestone in the development of the subject.

In the lecture, Titmuss sought to explore some of the major questions that might be asked about the role of the subject, including why there was a need for the establishment of an Association. It is interesting that, in doing this, he wanted to be as clear about what social policy was *not* as he was about what it should be. In particular, social policy was not simply the pursuit of political ideology (or ideologies). Of course, social policy academics sought to inform political debate and to influence policy development, as Titmuss did himself; but this they did through a commitment to social science, through a duty, 'first and last', to pursue the truth. This concern with academic rigour and academic independence was important in setting out the case for an academic subject association then and remains central to our conception of ourselves as academics today.

Titmuss also wanted to distinguish social policy from social work. The teaching of social policy in many universities had often been closely linked with the training of social workers. This was the legacy which Titmuss had inherited when he first took up his Chair at the LSE, and which he wanted to challenge by marking out a distinctive role for the study of social policy. Of course, a knowledge of social policy was, and remains, an essential element in social work education; and in the 1960s was also a source of the broadening interest in the subject in technical colleges (later polytechnics) and further education colleges participating in the expansion of social work education. However, social policy had sometimes been misunderstood as merely the academic element of social work training, and Titmuss saw the establishment of the new Association as a way of making it clear that there was a distinct and separate academic enterprise of social policy which, though contributing to the education of social workers (and other welfare professionals), was both organisationally and theoretically discrete. Today, many university departments (including my own) continue to teach social policy and social work alongside each other, but programmes of study, learning objectives and final qualifications are quite different.

It is significant that Titmuss devotes much of his time in this lecture to discussing the learning and teaching of social policy in universities. Although he was keen to ensure that academic research should seek to influence policy debate, Titmuss was at all times committed to the role of the academic as teacher; and he expected the professional association to play a major role in developing and promoting the teaching of social policy. In teaching the subject of social policy, academics should not just be concerned with ensuring the creation of a future cadre of researchers and tutors ("the next generation" as he puts it), but should also be concerned with the expansion of learning as an end in itself for the widest possible range of students. This is a theme which the current rhetoric of 'lifelong learning' continues to echo, but which sometimes seems to get lost in the drives for vocationalism and 'relevance'.

Towards the end of this first extract, Titmuss attempts to categorise the major fields of teaching and research in social policy. It is interesting to compare this brief list with the benchmark statement on social policy produced in 2000 as part of the Quality Assurance Agency's procedures for assessing the content of social policy degree programmes. Titmuss's list may not emphasise the theoretical and comparative dimensions of the subject as strongly as the modern statement does (although his commitments to these dimensions are clear from this book), but in this succinct statement in 1967 he captured much of what remains at the heart of the subject over thirty years later.

* * * * *

The second extract is taken from Titmuss's lectures to social policy
students at the LSE published posthumously in 1974. Here he adopts
a broader approach to a discussion of what is involved ideologically
and politically in the study of social policy. Titmuss's aim here was to
engage students and to inspire a commitment to the subject whilst
also mapping out its boundaries. He does this by focusing upon the
words themselves. 'Policy' implies a concern with action and with
the achievement of change. 'Social' reminds us that change takes
place within society; it is achieved collectively and structures social
relations. These two aspects of collectivity and change continue to
be the major attractions of the subject today for students, who wish
both to understand their world and to change it.

The lecture also addresses some of the theoretical and conceptual
issues underlying the study of social policy. Titmuss warns against
functionalism and teleology. There is no natural order to the social
world and no inevitable progress towards a given goal. He also points
out that social policy does not always benefit all people. Policies can
divide and discriminate; they can also support oppressive and
exploitative political regimes. These are important messages, for,
though Titmuss was widely known for his promotion of the need for
altruism to support welfare services and advantages of universalism
in ensuring high quality provision for all (as we have seen in this
book), it is significant that he wanted to ensure that students
understood both the positive and negative dimensions of the subject.
Here again the breadth of his vision remains relevant to modern
students coming to the subject many years after these early lectures.

Titmuss's lecture on social policy ended with a summary of the
three models of welfare which he developed to summarise the different
approaches which might underlie the structure and development of
social services. These are dealt with in more detail in Part 5, Chapter
One and so have been omitted from this extract. They are clear
evidence of the theoretical structure which Titmuss had developed
to support his broad analysis of trends within welfare policy; and, as
we saw in Part 5, they provide a framework for comparative analysis
which has been widely drawn on by scholars around the world since.
They underline the point that, in answering his own question –
'What is social policy?'– Titmuss was concerned to emphasise the
role of theory and comparison.

* * * * *

The final extract is also taken from the posthumous collection of
LSE lectures, here focusing on the role of values in the study of social
policy. For Titmuss, an investigation of the place of values in academic
study and research was essential to a proper understanding of the
subject. Values underpinned his own work; but not in the glib way

in which some critics, both contemporary and subsequent, have suggested. Titmuss recognised that both the practice and the study of social policy were about means and ends. We study policy in order to change it; policy change seeks to achieve particular goals; and goals are determined by the values that underpin them. Values are therefore intrinsic to study and research in social policy. However, academic study of social policy is not a licence to be prescriptive or judgemental, nor, importantly, can it tell us the 'right' answer. Titmuss's message was that we should be clear and explicit about the value base of our studies, but we cannot and should not impose our values through academic study. Rather by making clear the value bases of different policies we can then leave the choices between different policies and values to others. The aim of subject of social policy was to influence, but not to impose.

This extract also originally included a summary of Titmuss's analysis of the three divisions of social welfare discussed in Part 2, Chapter Three. His reference to it, however, made clear his more general point that different values did underpin different aspects of welfare provision in contemporary society, that choices had been made to pursue policies in support of these values, and that alternative choices could be made. Furthermore, he argued, the choices that had been made had affected existing social relations. In some cases, this had divisive consequences. It also changed perceptions of social obligation. Policy planning does change the world and that includes our perceptions of that world. It is significant therefore that, at the end of the lecture, he returned to the fundamental choices that face us in addressing questions about the role of policy in pursuing distributive justice – and pointed out that the choices to be made are socially determined.

* * * * *

As we have seen in this book, Titmuss's work championed the values of altruism and universalism in the provision of welfare services. It also explored the alternatives to these approaches and amassed evidence to demonstrate the advantages and disadvantages of these. Values and choices were at the centre of all of this, and it is fitting that they should be the final words here on the very nature of social policy itself. Social policy is the study of the decisions which society makes to promote welfare and wellbeing and of the values and the choices that lie behind these. Titmuss believed that, if we studied these values and choices more clearly, we would reach better decisions in policy planning. Students of social policy still choose the subject today because they believe that it offers such a basis for future social planning. They, and those that follow them, would still do well to follow his guidance on it.

The subject of social administration

In 1950, I was struggling to write something of interest about the subject of social administration for an inaugural lecture at the London School of Economics and Political Science. From a few notes I still have about that anxious summer, I can see that I did not want to claim too much for the subject. Generalists, and those who conceive their subject as having an integrative function in teaching and research, are confronted with a particular occupational hazard in attempting to give reasons for their existence. In the eyes of others, they may seem to be saying, 'Why then, the world's mine oyster'. This impression may also be supported at times by the tendency of social administrators to work in areas of thought and action neglected by other social scientists; they become interested in, for example, organisation, structure and development relating to the roles of family planners, town planners, architects, lawyers, nurses, doctors and other professional groups, and they start asking economic, social or administrative questions about institutions and systems which might properly be thought, on a strictly departmental view of the social sciences, to be infringing the unwritten rules of academic trespass.

Understandably then, I was cautious in 1950. For a relatively new subject, amorphous and obviously capable of territorial expansion, there were dangers of being accused of trespass in the even broader acres of sociology, economics or public administration. At the same time, there were others in the social sciences, sociologists and economists in particular, who were claiming that their subjects could, given adequate support by society, unlock the doors to rational decision-making in certain areas of social policy and resource allocation. There were, as Sprott (1962) subsequently described them, the 'fact-gatherers' (an industrious but rather grubby group), the 'method-men' (a somewhat sinister statistical brigade), the 'sociological bird-watchers' (with muddy boots and rural lisps) and, in the rear, a varied collection of aloof and straggling theorists.

One could be equally amusing about social administrators: the pragmatic engineers of incremental change (addicted to lonely short-distance running), the politicians in academic disguise (frequenting the murky corridors of power), the income-maintenance men (a particularly earnest lot), the illegitimate social historians, and so on.

There are occasions when teachers should not take themselves and their subjects too seriously. It is good for our students as well as for ourselves. On an occasion like this one, to launch the Social

Administration Association, it is perhaps appropriate to strike a self-critical note. Some of us are so busily engaged with the 'ought' as well as the 'why' that we need to remind ourselves from time to time that we are no more than assistant servants in the struggle against irrationality and obscurantism.

Why, then, if we divest ourselves of any illusions of expertise grandeur, do we need a Social Administration Association?

First, I would like to say something about certain reasons which cannot justify the establishment of this Association. We are not here to found a branch of the Conservative, Labour or Liberal parties. While the nature of our subject, including as it does the formation and development of social policies, may lead us to be much concerned with the contemporary human condition, it does not follow that we should see ourselves (or others should see us) as advancing any particular political ideology. Our first duty and our last duty is to the truth. It is because I am sceptical of the claims that are sometimes made for a value-free social science that I restate this fundamental allegiance. The values that we hold should be clear to our students; the evidence on all sides should also be clear. It is part of our responsibilities to expose more clearly the value choices that confront societies in the arena of social welfare.

In saying this, I would not wish it to be thought that in my view social administrators are more likely to be culpable of misrepresentation, bias and prejudice than political scientists, economists, sociologists, social psychologists, and members of the Social Medicine Association and similar groupings of teachers and research workers. But we do have a particular public image associated perhaps with the work of reformers from Booth to Beveridge. Sometimes it assumes a curious shape. In 1950, I was thought by one of my most distinguished professorial colleagues at the London School of Economics to be actively concerned with the training of midwives. I had to confess that I had no competence in that area although I respected the contribution that that profession had made to human progress in rescuing doctors (as well as parents) from obscurantism and in raising standards of maternal and child health.

Social administration is not alone in having difficulties in its external relationships. Sociology has to bear the cross of being associated both with socialism and social work. Tom Marshall (1947) in his inaugural lecture 'Sociology at the crossroads' found it necessary, while remarking that "sociology need not be ashamed of wishing to be useful", to comment on the implication that sociology had some connection with socialism. Others and members of the British Sociological Association have since expressed anxiety about being seen walking out in the company of social workers. This, of course, is understandable behaviour in the search for professional standards and exclusiveness and the wish to effect a monogamous alliance with a beautiful natural scientist. It becomes even more understandable if there is any validity in Edward Shil's comment (1967, p 90) that "sociology is becoming a mild surrogate religion ... replacing prayer as a source of guidance".

Now I must turn to other reasons which, in my view, do not justify the formation of a Social Administration Association. First, a word about relationships with the social work profession. The decision to establish a Social Administration Association should not be interpreted as a retreat from our traditional connections with the education and training of social workers; nor, on the other hand, does it indicate any move towards a centralising takeover bid. The study of social administration in most of its ramifications, theoretical and applied, forms an essential part of the education of social workers. This must be continued and strengthened.

In the past, the connections between the subject of social administration and the content of casework courses (or, to employ a medical analogy, the connections between the basic scientific courses and clinical teaching) have not been as close or as integrated as they might have been. There is a need to build more bridges if students are to be helped to see the relationships between structure and function, and between the administrative behaviour of human organisations and the roles of professional workers.

It is one of the aims of the Social Administration Association to provide a forum for discussion and study for those who have teaching and research responsibilities in this field. The formation of the Association should also make it possible to further the discussion of common teaching problems between social administrators and those more directly concerned with the content of social work training. Social workers are not, however, the only professional group whose basic education calls for the study of social policy and administration.

One of the more interesting trends in British society has been the growing concern about the education, vocational equipment and in-training of those responsible for the administration and management of the social services, and also with the education of many groups of specialist workers in schools, hospital offices, town planning departments, trade unions, central and local government, and other institutions. It is coming to be recognised that many of these workers require for the better management of their organisations an introduction to the study of social administration. This is not a matter of teaching techniques of management. It is largely a question of providing administrators with a broader and historical understanding of institutions and systems affecting the operations of the social services, and providing it in such a non-specialist way that students are not led to think of themselves as failures in not aiming to be research workers, professional sociologists or BBC *Panorama* experts.

Obviously, there are tasks ahead for social administrators; not only in research and evaluation but in examining the organisation, scope and content of teaching for different categories of workers at different levels in different specific and general settings. These tasks would be relatively uncomplicated if we aimed principally or solely at reproducing ourselves.

But this, as I see it, is not our aim. Unashamedly, we can say that we have broader, extra-mural, worker education, liberalising responsibilities and objectives. In this sense, we reject the philosophy of the Robbins Committee Report on Higher Education (1964). What fundamentally the Committee recommended was an extension and expansion of élitest education. Learning to think was conceived as the end in itself. Ability to reason and act effectively in a situation was not considered a criterion of academic success or intellectual competence and it was assumed that any element of education directed towards action was necessarily specific and technical and not abstract or imaginative.

This philosophy of higher education was the reverse of that propounded by Alexander Carr-Saunders (1959, p 14), a former director of the London School of Economics, when he wrote: "The young are anxious to think about and discuss general questions affecting the human situation; thus general education, as well as specialised preparation for a particular career, is within the ambition of students; it is the task of the university to unite them".

With due modesty, I suggest we apply this thought to the tasks that lie ahead in the teaching of social administration. In helping to unite the educational and vocational ambitions of students, the mature as well as the immature, the middle-aged as well as the young, we aim as an association to unite all those teachers concerned with the subject in all institutions of higher and further education, and not just those teachers who happen to find themselves in those places we call 'universities'. We thus launch the Association not as an exclusive, protective, élitest admiration club, but as a means of building bridges and fostering communications between teachers in different sectors of our hierarchical system of higher education. Our situations and our roles may vary but we have interests in common.

The primary one is teaching; this to me, the advancement of teaching, is the primary aim in the launching of the Social Administration Association. The subject, seen as an integrative, analytical area of study, is difficult to teach well. We all, I am sure, have experiences and memories of dull, descriptive monologues. But these and similar viruses are the cause of much specialised diseased teaching to undergraduates in all the social sciences; in psychology, in economics and in the endless thematic orchestrations of role theory. Social administration is thus not peculiar in this respect. It has, in common with social science disciplines, experienced an 'information explosion' in all its branches or sub-specialisations. This explosion and accumulation of information, empirical studies and untested (and perhaps untestable) hypotheses has exacerbated the problem of how to teach and what, selectively, to teach. As a result, we may at present be over-teaching information and under-teaching the imaginative excitements of unifying perspectives and principles.

But this only adds to my conviction that the primary function of the university is to teach; secondly, and complementarily, to advance knowledge. I do not therefore subscribe to what Ashby (1958) has described as 'the academic Arian heresy' which holds to the concept of the university as a research institute. This concept, which came to England and Germany in the 19th century, has done and is doing much harm to the system of higher education in this country. The academic, with a research team, questionnaires and computers, governmental and foundation infrastructure of resources, should be left alone – relieved from the 'burden' of teaching – to do 'useful' research. No longer is it argued that, as a person of leisured erudition, such a person should be left alone with useless philosophic doubts.

The case is attractively presented in de Jouvenel's book *The art of conjecture* (1967). The author seeks to demonstrate the great importance, indeed the social duty of academics, of attempting to make forecasts with maximum coherence and effectiveness:

> The common task of forecasting will cause [the social sciences] to converge again. None of these human disciplines, each fixed on one aspect of human behaviour and relations, can make forecasts in its field without drawing support from the other disciplines. As data are compiled and methods compared, each discipline will undergo an internal transformation arising from the new orientations towards forecasting. In each, research capable of shedding light on the dynamics of change will be of primary importance, and we shall see few talents devoted to pure erudition (that which cannot conceivably affect our decisions).

Seen in its essentials, this is the case for a technocratic society. It is based on the premise that modern civilisations have repudiated the sacredness of institutions and commitments, and therewith the means of achieving a known future. We are thus faced with more uncertainty and, at the same time, we want things to change more rapidly. Inter-disciplinary forecasting is the answer. There is no room for radical political choices, another way of pronouncing the demise of the political dialogue. Thus, the academic becomes the master forecaster in a technocratic society. In the past, people fought their misery with dreams; now, in an affluent age, they must fight anxiety with slide rules.

I should not, however, involve you in this controversy. Whatever the implications of this particular thesis for our subject, I want to reaffirm the need for useful education as well as useful research; that is to say, for education which furthers the abilities of men and women to reason and act effectively in a variety of vocational situations.

Most of these situations for most of our students, whether they be overseas students or British students, whether they come from developed or developing countries, will be non-market situations. In other words, we are concerned primarily, though not exclusively, with the imaginative education of men and women who either will be or are employed in the public and voluntary services as administrators, professionals, research workers or in other vocational roles, and who may, in the future contribute, politically and in other ways, to the working of democratic institutions. There is nothing very original in this statement; in the year 1316 a college was founded in Cambridge for the special purpose of providing 'Clerks for the King's service' (Whitehead, 1929). The interests of our students, educational and vocational, thus determine to some extent how we define, study and teach the subject of social administration.

Our problems, as teachers of social administration, are not so dissimilar from those that faced teachers of the subject of history in the 19th century when it had barely attained academic status in England. For the first seventeen years of its academical existence, said Green, writing in 1867, "history was struggling out of that condition in which it was looked on as no special or definite study, but as part of that general mass of things, which every gentleman should know"; Freeman pronounced that the History School in those years was "an easy school for rich men" (Southern, 1961, p 11).

This is familiar stuff. Who has not heard it said that social administration is no special or definite study but a part of that general mass of things which every earnest young man or woman should know? And that social administration is a soft option, which begs the question whether all subjects can be equally hard options for all students in an equally hard social science world.

Because I have drawn on the experience of the history school in the 19th century, it must not be concluded that I am predicting an analogous future for the Social Administration School. I feel no need to predict. That part of the general mass of things in the social sciences with which we, as social administrators, are concerned is, I have no doubt, a part that can be studied and taught in the best traditions of academic scholarship and detachment. What matters is how we teach and how we study; if we bring to these tasks that uncommon mixture of intellectual excitement and practical usefulness, we need not worry about the status ranking of social administration in the world of the social sciences.

Now I must say something about the unsoluble problem of defining 'social administration'. It would be possible to begin by embarking on a content analysis of inaugural lectures on the subject or by examining the variety of definitions of 'social policy and administration' offered in the growing volume of textbooks and essays in Britain and other countries. This could be invidious or boring or both. But at least I can point out that the term 'social administration' is a misleading one; we are not experts in office management and social book-keeping, nor are we technicians in man-manipulation. One reason for the term we carry around and which creates so much confusion is that the social sciences have consumed, tainted and spoiled collective nouns in the English language at such a rate in recent decades that hardly any other options now remain. In accepting these difficulties, as we must, we can remember Edmund Burke's consolation, "Custom reconciles us to everything". And we can also draw some shreds of compensation from the thought that, unlike some who teach in other fields of the social sciences, we do not have continually to look over our shoulders and ask ourselves whether we are behaving, teaching and researching like professional social administrators. There is no such animal.

If, like others before me, I refuse to offer a definitive explanation of the subject I will nevertheless attempt briefly to say something about our interests and our perspectives.

Basically, we are concerned with the study of a range of social needs and the functioning, in conditions of scarcity, of human organisations, traditionally called 'social services' or 'social welfare systems', to meet these needs. This complex area of social life lies outside or on the fringes of the so-called free market, the mechanisms of price and tests of profitability. Although this area has some of the characteristics of the market-place – for example, all social services are allocative systems and ration demand and supply – there are many other characteristics which relate to the non-economic elements in human relations.

Social administration is thus concerned, for instance, with different types of moral transactions, embodying notions of gift-exchange, or reciprocal obligations, which have developed in modern societies in institutional forms to bring about and maintain social and community relations. Mauss, the French sociologist, depicted in his book *The gift* (1966, pp 66-7), the growth of social insurance, of what he called "solicitude in mutuality and cooperation", as an expression of need and response to group relationships. "The theme of the gift", he wrote, "of freedom and obligation in the gift, of generosity and self-interest in giving, reappear in our own society like the resurrection of a dominant motif long forgotten."

Many of the services, transactions and transfers, we study, whether they are classified as social, public, occupational, voluntary or fiscal, contain both economic and non-economic elements. It is the objectives of these services, transactions and transfers in relation to social needs, rather than the particular administrative method or institutional device employed to attain objectives, which largely determine our interests in research and study and the categorisation of these activities as social services. The study of welfare objectives and of social policy thus lies at the centre of our focus of vision. We may bring to this focus, singly or in combination, the methods, techniques and insights of the historian, the economist, the statistician, the sociologist or, on occasion, some of the perspectives of the philosopher.

Kenneth Boulding, the economist, is one of the few writers that have attempted to answer the question: what distinguishes social policy from economic policy? In the context in which he uses the word, 'policy' embraces not only goal-formulation but administrative processes, historical change and methods of delivering, measuring and evaluating services and systems.

After despairing, as I do, of finding any clear definition or clean boundaries, he arrives at the conclusion (1967, pp 3-11):

> If there is one common thread that unites all aspects of social policy and distinguishes them from merely economic policy, it is the thread of what has elsewhere been called the 'integrative system'. This includes those aspects of social life that are characterised not so much by exchange in which a quid is got for a quo [theoretically the basis of private risk insurance] as by unilateral transfers that are justified by some kind of appeal to a status or legitimacy, identity, or community. The institutions with which social policy is especially concerned, such as the school, family, church, or, at the other end, the public assistance office, court, prison, or criminal gang, all reflect degrees of integration and community. By and large it is an objective of social policy to build the identity of a person around some community with which he is associated.

Boulding and Mauss, from different approaches and different disciplines, have thus helped to clarify our perspectives. The grant, or the gift or unilateral transfer – whether it takes the form of cash, time, energy, satisfaction, blood or even life itself – is the distinguishing mark of the social (in policy and administration) just as exchange or bilateral transfer is a mark of the economic. In an extravagant mood, I suppose, we might think of conceptualising this area as the 'social market' in contradistinction to the 'economic market'.

What this implies, of course, as Boulding rightly points out, is that social policy has to concern itself with questions of identity and alienation, for alienation threatens or destroys the system of unilateral transfer. It follows that, if social administrators share this perspective of concern, then they are problem-oriented. But to be problem-conscious in this sense is a far cry from the image of the social administrator as a technical problem-solver seeking solutions to the dilemmas of the earnings rule, adoption regulations and the eleven-plus. As Wright Mills (1959, p 178) once observed: "All social scientists, by the fact of their existence, are involved in the struggle between enlightenment and obscurantism". Social administrators are no exception.

* * * * *

I reach the conclusion therefore that social administration as a subject is not a messy conglomeration of the technical ad hoc. Its primary areas of unifying interest are centred on those social institutions that foster integration and discourage alienation. In a universe of change, this explains and unites our concern with the 'ends' (the objectives of social policy) and the 'means' (the development and administration of particular public and voluntary organisations).

It also explains why in recent years the subject has in an empirical and confused way been slowly conceptualising its major fields of research and teaching. These, I suggest, may broadly be categorised as follows:

- the analysis and description of policy formation and its consequences, intended and unintended;
- the study of structure, function, organisation, planning and administrative processes of institutions and agencies, historical and comparative;
- the study of social needs and of problems of access to, utilisation and patterns of outcome of services, transactions and transfers;
- the analysis of the nature, attributes and distribution of social costs and diswelfares;
- the analysis of distributive and allocative patterns in command-over-resources-through-time and the particular impact of the social services;
- the study of the roles and functions of elected representatives, professional workers, administrators and interest groups in the operation and performance of social welfare institutions;
- the study of the social rights of the citizen as contributor, participant and user of social services;
- the study of the role of government (local and central) as an allocation of values and of rights to social property as expressed through social and administrative law and other rule-making channels.

If one surveys the interests, activities and writings of social administrators (as Professor Kay Jones attempted for the Social Science Research Council), I think one would find that most of them would fall within one or other of these eight headings. Stated in this extremely generalised form and remembering, of course, that all require to be viewed in the context of 'social administration as the study of social needs', nevertheless, the range seems immodestly broad; but that is not my intention as it is the price of most attempts to generalise. Even so, there is much that I have omitted in this broad appraisal. I have, for example, largely confined my observations to the study of social administration in our own society. Its relevance to other societies and cultures is a matter which should be discussed on another occasion.

Despite all the gaps and ambiguities of which I am very conscious, I would like to end on a coherent note. I happen to believe that, as a subject, social administration has begun to develop a body of knowledge and a related set of concepts and principles. It is in the process of knowledge-building which is one of the attributes of science. In doing so, it has borrowed heavily from different disciplines in the social sciences and now faces the tasks of refining, extending and adapting insights, perspectives and methods so as to further our understanding of, and to teach more imaginatively about, the roles and functions of social services in contemporary society.

What is social policy?

In this chapter, we look at the term 'social policy' and ask a good many questions about it. In doing so, we shall inevitably have to consider various definitions of associated concepts and categorised labels: social administration, social services, social welfare, social security, welfare states and so forth. We will have to ask ourselves why we should study social policy at all or, for that matter, society's response as it identifies or fails to identify social needs and problems. Are we concerned with principles and objectives about certain areas of social life and organisation or with social engineering, that is, with methods and techniques of action, management, organisation and the application of games theory?

Whatever the answer we arrive at, we cannot fail to become heavily involved in the issues of moral and political values. Indeed, political propaganda frequently masquerades under social policy labels.

* * * * *

What do we mean by 'social policy'? Connected with this is the equally important question: whose social policy? For our purposes the word 'policy' can be taken to refer to the principles that govern action directed towards given ends. The concept denotes action about means as well as ends and it therefore implies change: changing situations, systems, practices and behaviour. And here we should note that the concept of policy is only meaningful if we (society, a group, or an organisation) believe we can affect change in some form or another. We do not have policies about the weather because, as yet, we are powerless to do anything about the weather. But we do have policies (or we can have policies) about illegitimate children because we think we have some power to affect their lives – for better or worse, depending on whether you are the policy maker or the illegitimate child.

The word 'policy' is used here in an action-oriented and problem-oriented sense. The collective 'we' is used to refer to the actions of government in expressing the 'general will' of the people, whether of Britain, Nigeria or China. The meaning and validity of a concept of the 'general will' is, of course, hotly debated.

The greatest semantic difficulty arises, inevitably, with the word 'social'. Nor is it made any easier by the fact that so many disciplines, professions and groups claim it as a forename and, indeed, flourish it about as something distinctly different. We have, for example, social geography, social planning, social psychology, social psychiatry, social administration, social work, social law, social linguistics, social history, social medicine, social pathology and so on. Even the Bank of America created in January 1972 a new post of executive vice-president in charge of social policy! Why not social theology? Is it really necessary to drive home so ponderously the fact that all these subjects and groups are concerned in some way with man in society and particularly with the non-economic factors in human relations? Are they not all, in short, emphasising that man is a social being; that he is not solely economic man; and that society cannot be thought of in terms of mechanistic–organic models or physiological models? It may well be that much of the current fashion for 'social' is a reaction against the sillier models of man in society constructed in the past by economists, political philosophers, experimental psychologists and sociologists.

Take, for example, the attempts of the Victorian economists to establish a competitive, self-regulating total market economy, or Radcliffe-Brown's doctrine (as one of the 'fathers' of modern anthropology) that the organic nature of society is a fact. Such a doctrine implies that integration and solidarity must be 'natural' attributes of all social systems. "Social structures", he wrote (1952), "are just as real as are individual organisms. A complex organism is a collection of living cells and interstitial fluids arranged in a certain structure...." This is what another anthropologist, a *social* anthropologist, Edmund Leach in *New Society* (14 May 1964), had to say about this doctrine: "If you feel certain, on a *priori* grounds, that all forms of social stress must produce a reaction which will tend to restore or even reinforce the solidarity (ie organic health) of society then you will quickly persuade yourself that war is peace and conflict harmony."

You might argue, if social stresses correct themselves automatically (on the analogy of the self-regulating market economy), then there is no place for an unpredictable concept like social policy.

But it can, of course, be argued that social policy (or, to be more precise, a system of social welfare) is simply part of the self-regulatory mechanisms built into a 'natural' social system. This would mean that the history of the development of the social services in Britain since the beginning of 20th century was, in a sense, predetermined; that it was bound to happen because of a 'natural' tendency in the social system toward equilibrium and order. Some part of the theory of Talcott Parsons (1949, 1964) sustains this equilibrium-order concept. Fundamentally, it is a conservative ideology akin to the philosophy that "all is for the best in this best of all possible worlds"; or akin, to take another analogy, to neo-classical economic theory with its conception of the best possible self-regulating supply and demand private market (largely, as the Women's Liberation Movement has pointed out, a private market for men).

All this is a rather roundabout way of saying that these mechanistic theories of orderly man and society consign a minor subsidiary role to social policy; indeed, not a 'policy' role at all; a role similar to that assigned to the state in 19th century Britain by Lassalle when he wrote about the 'Night Watchman State' (the 'law and order state' in the language of the 1970s). Only in a very restricted and contradictory sense could it be said that night watchmen have policies, unless it can be argued that to watch and keep order and not to act and change is a policy.

At the other end of the spectrum of values is the rejection of the notion of a mechanistic or residual role for social policy. Social policy can be seen as a positive instrument of change; as an unpredictable, incalculable part of the whole political process.

We must not, however, jump to the conclusion that social policy as conceived in this or any other way is necessarily beneficent or welfare-oriented in the sense of providing more welfare and more benefits for the poor, the so-called working classes, old-age pensioners, women, deprived children and other categories in the catalogue of social poverty. A redistributive social policy can redistribute command over material and non-material resources from the poor to the rich; from one ethnic group to another ethnic group; from working life to old age within income groups and social classes as, for example, in middle-class pension schemes and in other ways.

There have existed social policies in South Africa under apartheid which many people would not regard as being beneficent or welfare-oriented. There are social insurance programmes in some Latin American countries, Brazil in particular, which function as concealed multipliers of inequality; they transfer resources from the poor to the rich. Hitler developed social policies in Nazi Germany, which were in fact called 'social policies', concerning the mentally ill and retarded, the Jews and other ethnic groups. World public opinion condemned these instruments of social policy which had as their ultimate ends the use of human beings for medical research, sterilisation and the gas chamber.

When we use the term 'social policy', we must not therefore automatically react by investing it with a halo of altruism, concern for others, concern about equality and so on. Nor must we unthinkingly conclude that because Britain, or any other country, has a social policy or has developed social services, that they actually operate in practice to further the ends of progressive redistribution, equality and social altruism. What is 'welfare' for some groups may be 'illfare' for others.

And, lastly, in guarding against the value implications of 'social policy', I should point out that it does not imply allegiance to any political party or ideology. We all have our values and our prejudices; we all have our rights and duties as citizens, and our rights and duties as teachers and students. At the very least, we have a responsibility for making our values clear and we have a special duty to do so when we are discussing such a subject as social policy which, quite clearly, has no meaning at all if it is considered to be neutral in terms of values. Or as Nye Bevan, the architect of the British National Health Service was so fond of saying, "This is my truth, now tell me yours".

Gunnar Myrdal (1970) had much to say on economic and social policy about the dangers of deceiving ourselves and others about our values and biases. He criticised sociologists and anthropologists for believing in the possibility of a value-free approach in their studies of social organisation.

Hume once said that the true sceptic should be as diffident of his philosophical doubts as of his philosophical convictions. Can we then say that a true believer should be as diffident of his philosophical convictions as of his philosophical doubts, so a true sceptic and a true believer would be one and the same? Is such a paragon possible? Can a man temper his doubts with assertion and his assertions with doubt, and yet act in pursuit of certain social policy goals? Is this what in the ordinary life of decision-making some people call 'wisdom', the power to be both critical and practical, both speculative and pragmatic?

* * * * *

To return, however, to this tiresome business of defining social policy. Let us consider what some other writers have said on the subject. At one extreme, we can find the most comprehensive definition in the statement by Macbeath in his 1957 Hobhouse Lecture: "Social policies are concerned with the right ordering of the network of relationships between men and women who live together in societies, or with the principles which should govern the activities of individuals and groups so far as they affect the lives and interests of other people."

It would be difficult to be more sweeping than that. It could easily be read as a grand definition of the scope of sociology; indeed, a definition that includes economics and all the social science disciplines. However, one should point out that it was Professor Macbeath's purpose to state the central issue in social policy or any policy determined by government to intervene in the life of the community. As he saw it, the central issue was between the self-regarding (egotistical) activities of man and the other-regarding (altruistic) activities. Ginsberg (1953, p 24) took much the same position. Arguing that some forms of social policy are based on the notion of moral progress, he then used criteria of moral progress which are to be found "in the growing power of altruism over egoism" brought about by a fusion of intelligence and concern for social justice and equality. My book, *The gift relationship* (1970), was an attempt to provide a concrete illustration of this philosophical view from an international study of blood donor systems.

At the other extreme, let us take Hagenbuch's (1958, p 205) definition of social policy. "Stated in general terms, the mainspring of social policy may be said to be the desire to ensure every member of the community certain minimum standards and certain opportunities." This I think is typical of many definitions offered by other writers in a large number of Western countries. It is similar also to the views expressed by the United States in a series of studies and reports.

These and similar definitions, whether one views them as limited or broad, all contain three objectives and, of course, value judgements. First, they aim to be beneficent; policy is directed to provide welfare for citizens. Second, they include economic as well as non-economic objectives: for example, minimum wages, minimum standards of income maintenance and so on. Third, they involve some measure of progressive redistribution in command-over-resources from rich to poor.

Dissenting somewhat from these views is François Lafitte (1962) who sees social policy as being more concerned with the communal environments; that is, the provision of social amenity (urban renewal and national parks, for example, and measures against pollution, noise, etc) which the individual cannot purchase in the market as a lone individual. He puts less emphasis on individual transfer payments (like pensions) and argues that "in the main, social policy is an attempt to steer the life of society along channels it would not follow if left to itself". This is in some senses a more limited definition, but it does imply a substantial interventionist role by government in the provision of a wide range of community facilities and safeguards.

Marshall (1965, p 7) is more practical and down-to-earth:

> 'Social Policy' is not a technical term with an exact meaning ... it is taken to refer to the policy of governments with regard to action having a direct impact on the welfare of the citizen, by providing them with services or income. The central core consists, therefore, of social insurance, public (or national) assistance, the health and welfare services, housing policy.

Again, social policy is seen to be beneficent, redistributive and concerned with economic as well as non-economic objectives. Like many of the other definitions, social policy (as with economic policy) is all about 'what is and what might be'. It is thus involved in choices in the ordering of social change.

Values and choices

Chapter Three

There is no escape from value choices in welfare systems. The construction of any models or the elaboration of any theories which have anything to do with policy must inevitably be concerned with 'what is and what might be'; with what we (as members of a society) want (the ends); and with how we get there (the means).

Not only is policy all about values but those who discuss problems of policy have their own values (some would call them prejudices). But, whatever they are called, it is obvious that the social sciences, and particularly economics and sociology, are not, nor can ever be, 'value-free'. No doubt there are some practitioners, concerned about the professional status of their subject or discipline (which in itself is an odd word suggestive of a master–servant relationship), who like to think they are value-free, floating in an abstracted social world of an exact Robinson Crusoe science. They take refuge in the description of facts, or in mathematical model-building, or in a mystique of casework or psychoanalysis. But even the labelling of one's subject or the choice of topics for research or for teaching in the social sciences can reveal the existence of value premises. Consider the use of such terms as 'race relations'. Does it not imply certain judgements about the unscientific concept of race? Or the use of such valuative and emotive terms as 'economic growth', 'progress', 'productivity', 'health', 'social mobility' and 'equality'.

There are, of course, some social phenomena that may be studied with a certain degree of cold rational disinterestedness while never achieving the lack of involvement displayed by a mathematician analysing a quadratic equation. But this is not possible with the study of social policy or, to take another example, social deviation, which is a concept inextricably mixed up in all fields of social policy, medical care, social work and psychiatry. One of the value assumptions, for instance, is that the residual non–market sector (the public social policy sector) should concern itself with the social deviants; the 'bad actuarial risks', those who are unwilling or unable to provide for their own needs and the needs of their families through the normal mechanisms of the market.

The definition of deviation means an aberration, turning from the right course, obliquity of conduct. Language is not a mere symbolic tool of communication. By describing people as deviant we express an attitude; we morally brand them and stigmatise them with our value judgement. Social deviation, like crime, is a social ill or a 'social problem'. The ultimate aim of some people who study the aetiology and pressures leading to crime and deviation is to devise better ways and means to combat and prevent them. This stems from a clear-cut value involvement.

The investigators of *The power elite* (Mills, 1956), *The status seekers* (Packard, 1971) and *The hidden persuaders* (Packard, 1970) were hardly neutral towards their subjects. Less obvious is the higher proportion of Jews to non-Jews among the investigators of anti-Semitism. Merton (1957) may have partially escaped the perils of value judgement because he was mainly concerned with the schematic description and typology of deviants; but many others have not. They have followed the original Durkheimian conception of deviance according to which the unadjusted, the pariahs, the outsiders, are by definition detrimental to the interests of the group and their faulty solidarity invariably injures the group itself.

Consequently, one of the vital norms of every group is that the individuals comprising it should 'adjust' or conform to its normative system and values. The term 'adjustment' in itself is associated immediately with the use of power and pressure to chip off the corners of a square peg so that it fits into a round hole.

Actually, 'adjustment' is a virtue prescribed by the group whose interest (that is, solidarity) it serves, which has the power to enforce it and apply sanctions to those who are maladjusted. The analysis of the processes leading to deviation in the Durkheimian tradition is necessarily based on an axiomatic value judgement: that group cohesion, solidarity and following group norms is 'functional', social (as opposed to anti-social) and therefore *good*!

The whole 'adjustment' literature in the socio-psychological, psychiatric and educational fields is based on this axiomatic premise. The image of a balanced personality, one who 'plays according the to rules of the game' prescribed by the group norms, is a direct corollary of this premise.

'The rules of the game', explicit or implicit in our three different models of social policy, are values which we all have to think about, criticise and argue about. There is no imperative 'ought' or 'should' or 'rightness' about any one of them. The social sciences cannot give a final answer to the question whether any given policy is 'right'. On the other hand, the social scientist can study what people say they want, what they think they want, and may even infer from their behaviour what they 'really' want, but it is not the business of science to say whether people want the *right* things. The critique of ends – that is, the discussion of what are the right things to want – is more in the province of the philosopher or the theologian. But who these days qualifies as a philosopher – people like Sartre who summed up, in his play *No Exit*, 'Hell is other people'?

This, however, is not to say that those who study social policy cannot make any contribution at all to the discussion of objectives. They can point out, for instance, that many things that people think are ends are in fact means to some further end and that a discussion that seems to be about ends (like our models of social policy) may be more easily resolved if it can be stated in terms of a choice of means to some further end. They may also point out that human activity seldom has but one objective and that there are many ends, some of which may not be compatible.

The Americans want safe and effective surgical operations, but they do not want to support free and anonymous blood donations to minimise the risk of serum hepatitis. We (as well as the Americans) want to diminish colour prejudice but we do not always want social policies that are non-discriminatory in character. We want riches but we also want the things that make for poverty; that is, the social costs, damages and disservices of economic growth. We want equality but we also want wage and salary differentials. We want to be paid more when we are working than when we are not working, yet at the same time we want to abolish the wage-stop. And who are the 'we' in all this? What are the boundaries of my and other people's welfare: the family, the kin, the village, the state or the world? Where does egoism end and altruism begin? Should we import human blood from other societies or even recruit doctors from poorer nations because we (or the United States or Canada) have discovered that, in the international medical market place, it is now cheaper to import doctors than to train them?

* * * * *

So far as the study of these social policy questions is concerned, all we can do is to expose more clearly the value choices confronting society; whether they relate to medical care, social security, education and other services which, in essence, involve social relations and systems of belief. As Joan Robinson (1962, p 4) once said in discussing the value premises of economics, "without ideology we would never have thought of the question(s)". And so it is with social policy models which, with all their apparent remoteness from reality, can serve a purpose in providing us with an ideological framework which may stimulate us to ask the significant questions and expose the significant choices.

We will not be led to ask the significant questions if we view the area of social policy as (so to speak) a closed and separate system of welfare for a particular group or groups in society. Or as a technical exercise in social engineering in which a power elite decides, in a closed system, how much welfare poor people need and how it should be provided. As soon as we narrow our vision in this way, we are at once in danger of being imprisoned in one of the stereotypes associated with the notion of 'the welfare state' or a 'war on poverty'. Assumptions here include those that 'welfare' is necessarily and inevitably improving (as the Victorians would have said), or wholly beneficient (as some left-wing politicians believe) or an adjustable fringe donation (as some right-wing politicians believe). Or again, that what *we* do for *poor* people or *to* poor people (which in itself raises the question of how we identify the poor and how we discriminate in their favour) will inevitably lead us, if we win the poverty war, to some sort of final welfare destination. It sounds simple, too simple: the conversion of the poor into the non-poor.

This is, perhaps, an unjust criticism, because all generalisations, like generalisations about the welfare state or wars on poverty, have a common drawback: both ends and means are made to appear deceptively simple. It is when we move from abstract generalisation to the precise diagnosis of social problems that the trouble begins. It is at this point we have to ask the significant questions and we are unlikely to do so unless our conceptual frame of reference (as well as our world of reality) includes the non-poor as well as the poor; the uncertainties of social change as well as the certainties; the past and the future in the spectrum of social time as well as the present.

* * * * *

We cannot generalise in any rational way about the respective roles and functions of government and the private sector unless we have first considered questions of this kind.

Among all the theories and principles relating to social policy, perhaps the most fundamental ones centre round the historic problems of distributive justice. They embrace four well-known maxims:

- to each according to individual *need*
- to each according to individual *worth*
- to each according to individual *merit*
- to each according to individual *work*

To these four we might add a fifth: to each according to *our needs*. In other words, if it is the will of society to move towards a more equal society, which of these four maxims should determine the provision of welfare?

Bibliography

Abel–Smith, B. (1958) 'Whose welfare state?', in N. Mackenzie (ed) *Conviction*, London: MacGibbon & Kee.

Abel–Smith, B. and Titmuss, R. (eds) (1974) *The cost of the National Health Service in England and Wales*, Cambridge: Cambridge University Press.

Abel–Smith, B. and Titmuss, R. (eds) (1974) *Social policy: An introduction*, London: Unwin Hyman.

Abel–Smith, B. and Townsend, P. (1965) *The poor and the poorest*, London: G. Bell and Sons.

Abel–Smith, B., Macdonald, G., Titmuss, R., Williams, A. and Ward, C. (1964) *The health services of Tanganyika*, London: Pitman Medical Publishing Co.

Abramowitz, M. (1988) *Social welfare policy from colonial times to the present*, Boston, MA: South End Press.

Acheson Report (1998) *Independent Inquiry into Inequalities in Health*, London: The Stationery Office.

Agulnik, P. and LeGrand, J. (1998) 'Tax relief and partnership pensions', *Fiscal Studies*, vol 19, no 4, pp 403-28, November.

Alcock, P. (1998) 'The discipline of social policy', in P. Alcock, A. Erskine and M. May (eds) *The student's companion to social policy*, Oxford: Blackwell.

Anderson, M., Bechhofer, F. and Gershuny, J. (eds) (1994) *The social and political economy of the household*, Oxford: Oxford University Press.

Andreski, S. (1954) *Military organization and society*, London: Routledge & Kegan Paul.

Ansell, C. (1874) 'Vital statistics of families in the upper and professional classes', *Journal of the Royal Statistical Society*, vol 37.

Arrow, K. (1963) 'Uncertainty and the welfare economics of medical care', *American Economic Review*, vol 53, pp 941-73.

Ashby, E. (1958) *Technology and the academics*, London: Macmillan.

Atkinson, A.B. (1969) *Poverty in Britain and the reform of social security*, Cambridge: Cambridge University Press.

Atkinson, A.B. (1975) 'Income distribution and social change revisited', *Journal of Social Policy*, vol 4, no 1, pp 57-68.

Atkinson, A.B. (1983) (2nd edn) *The economics of inequality*, Oxford: Clarendon Press.

Atkinson, A.B. (1995) *Incomes and the welfare state: Essays on Britain and Europe*, Cambridge: Cambridge University Press.

Atkinson, A.B. (1999) *Is rising inequality inevitable? A critique of the transatlantic consensus*, WIDER, Annual Lectures 3, Helsinki: United Nations University World Institute for Development Economics Research (UNU/WIDER).

Atkinson, A.B. (2000) 'Distribution of income and wealth', in A.H. Halsey with J. Webb (eds) *Twentieth-century British social trends*, Houndmills: Macmillan (3rd edn), pp 348-81.

Bailey and Day (1861) 'On the rate of mortality prevailing amongst the families of the peerage during the nineteenth century', *Journal of the Institute of Actuaries*, vol 9.

Barnett, C. (1986) *The audit of war: The illusion and reality of Britain as a great nation*, London: Macmillan.

Barr, N. (1998) *The economics of the welfare state* (3rd edn), Oxford: Oxford University Press.

Bell, D. (1960) *The end of ideology: On the exhaustion of political ideas in the fifties*, Glencoe, IL: Free Press.

Benn, M. (1999) *Towards a new politics of motherhood*, London: Vintage.

Berlin, I. (1969) *Four essays on liberty*, Oxford: Oxford University Press.

Beveridge Report (1942) *Social insurance and allied services*, London: HMSO.

BIR (Board of Inland Revenue) (1950) *Annual Report of the Board of Inland Revenue*, London: HMSO.

Booth, P. and Dickinson, G. (1997) *The insurance solution*, London: European Policy Forum.

Boulding, K.E. (1967) 'The boundaries of social policy', *Social Work*, vol 12, no 1, January.

Boulding, K.E. (1968) *Principles of economic policy*, London: Staples.

Bradshaw, J. (2000) 'Child poverty in comparative perspective', in D. Gordon and P. Townsend (eds) *Breadline Europe: The measurement of poverty*, Bristol: The Policy Press.

Bryson, L. (1992) *Welfare and the state*, Basingstoke: Macmillan.

Burchardt, T. (1997) *Boundaries between public and private welfare: A typology and map of services*, CASE Paper 2, London: Centre for Analysis of Social Exclusion, London School of Economics and Political Science.

Burchardt, T., Hills, J. and Propper, C. (1999) *Private welfare and public policy*, York: York Publishing Services.

Campion, H. (1939) *Public and private property in Great Britain*, London: Oxford University Press.

Caplovitz, D. (1963) *The poor pay more*, Glencoe, IL: Free Press.

Carr-Saunders, A. (1959) *English universities today*, London: London School of Economics and Political Science.

Cartter, A. (1953) 'Income-tax allowances and the family in Great Britain', *Population Studies*, vol 6, no 3, March.

Clark, C. (1954) *Welfare and taxation*, Oxford: Catholic Social Guild.

Cole, D. with Utting, J.E.G. (1962) *The economic circumstances of old people*, Occasional Papers on Social Administration, no 4, London: London School of Economics and Political Science.

Commisioners for Inquiry (1844) *First report of the Commissioners for Inquiry into the state of large towns and populous districts, London.*

Conservative Political Centre (1950) *One nation*, London: Conservative Political Centre.

Cook, D. (1989) *Rich Law, Poor Law: Different responses to tax and supplementary benefit fraud*, Milton Keynes: Open University Press.

Costello, C.B., Miles, S. and Stone, A.J. (eds) (1998) *The American woman 1999-2000*, New York, NY: W.W. Norton.

Coward, R. (1999) *Sacred cows: Is feminism relevant to the new millennium?*, London: HarperCollins.

CSO (Central Statistical Office) (1955) *Monthly Digest of Statistics (May)*, London: HMSO.

Crossman, R.H.S. (1955) *Socialism and the new despotism*, Fabian Tract 298, London: Fabian Society.

Crowther Report (1959) *Central Advisory Council for Education (England)*, London: HMSO.

Davies, J.N.P. (1944) *British Medical Journal*, vol 2.

De Jouvenal, B. (1951) *The ethics of redistribution*, Cambridge: Cambridge University Press.

De Jouvenal, B. (1967, translated by N. Lavy) *The art of conjecture*, London: Weidenfield & Nicholson.

Delphy, C. and Leonard, D. (1992) *Familiar exploitation*, Cambridge: Polity Press.

DHSS (Department of Health and Social Security) (1972) *Supplementary Benefits Handbook (November)*, London: HMSO.

Dicey, A.V. (1905) *Lecture on the relation between the law and opinion in England during the nineteenth century*, London: Macmillan & Co.

Donnison, D. (1967) *The government of housing*, Harmondsworth: Penguin.

Donnison, D. (1973) 'Richard Titmuss', *New Society*, 12 April, p 81.

Donnison, D. (1994) 'Social policy studies in Britain: retrospect and prospect', in J. Ferris and R. Page (eds) *Social policy in transition*, Aldershot: Avebury.

DSS (Department of Social Security) (2000) *Pensioners' Income Series 1998/99*, London: Analytical Services Division, DSS.

Dublin, L.I. (1928) *Health and wealth: A survey of the economics of world wealth*, New York, NY: Harper & Bros.

Durham, W. (1958) *The LSD of welfare in industry*, London: Industrial Welfare Society.

Durkheim, E. (1904, translated by G. Simpson, 1933) *The division of labour in society*, New York, NY: Free Press of Glencoe.

Erskine, A. (1998) 'The approaches and methods of social policy', in P. Alcock, A. Erskine and M. May (eds) *The student's companion to social policy*, Oxford: Blackwell.

Esping-Andersen, G. (1990) *The three worlds of welfare capitalism*, Cambridge: Polity Press.

Esping-Andersen, G. (1999) *Social foundations of postindustrial economies*, Oxford: Oxford University Press.

Falls, C.B. (1941) *The nature of modern warfare*, London: Methuen & Co.

Farr, W. (1843) Appendix to Registrar-General's fifth annual report, London.

Fontaine, P. (2000) 'Blood, politics and economic man: Richard Titmuss and economists on Altruism, 1957-1973', Mimeo, Cachan: École Supérieure de Cachan.

Friedmann, G. (1952) 'The social consequences of technical progress', *International Social Science Bulletin*, vol 4, no 2.

Friedmann, W. (1951) *Law and social change in contemporary Britain*, London: Stevens & Sons.

Fromm, E. (1965) *Socialist humanism*, New York, NY: Doubleday.

Galbraith, J.K. (1958) *The affluent society*, Boston, MA: Houghton Mifflin Co.

Galton, F (1883) *Inquiries into human faculty and its development*, London: Macmillan.

Gellner, E. (1959) *Words and things*, London: Victor Gollancz.

Gerth, H.H. and Mills, C.W. (1946) *From Max Weber: Essays in sociology*, London/Trends: Kegan Paul/Trubner & Co.

Gerth, H.H. and Mills, C.W. (1954) *Character and social structure*, London: Routledge & Kegan Paul.

Gilbert, B.B. (1966) *The evolution of national insurance: The origins of the welfare state*, London: Michael Joseph.

Ginsberg, M. (1953) *The idea of progress: A revaluation*, London: Methuen.

Glass, D.V. and Grebnick, E. (1954) *The trend and pattern of fertility in Great Britain: A report on the family census of 1946*, London [publisher unknown].

Glennerster, H. (1988) 'Requiem for the Social Administration Association', *Journal of Social Policy*, vol 17, no 1.

Glennerster, H. (2000) *British social policy since 1945* (2nd edn), Oxford: Blackwell.

Glennerster, H. and Hills, J. (eds) (1998) *The state of welfare* (2nd edn), Oxford: Oxford University Press.

Gornick, J.C., Meyers, M.K. and Ross, K.E. (1997) 'Supporting the employment of mothers: policy variation across fourteen welfare states', *Journal of European Social Policy*, vol 7, no 1, pp 45-70.

Gowing, M. (1975) 'Richard Morris Titmuss', *Proceedings of the British Academy*, vol LXI.

Greenwood, M. (1942), 'British loss of life in the wars of 1794-1815 and 1914-18', *Journal of the Royal Statistical Society*, vol 105, part 1.

Graham, H. (1984) *Women, health and the family*, Brighton: Harvester Wheatsheaf.

Greve, B. (1994) 'The hidden welfare state: tax expenditure and social policy', *Scandinavian Journal of Social Welfare*, vol 3, no 4, pp 203-11.

Guillebaud Committee (1956) *Committee of Enquiry into the cost of the National Health Service*, London: HMSO.

Hagenbuch, R. (1953) *Lloyds Bank Review* (July).

Hagenbuch, W. (1958) *Social economics*, Welwyn: Nisbet.

Hailsham, Lord (1959) *The Conservative case*, London: Penguin.

Hakim, C. (1995) 'Five feminist myths about women's employment', *British Journal of Sociology*, vol 46, no 3, pp 429-55.

Hall, M.P. (1952) *The social services of modern England*, London: Routledge.

Hanmer, J. and Hearn, J. (1999) 'Gender and welfare research', in F. Williams, J. Popay and A. Oakley (eds) *Welfare research: A critical review*, London: UCL Press.

Hannah, L. (1986) *Inventing retirement: The development of occupational pensions in Britain*, Cambridge: Cambridge University Press.

Hansson, K. (1958) 'Life assurance in Sweden', *The Policy-Holder Journal*, 20 November.

Harrington, M. (1962) *The other America: Poverty in the United States*, New York, NY: Macmillan & Co.

Harris, J. (1992) 'Political thought and the welfare state 1940-1970: an intellectual framework for British social policy', *Past and Present*, no 135, pp 116-41.

Harris, J. (1997) *William Beveridge: A biography*, Oxford: Oxford University Press.

Hazen, C.A. and Frinking, G.A.B. (eds) (1990) *Emerging questions in demographic research*, Amsterdam/Oxford: Elsevier.

Hills, J. (ed) (1996) *New inequalities: The changing distribution of income and wealth in the United Kingdom*, Cambridge: Cambridge University Press.

Hills, J. and Lelkes, O. (1999) 'Social security, selective universalism and patchwork redistribution', in R. Jowell, J. Curtice, A. Park and K. Thomson (eds) *British Social Attitudes: The 16th report*, Aldershot: Ashgate.

Hodson, J. (1952) *Royal Commission on Marriage and Divorce*, MDP/1952/337, London: HMSO.

Hoffer, W. (1954) *Lancet*, vol 2, p 1234.

Howard, C. (1997) *The hidden welfare state: Tax expenditures and social policy in the United States*, Princeton, NJ: Princeton University Press.

Hutchins, R.M. (1959) 'Is democracy possible?', *Bulletin of the Fund for the Republic*, February.

Inland Revenue (1950) *Ninety-second report of the Commission of His Majesty's Inland Revenue for the year ended 31 March 1949*, London: HMSO.

IPPR (Institute for Public Policy Research) (2001) *Building better partnerships: Final report of the Commission on Public Private Partnerships*, London: IPPR.

Jay, D. (1962) *Socialism in the new society*, London: Longmans.

Jenkins, D. (1961) *Equality and excellence*, London: SCM Press for the Christian Frontier Council.

Jephcott, P. with Seear, N. and Smith, J.H. (1962) *Married women working*, London: Allen & Unwin.

Jewkes, J. (1939) 'Introduction' to H. Campion (1939) *Public and private property in Great Britain*, London: Oxford University Press.

Jolly, R. and Cornea, G.A. (eds) (1984) *The impact of world recession on children: A study prepared for UNICEF*, Oxford: Pergamon Press.

Joseph Rowntree Foundation (1995) *Inquiry into income and wealth*, vol 2, York: Joseph Rowntree Foundation.

Kaldor, N. (1955) *An expenditure tax*, London: Allen & Unwin.

Keynes, J.M. (1930) *A treatise on money*, London: Macmillan.

Keynes, J.M. (1936) *The general theory of employment, interest and money*, London: Macmillan & Co.

Keyserling Report (1961) *Poverty and deprivation in the United States*, Report on the Conference on Economic Development, Washington, DC: US Government Printing Office.

Kvist, J. and Sinfield, A. (1997) 'Comparing tax welfare states', *Social Policy Review 9*, ch 14, pp 249-75.

Lafitte, F. (1962) *Social policy in a free society*, Birmingham: Birmingham University Press.

Lakin, C. (2001) 'The effects of taxes and benefits on household income, 1999-2000', *Economic Trends*, no 569, pp 35-74, April.

Lampman, R.J. (1959) *Review of Economic Statistics*, vol 41, pp 379-92, November.

Lampman, R.J. (1962) *The share of top wealth-holders in national wealth, 1922-56*, Princeton, NJ: Princeton University Press.

Land, H. (1978) 'Who cares for the family?', *Journal of Social Policy*, vol 7, no 3, pp 257-84.

LeGrand, J. (1982) *The strategy of equality*, London: Allen & Unwin.

LeGrand, J. and Bartlett, W. (eds) (1993) *Quasi-markets and social policy*, Basingstoke: Macmillan.

Levitt, T. (1958) *Harvard Business Review*, September-October.

Lewis, J. (1992) 'Gender and the development of welfare regimes', *Journal of European Social Policy*, vol 2, no 3, pp 175-97.

Lewis, R. (1955) 'A socialist economic policy', *Socialist Commentary*, June.

Lewis, R. and Maude, A. (1949) *The English middle classes*, London: Phoenix House.

Lewis, R. and Maude. A. (1952) *Professional people*, London: Phoenix House.

Lindsey, A. (1962) *Socialized medicine in England and Wales*, North Carolina: University of North Carolina Press.

Lipset, S.M. (1960) *Political man: The social bases of politics*, New York, NY: Doubleday.

Loutfi, M.F. (ed) (2001) *Women, gender and work*, Geneva: International Labour Office.

Lowe, R. (1990) 'The Second World War: consensus and the foundation of the welfare state', *Twentieth Century British History*, vol 1, no 2, pp 152-82.

Lydall, H.F. and Tipping, D.G. (1961) 'The distribution of personal wealth in Britain', *Oxford Institute of Statistics Bulletin*, vol 23, no 1, pp 83-104.

Lynes, T.A. (1962) *National assistance and national prosperity*, Occassional Papers on Social Administration, no 5, London: London School of Economics and Political Science.

Lynes, T.A. (1963) 'Poverty in the welfare state', *Aspect*, no 7, August.

Macbeth, G. (1957) 'Can social policies be rationally tested?', *Hobhouse Memorial Trust Lecture*, Oxford: Oxford University Press.

McGregor, D.R. (1955) 'The social position of women in England, 1850-1914', *British Journal of Sociology*, vol 6, no 1, March.

McKeown, T. (1976) *The modern rise of population*, London: Edward Arnold.

Macleod, I. and Maude, A. (eds) (1950) *One nation*, London: Conservative Political Centre.

Macleod, I. and Powell, J.F. (1952) *The social services: Needs and means*, London: Conservative Political Centre.

McRae, S. (ed) (1999) *Changing Britain: Families and households in the 1990s*, Oxford: Oxford University Press.

Mann, K. (1992) *The making of an English 'underclass'*, Milton Keynes: Open University Press.

Marshall, A. (1949, 8th edn; first published 1892), *Principles of economics*, London: Macmillan.

Marshall, T.H. (1947) *Sociology at the crossroads*, London: Longmans.

Marshall, T.H. (1950) *Citizenship and social class, and other essays*, Cambridge: Cambridge University Press.

Marshall, T.H. (1965) *Social policy*, London: Hutchinson.

Mauss, M. (1966) *The gift*, London: Cohen & West.

May, M. and Brunsdon, E. (1994) 'Workplace care in the mixed economy of welfare', *Social Policy Review 6*, ch 8.

May, M. and Brunsdon, E. (1999) 'Commercial and occupational welfare in the twentieth century', in R.M. Page and R. Silburn (eds) *British social welfare in the twentieth century*, Basingstoke: Macmillan.

Meade, J.E., Foggon, G., Houghton, H., Lees, N., Marshall, R.S., Roddan, G.M. and Selwyn, P. (1960) *The economic and social structure of Mauritius*, London: Methuen.

Mencher, S. (1963) 'Perspectives on recent welfare legislation', *Social Work*, vol 8, no 3.

Merton, R.K. (1957) *Social theory and social structure*, Glencoe, IL: Free Press.

Midgley, J. (1997) *Social welfare in global context*, Thousand Oaks, CA/London/Delhi: Sage Publications.

Miller, S.M. (1987) 'Introduction: the legacy of Richard Titmuss', in A. Abel-Smith and K. Titmuss (eds) *The philosophy of welfare: Selected writings of Richard M. Titmuss*, London: Allen & Unwin.

Miller, S.M. and Roby, P. (1970) *The future of inequality*, New York, NY: Basic Books.

Mill, J.S. (1869) *The subjection of women*, London [publisher unknown].

Mills, C.W. (1956) *The power elite*, Oxford: Oxford University Press.

Milne, J. (1815) *A treatise on the valuation of annuities and assurances in lives and survivorships*, London [publisher unknown].

Ministry of Pensions and National Insurance (1955) *Report of the National Insurance Advisory Committee on the question of benefit for short spells of unemployment or sickness*, London: HMSO.

Minns, R. (2001) *The cold war in welfare: Stock market versus pensions*, London: Verso.

Mirsky, J. and Radlett, M. (eds) (2000) *No paradise yet*, London: Zed Books.

Moloney, J.C. (1950) in M.J.E. Senn (ed) *Symposium on the healthy personality*, New York, NY [publisher unknown].

Morris, J.N. (1957) *Uses of epidemiology*, Edinburgh/London: E & S Livingstone.

Myrdal, G. (1960) *Beyond the welfare state*, Yale, MA: Yale University Press.

Myrdal, G. (1970) *The challenge of world poverty*, London: Allen Lane.

Nevitt, D. (1964) *Essays on housing*, Occassional Papers on Social Administration, no 9, London: London School of Economics and Political Science.

Newsholme, A. (1909-10) Supplement to 39th annual report of the Local Government Board, London.

Newsom Report (1959) *Report of the Central Advisory Council for Education: England*, vol 1, London: HMSO.

Nicholson, R.J. (1967) 'The distribution of personal income', *Lloyds Bank Review*, January.

Nyerere, J.K. (1968) *Ujamaa: Essays on socialism*, Dar Es Salaam: Oxford University Press.

Oakley, A. (1991) 'Eugenics, social medicine and the career of Richard Titmuss in Britain 1935-50', *British Journal of Sociology*, vol 42, no 2, pp 165-94.

Oakley, A. (1996) *Man and wife: Richard and Kay Titmuss, my parents' early years*, London: HarperCollins.

Oakley, A. (2001: forthcoming) *Aliens and outsiders: Gender and public policy*, Cambridge: Polity Press.

Orloff, A.S. (1993) 'Gender and the social rights of citizenship: the comparative analysis of gender relations and welfare states', *American Sociological Review*, vol 58, pp 303-28.

Orwell, G. (1941) *The lion and the unicorn: Socialism and the English genius*, London: Secker and Warburg.

Packard, V.O. (1970) *The hidden persuaders*, London/Harmondsworth: Longman/Penguin.

Packard, V.O. (1971) *The status seekers*, London/Harmondsworth: Longman/Penguin.

Papadakis, E. and Taylor-Gooby, P. (1987) *The private provision of public welfare: State, market and community*, Brighton: Wheatsheaf.

Parsons, T. (1949) *The structure of social action*, London: Allen & Unwin.

Parsons, T. (1964) *The social system*, London: Routledge & Kegan Paul.

Parsons, T. and Bales, R.F. (1956) *Family, socialisation and interaction process*, London: Routledge & Kegan Paul.

Peacock, A. (1960) *The welfare society*, London: Liberal Publication Department.

Piel, G. (1961) *Consumers of abundance*, Santa Barbara, CA: Center for the Study of Democratic Institutions.

Pigou, K.C. (1932, 4th edn) *The economics of welfare*, London: Macmillan & Co.

Pinker, R. (1971) *Social theory and social policy*, London: Heinemann.

Polanyi, K. (1945) *Origins of our time*, London: Beacon Paperbacks.

Pound, R. (1930) *Kentucky Law Journal*, vol 19, no 1, p 14.

Powell, J.E. (1960) *Saving in a free society*, London: Hutchinson (for the Institute of Economic Affairs).

Powell, J.E. (1966) *Medicine and politics*, London: Pitman.

President's Advisory Panel (1968) *Meeting the insurance crisis of our cities: A report by the President's Advisory Panel*, Washington, DC: US Government Printing Office.

Pusic, E. (1971) 'Levels of social and economic development as limits to welfare policy', *Social Services Review*, vol 45, no 4, December.

Radcliffe-Brown, A.R. (1952) *Structure and function in primitive society*, London: Cohen and West.

Registrar-General (1914) *Registrar-General's 75th statistical review, England and Wales*, London: HMSO.

Registrar-General (1910-15) *Registrar-General's statistical review, England and Wales*, London: HMSO.

Registrar-General (1946-50), *Registrar-General's statistical review, England and Wales*, London: HMSO.

Registrar-General (1951) *Registrar-General's dicennial supplement, England and Wales*, London: HMSO.

Registrar-General (1954) *Registrar-General's statistical review, England and Wales*, London: HMSO.

Registrar-General (1955) *Registrar-General's quarterly return, England and Wales (December)*, London, HMSO.

Registrar-General (1955) *Registrar-General's statistical review, England and Wales*, London: HMSO.

Registrar-General (1956) *Registrar-General's quarterly return, England and Wales (September)*, London: HMSO.

Registrar-General for Scotland (1950-52) *Registrar-General's statistical review*, London: HMSO.

Reisman, D.A. (1977) *Richard Titmuss: Welfare and society*, London: Heinemann.

Riley, D. (1983) *War in the nursery*, London: Virago.

Robbins, L. (1955) 'Notes on public finance', *Lloyds Bank Review*, October.

Robbins Committee (1964) *Report on higher education*, London: HMSO.

Roberts, F. (1952) *The cost of health* [publisher unknown].

Roberts, H. (2000) *What works in reducing inequalities in child health*, Ilford: Barnardo's.

Roberts, I. and Power, C. (1996) 'Does the decline in child mortality vary by social class? A comparison of class-specific mortality in 1981 and 1991', *British Medical Journal*, vol 313, pp 784-6.

Robinson, J. (1962) *Economic philosophy*, London: Watts.

Root, L.S. (1982) *Fringe benefits: Social insurance in the steel industry*, Beverley, CA: Sage Publications.

Rose, H. (1981) 'Rereading Titmuss: the sexual division of welfare', *Journal of Social Policy*, vol 10, no 4, pp 477-502.

Rostow, W.W. (1960) *The stages of economic growth*, Cambridge: Cambridge University Press.

Royal Commission on Marriage and Divorce (1951-55) *Report of the Royal Commission on Marriage and Divorce*, London: HMSO.

Royal Commission on Population (1949) *Report of the Royal Commission on Population*, London: HMSO.

Royal Commission on Taxation (1955) *Final report of the Royal Commission on Taxation*, London: HMSO.

Sand, R. (1935) *Health and human progress*, London: Kegan Paul & Co.

Schumpeter, J.A. (1950) *Capitalism, socialism and democracy*, London: Allen & Unwin.

Scott-Samuel, A. (1989) 'Building the new public health: a public health alliance and a new social epidemiology', in C.J. Martin and D.V. McQueen (eds) *Readings for a new public health*, Edinburgh: Edinburgh University Press.

Seers, D. and Joy, L. (1971) *Development in a divided world*, Harmondsworth: Penguin.

Sefton, T. (1997) *The changing distribution of the social wage*, STICERD Occasional Paper No 21, London: London School of Economics.

Selvin, H.C. and Hagstrom, W.C. (1960) 'Determinants of support for civil liberties', *British Journal of Sociology*, vol 11, no 1.

Sewill, B. (1958) *Taxes for today*, London: The Bow Group.

Shalev, M. (ed) (1996) *The privatization of social policy? Occupational welfare and the welfare state in America, Scandinavia and Japan*, Basingstoke: Macmillan.

Shils, E. (1967) 'The ways of sociology', *Encounter*, vol 28, no 6, p 90, June.

Simon, J. (1890) *English sanitary institutions*, London: Cassell & Co.

Sinfield, A. (1978) 'Analyses in the social division of welfare', *Journal of Social Policy*, vol 7, no 2, pp 129-56, April.

Sinfield, A. (2000) 'Tax benefits in non-state pensions', *European Journal of Social Security*, vol 2, no 2, pp 137-67.

Singer, H.W. (1971) 'A new approach to the problems of the dual society in developing countries', *International Social Development Review*, no 3, New York, NY: United Nations.

Slater, E.T.O. and Woodside, M. (1951) *Patterns of marriage*, London: Cassell & Co.

Smith, G. (1988) 'A paean for the Social Policy Association: a response to Glennerster', *Journal of Social Policy*, vol 17, no 3.

Society for International Development (1972) *Survey of international development*, vol 9, no 4, April.

Southern, R.W. (1961) *The shape and substance of academic history*, Oxford: Oxford University Press.

Sprott, W.J.H. (1962) *Sociology at the seven dials*, London: The Athlone Press.

Stevens, B. (1986) *Complementing the welfare state: The development of private pensions, health insurance and other employee benefits in the United States*, Geneva: ILO.

Stocks, P. (1934) 'The association between mortality and density of housing', *Proceedings of the Royal Society of Medicine*, vol 27, no 2, p 1127.

Stocks, p. (1943) *Lancet*, vol 1, p 543.

Strachey, R. (1928) *The cause*, London: G Bell & Sons.

Surrey, S. (1973) *Pathways to tax reform: The concept of tax expenditures*, Cambridge, MA: Harvard University Press.

Tawney, R.H. (1921) *The acquisitive society*, Cheltenham: Cheltenham Press.

Tawney, R.H. (1934) 'The choice before the Labour Party', *The Attack* (1953).

Tawney, R.H. (1964) *Equality*, London: Allen & Unwin.

Teitelbaum, M.S. and Winter, J.M. (1985) *The fear of population decline*, New York, NY: Academic Press.

Temple, W. (1941) *Citizen and churchman*, London: Eyre & Spottiswoode.

Tilove, R. (1959) *Pension funds and economic freedom: A report to the Fund for the Republic*, New York, NY.

Titmuss, R.M. (1938) *Poverty and population*, London: Macmillan.

Titmuss, R.M. (1942) *Parents revolt*, London: Secker & Warburg.

Titmuss, R.M (1943) *Birth, poverty and wealth*, London: Hamish Hamilton Medical Books.

Titmuss, R.M. (1950) *Problems of social policy*, London: HMSO.

Titmuss, R.M. (1958) *Essays on 'The welfare state'*, London: Allen & Unwin.

Titmuss, R.M. (1962) *Income distribution and social change*, London: Allen & Unwin.

Titmuss, R.M. (1963) *Essays on 'The welfare state'* (2nd edn), London: Allen & Unwin.

Titmuss, R.M. (1963) 'Ethics and economics of medical care', *Medical Care*, vol 1, pp 16-22.

Titmuss, R.M. (1964) 'Introduction', in R.H. Tawney (ed) *Equality*, London: Unwin Books, pp 9-24.

Titmuss, R.M. (1968) 'Choices and the welfare state', in R.M. Titmuss, *Commitment to welfare*, London: Allen & Unwin.

Titmuss, R.M. (1968) 'Universal and selective social services', in R.M. Titmuss, *Commitment to welfare*, London: Allen & Unwin.

Titmuss, R.M. (1968) 'Social policy and economic progress', in R.M. Titmuss, *Commitment to welfare*, London: Allen & Unwin.

Titmuss, R.M. (1968) *Commitment to welfare*, London: Allen & Unwin.

Titmuss, R.M. (1970) *The gift relationship*, London: Allen & Unwin, reprinted 1997, London: LSE Books.

Titmuss, R.M., Abel-Smith, B. with Lynes, T. (1961) *Social policies and population growth in Mauritius*, London: Methuen.

Townsend, P. (1958) 'A society for people', in N. Mackenzie (ed) *Conviction*, London: MacGibbon & Kee.

Townsend, P. (1964) *The last refuge*, London: Routledge.

Townsend, P. (1967) *Poverty, socialism and Labour in power*, Fabian Tract 371, London: Fabian Society.

Townsend, P. (1979) *Poverty in the United Kingdom: A survey of household resources and standards of living*, Harmondsworth: Penguin.

Townsend, P., Davidson, N. and Whitehead, M. (1992) *Inequalities in health*, Harmondsworth: Penguin.

Toynbee, A. (1950) *War and civilisation*, New York, NY: Oxford University Press.

Trotter, W. (1916) *Instincts of the herd in peace and war*, London: T. Fisher Unwin.

United Nations (1961) *Report on the world social situation*, New York, NY: United Nations.

US Senate (1955) *Committee on Banking and Currency*, 84th Congress, 1st Sesssion, Washington, DC: US Government Printing Office.

US Senate (1959) *Hearings before the Sub-committee on the Aged and Ageing*, 86th Congress, Report 43350 (June), Washington, DC: US Government Printing Office.

Vaizey, J. (1983) *In breach of promise*, London: Weidenfeld and Nicolson.

Wallas, G. (1921) 'Professionalism', in *Our social heritage* (1921), London: Allen & Unwin.

Welshman, J. (1998) 'Evacuation and social policy during the Second World War: myth and reality', *Twentieth Century British History*, vol 9, no 1, pp 28-53.

Whitehead, A.N. (1929) *The aims of education*, London: Benn.

Whiting, R. (2000) *The Labour Party and taxation: Party identity and political purpose in twentieth century Britain*, Cambridge: Cambridge University Press.

Whittaker, E.B. (1957) *Transactions of XVth International Congress of Actuaries*, vol 4, p 155.

Wilensky, H.L. and Lebaux, C.N. (1958) *Industrial society and social welfare*, New York, NY: Free Press.

Wiles, P.J.D. and Markowski, S. (1971) 'Income distribution under communism and capitalism', *Soviet Studies*, nos 3 and 4.

Woodham Smith, C.B. (1950) *Florence Nightingale*, London: Constable.

Woodroffe, C., Glickman, M., Barker, M. and Power, C. (1993) *Children, teenagers and health*, Buckingham: Open University Press.

Woolf, V. (1938) *Three guineas*, London: Hogarth Press.

Wright Mills, C. (1959) *The sociological imagination*, Oxford: Oxford University Press.

Young, M. and Willmott, P. (1957) *Family and kinship in East London*, London: Routledge & Kegan Paul.

Index

NOTE: Page numbers in bold denote an extract from or reproduction of the work indexed; RT = Richard Titmuss.